iPad™

PORTABLE GENIUS

iPad™

PORTABLE GENIUS

by Paul McFedries

Wiley Publishing, Inc.

iPad™ Portable Genius

Published by
Wiley Publishing, Inc.
10475 Crosspoint Blvd.
Indianapolis, IN 46256
www.wiley.com

ISBN: 978-0-470-54096-1

Manufactured in the United States of America

10 9 8 7 6 5 4 3

For general information on our other products and services or to obtain technical support, please contact our Customer Care Department within the U.S. at (877) 762-2974, outside the U.S. at (317) 572-3993 or fax (317) 572-4002.

Wiley also publishes its books in a variety of electronic formats. Some content that appears in print may not be available in electronic books.

Library of Congress Control Number: 2010925244

About the Author

Paul McFedries is a full-time technical writer. Paul has been authoring computer books since 1991 and has more than 70 books to his credit. Paul's books have sold more than three million copies world-wide. These books include the Wiley titles *iPhone 3G S Portable Genius, Macs Portable Genius, MacBook Air Portable Genius, Switching to a Mac Portable Genius, Teach Yourself VISUALLY Macs, Teach Yourself VISUALLY Computers, Fifth Edition,* and *Internet Simplified*. Paul is also the proprietor

of Word Spy (www.wordspy.com), a Web site that tracks new words and phrases as they enter the language. Paul invites you to drop by his Web site at www.mcfedries.com and to follow him on Twitter at twitter.com/paulmcf.

Credits

Senior Acquisitions Editor
Stephanie McComb

Project Editor
Jama Carter

Technical Editor
G. Smith

Copy Editor
Gwenette Gaddis

Editorial Director
Robyn Siesky

Vice President and Executive Group Publisher
Richard Swadley

Vice President and Executive Publisher
Barry Pruett

Business Manager
Amy Knies

Senior Marketing Manager
Sandy Smith

Project Coordinator
Kristie Rees

Graphics and Production Specialists
Jennifer Henry
Andrea Hornberger

Quality Control Technician
Rebecca Denoncour

Proofreading
Shannon Ramsey

Indexing
BIM Indexing & Proofreading Services

To David, Kyra, and Greg, for being great friends in a time of need, to Karen, of course, and to Gypsy for having a big heart.

Acknowledgments

Being a freelance technical writer is an awesome vocation: You get to work at home; you get to set your own schedule; and you get to help other people understand and use technology, which is a big warm-fuzzy-feeling generator. But perhaps the best part of technical writing is getting to be among the first not just to use but to really *dive into* the latest and greatest software and hardware. The hardware side is often the most fun, because it means you get to play with gadgets, and that's a gadget geek's definition of a dream job. So to say I had a blast researching and writing about the iPad redefines the word *understatement*. What self-respecting gadget guy wouldn't have a perma-grin while poking and prodding the iPad to see just what it can do?

And what self-respecting technical writer wouldn't be constantly shaking his head in admiration while working with the amazing editorial team at Wiley? Skip back a couple of pages to see the complete list of the team who worked so hard to bring you this book. The people I worked with directly included Senior Acquisitions Editor Stephanie McComb, who found a way for me to realize my dream of writing an iPad book; Project Editor Jama Carter, who not only has the coolest name on the planet, but is bursting with great ideas and infectious energy; Copy Editor Gwenette Gaddis, whose super-human attention to the all-important details and deft editing touch brought this book up a notch or three; and Technical Editor G. Smith, who made sure I didn't lead you astray with my information or my instructions. Many heartfelt thanks to all of you for outstanding work on this project.

Contents
at a Glance

Contents

How Do I Manage My eBook Library on My iPad? 158

Introduction

There are many reasons behind the success of the iPad, and its smaller cousins, the iPhone and iPod touch, but if you polled fans of these devices I bet one reason would quickly bubble up to the top spot: the touch interface. It's slick, elegant, and just so easy: a tap here, a tap there, and away you go.

Using the iPad's touch interface is like playing in one of those seaside areas where the water is only a couple of feet deep no matter where you go: You can still have all kinds of fun, but you never have to swim hard and there's little chance of drowning. However, if you walk out far enough in many of those ocean areas, you suddenly come to the edge of an underwater shelf, where the sandy bottom gives way to the inky ocean depths.

Your iPad, too, has its unexplored depths: hidden settings, obscure features, out-of-the-way preferences, and little-known techniques. The usefulness of some of these features is debatable, at best, but many of them can help you work faster, easier, and more efficiently. Rather than swimming blindly through the murky waters of your iPad's deep end, you might consider making an appointment with your local Apple Store's Genius Bar. And, more often than not, the on-duty genius will give you good advice on how to get more out of your iPad investment. The Genius Bar is a great thing, but it isn't always a convenient thing. You usually have to make an appointment, drag yourself down to the store, perhaps wait for your genius, get the advice you need (or the problem looked at, or whatever), and then make your way back home; and in some cases, you may need to leave your iPad for a while (the horror!) to get a problem checked out and hopefully resolved.

What you really need is a version of the Genius Bar that's easier to access, more convenient, and doesn't require tons of time or leaving your iPad in the hands of a stranger. What you really need is a "portable" genius that enables you to be more productive and solve problems wherever you and your iPad happen to be hanging out.

Welcome to *iPad Portable Genius*. This book is like a mini Genius Bar all wrapped up in an easy-to-use, easy-to-access, and eminently portable format. In this book, you learn how to get more out of your iPad by learning how to access all the really powerful and timesaving features that aren't obvious at a casual glance. In this book, you learn how to avoid your iPad's occasional annoying character traits, and in those cases where such behavior can't be avoided, you learn how to work around it. In this book, you learn how to prevent iPad problems from occurring, and just in case your preventative measures are for naught, you learn how to fix many common problems yourself.

This book is for iPad users who know the basics but want to take their iPad education to a higher level. It's a book for people who want to be more productive, more efficient, more creative, and more self-sufficient (at least as far as the iPad goes anyway). It's a book for people who use their iPads every day, but who would like to incorporate it into more of their day-to-day activities. It's a book I had a blast writing, so I think it's a book you'll enjoy reading.

You can do plenty of things locally on your iPad without having to reach out and touch some remote site or service. You can view the time, set an alarm, make some quick calculations, jot some notes, or just play around with your iPad's settings. Nothing wrong with any of that, but I'm willing to bet you didn't fork over the bucks for an IPad just so you could play around with the Calculator app. I didn't think so. After all, the iPad was engineered from the ground up to *connect*. Whether it's the Web to go on a surfin' safari, the App Store or iBookstore to grab some content, or Google Maps to find your way, the iPad comes alive when it's connected to a network.

Understanding Internet Access Networks

To get on the Web, your iPad must first connect to a network that offers Internet access. To make this easy and seamless, your iPad comes with internal hardware that enables it to detect and connect to available networks. Exactly how this happens and what kinds of networks your iPad can access depends on the type of iPad you own:

- **iPad with Wi-Fi.** This type of iPad can connect only to Wi-Fi wireless networks.

- **iPad with Wi-Fi + 3G.** This type of iPad can connect to Wi-Fi wireless networks and cellular networks.

The next couple of sections tell you more.

Understanding Wi-Fi networks

Wireless devices such as the iPad transmit data and communicate with other devices using *radio frequency* (RF) signals that are beamed from one device to another. Although these radio signals are similar to those used in commercial radio broadcasts, they operate on a different frequency. For example, if you use a wireless keyboard and mouse, you have an RF receiver device plugged into, usually, a USB port on your computer. The keyboard and mouse have built-in RF transmitters. When you press a key or move or click the mouse, the transmitter sends the appropriate RF signal; that signal is picked up by the receiver, and the corresponding keystroke or mouse action is passed along to Windows, just as if the original device had been connected to the computer directly.

A *radio transceiver* is a device that can act as both a transmitter and a receiver of radio signals. All wireless devices that require two-way communications use a transceiver, and your iPad is no exception.

The most common wireless networking technology is *wireless fidelity*, which is almost always shortened to *Wi-Fi* (which rhymes with *hi-fi*), and the generic Institute of Electrical and Electronics Engineers (IEEE) designation for this wireless networking standard is 802.11. There are four main types — 802.11a, 802.11b, 802.11g, and 802.11n — each of which has its own range and speed limits, as you see in the following list:

Caution

All wireless standard speeds are theoretical because interference and bandwidth limitations almost always mean that real-world speeds are slower than the optimum speeds. Bear that in mind as you read about the various Wi-Fi standards.

- **802.11b.** The original 802.11 standard was published by the IEEE in 1997, but few people took it seriously because it was hobbled by a maximum transmission rate of just 2 Mbps. By 1999, the IEEE had worked out not one but *two* new standards: 802.11a and 802.11b. The 802.11b standard became the more popular of the two, so I discuss it first. 802.11b upped the Wi-Fi data transmission rate to 11 Mbps. The indoor range of 802.11b is about 115 feet. 802.11b operates on the 2.4 GHz radio frequency, which is an unregulated frequency often used by other consumer products such as microwave ovens, cordless telephones, and baby monitors. This keeps the price of 802.11b hardware down, but it also can cause interference problems when you attempt to access the network near another device that's using the 2.4 GHz frequency.

Note

When you're talking about data communications, a *megabit* (Mb) is equal to one million bits. So, the 11 Mbps transmission speed of 802.11b means that it can (theoretically, of course) transfer 11 million bits of data per second. Just to confuse matters, if you're talking about memory or data storage, a megabit equals 1,048,576 bits.

- **802.11a.** The 802.11a standard was released at around the same time as the 802.11b standard. There are two key differences between these standards: 802.11a has a maximum transmission rate of 54 Mbps, and it operates using the regulated 5.0 GHz radio frequency band. This higher frequency band means that 802.11a devices don't have the same interference problems as 802.11b devices, but it also means that 802.11a hardware is more expensive, offers a shorter range (about 75 feet), and has trouble penetrating solid surfaces such as walls. So, despite its impressive transmission speed, 802.11a had too many negative factors against it, so 802.11b won the hearts of consumers and became the first true wireless networking standard.

- **802.11g.** During the battle between 802.11a and 802.11b, it became clear that consumers and small businesses really wanted the best of both worlds. That is, they wanted a WLAN technology that was as fast and as interference-free as 802.11a, but had the longer range and cheaper cost of 802.11b. Alas, "the best of both worlds" is a state rarely achieved in the real world. However, the IEEE came close when it introduced the next version of the wireless networking standard in 2003: 802.11g. Like its 802.11a predecessor, 802.11g has a theoretical maximum transmission rate of 54 Mbps, and like 802.11b, 802.11g boasted an indoor range of about 115 feet and was cheap to manufacture. That cheapness came from its use of the 2.4 GHz RF band, which means that 802.11g devices can suffer from interference from other nearby consumer devices that use the same frequency. Despite the possibility of interference, 802.11g quickly became the most popular of the Wi-Fi standards, and most WLAN devices sold today support 802.11g.

● **802.11n.** The latest wireless standard is called 802.11n. 802.11n implements a technology called *multiple-input multiple-output* (MIMO) that uses multiple transmitters and receivers in each device. This enables multiple data streams on a single device, which will greatly improve WLAN performance. For example, using three transmitters and two receivers (the standard configuration), 802.11n promises a theoretical transmission speed of up to 248 Mbps. 802.11n also promises to double the wireless range to about 230 feet.

How does your iPad fit into all this? I'm happy to report that the iPad supports 802.11n, which means it can take advantage of the fastest wireless networks out there, particularly those based on Apple's AirPort Extreme wireless access point. (*AirPort* is the name Apple uses instead of *Wi-Fi.*) However, the iPad actually comes with 802.11a/b/g/n support, which means it also understands older wireless networks that use the 802.11a, 802.11b, and 802.11g standards. In other words, your iPad works perfectly with *any* wireless network.

This is good news because although you may know what kind of Wi-Fi technology you have in your home or office, you'll likely not have a clue when it comes to the wireless networks that are popping up in cities all across the world: in coffee shops, cafes, restaurants, fast-food outlets, hotels, airports, trains, even dental offices. Some cities have even started offering universal Wi-Fi access in the downtown area. These wireless networks share an Internet connection, so you can connect to the network and then use it to surf the Web, check your e-mail, catch up on your RSS feeds, log on to the office network, and more. A public wireless network that shares an Internet connection is called a *wireless hot spot* (or just a hot spot). In some cases, the establishment offers Internet access free of charge as a perk for doing business with them. However, most hot spots charge a fee to access the network.

Because most wireless networks are connected to high-speed Internet connections, Wi-Fi is by far your best bet for an Internet connection on your iPad. You get fast downloads, and if you have an iPad with 3G support, you don't use up data transfers in whatever Internet connection plan you have with your cellular provider. As long as a Wi-Fi network is within range and you can connect to that network, your iPad always defaults to using Wi-Fi for Internet access.

Genius

Not sure if you've got any hot spots nearby? One easy way to find Wi-Fi near you is to open the Maps app on your iPad, display your current location (see Chapter 12), and type **wifi** into the search box. This gives you a map with pushpins representing Wi-Fi hotspots near you. The App Store also has lots of apps that can locate not only wireless hot spots, but also unsecured wireless networks within range. See, for example, Bitrino's WiFiTrak and JiWire's Free Wi-Fi Finder.

Understanding cellular networks

If your iPad is a Wi-Fi + 3G model, it means not only can your iPad connect to Wi-Fi networks and hot spots, but it also can make use of a cellular network if no Wi-Fi is within range. In fact, your iPad is social enough to be on friendly terms with not just one, but *two*, types of cellular networks:

- **3G.** Short for Third Generation, 3G is currently available in several hundred U.S. metropolitan areas. Most other countries offer widespread 3G coverage, so you won't often find yourself out of 3G service. The 3G network is a cellular network, so as long as you're in a 3G coverage area, you can access the Internet from anywhere, even a moving car. 3G is slower than Wi-Fi, but download speeds are anywhere from 2 to 2.5 times as fast as the notoriously pokey EDGE downloads (discussed next), so you won't grow old waiting for a Web site to open. If your 3G-enabled iPad has no Wi-Fi hot spot in range, it automatically switches to the 3G network, assuming you're in a coverage area.

- **EDGE.** This is short for Enhanced Data rates for GSM (Global System for Mobile communication) Evolution, an absurdly grandiose name for a rightfully maligned cellular network technology. Why the bad press for EDGE? Because it's, in a word, *slow*. Paint dries faster than most Web sites download over an EDGE connection. So why bother with EDGE at all? Mostly because although 3G is widespread, it doesn't have as much coverage as EDGE does. So if you don't have a Wi-Fi network nearby, and you're not in a 3G coverage area, your cellular-chip-equipped iPad drops down into EDGE mode so you can at least get a signal.

Unfortunately, although you can often ride the Wi-Fi train for free, there's no such luck when it comes to cellular networks. Your iPad's 3G chip won't work unless you plug a SIM (Subscriber Identity Module) card into the iPad's SIM slot (located on the top edge of the device). However, to get a SIM card, you must sign up for a data plan with a cellular provider.

Why not just pop out the SIM card in your existing phone and pop it into your iPad? Ah, that would be sweet, wouldn't it? Unfortunately, that's probably not going to work because most mobile phones today use regular SIM cards, while the iPad uses the fairly obscure (for now) *micro* SIM card, which is much smaller. So chances are good that your mobile phone's SIM is too big to fit into the iPad's SIM slot.

Inserting a micro SIM card into your iPad

After you've signed up for a data plan, or if you just happen to have a micro SIM card available through your existing cellular provider, then to use the cellular network, you must insert the SIM card into your iPad. Here's how it's done:

1. **Turn off your iPad.**

2. **Locate the SIM Removal Tool that came with your iPad.** The SIM Removal Tool is a long, thin piece of metal with a handle on one end.

3. **Stand up the iPad, and locate the SIM slot on the top edge of the device.** You're looking for a tiny hole beside the audio jack.

4. **Insert the end of the SIM Removal Tool (or paper clip) carefully into the SIM slot hole.** You don't need to go in very far — a sixteenth of an inch is plenty.

5. **Gently pull the SIM Removal Tool away from the iPad.** As you pull, the SIM tray should come along with the tool. If it doesn't, insert the tool a little farther.

6. **After you have the tray out, orient the micro SIM card with the edges of the tray, and then drop the card inside the tray.** Make sure the card is lying flat in the tray.

Genius

If you can't find the SIM Removal Tool, a paper clip will do in a pinch. Just take any medium-sized paper clip and straighten out one end.

7. **Insert the SIM tray back into the SIM slot.** Make sure you put the SIM tray back into the slot using the same orientation as when you removed it. Make sure the tray is fully inserted into the slot.

8. **Place a finger over the SIM tray to keep it in place, and then pull out the SIM Removal Tool.**

Connecting to a Wi-Fi Network

You see a bit later (in the section on working with cellular network connections) that a 3G-enabled iPad connects to cellular networks automatically. Things aren't immediately automatic when it comes to Wi-Fi connections, at least not at first. As soon as you try to access something on the Internet — a Web site, your e-mail, a Google Map, or whatever — your iPad scours the surrounding airwaves for Wi-Fi network signals. If you've never connected to a Wi-Fi network, or if you're in an area that doesn't have any Wi-Fi networks you've used in the past, you see the Select a Wi-Fi Network dialog, as shown in Figure 1.1. (If you don't see the Select a Wi-Fi Network dialog, you can still connect to a wireless network, see the section on stopping the incessant Wi-Fi network prompts later in this chapter.)

1.1 If you're just starting out on the Wi-Fi trail, your iPad displays a list of nearby networks.

This dialog displays a list of the Wi-Fi networks that are within range. For each network, you get three tidbits of data:

- **Network name.** This is the name that the administrator has assigned to the network. If you're in a coffee shop or similar public hot spot and you want to use that network, look for the name of the shop (or a variation on the name).

- **Password-protected.** If a Wi-Fi network displays a lock icon, it means the network is protected by a password, and you need to know that password to make the connection.

- **Signal strength.** This icon gives you a rough idea of how strong the wireless signals are. The stronger the signal (the more bars you see, the better the signal), the more likely you are to get a fast and reliable connection.

Making your first connection

Follow these steps to connect to a Wi-Fi network:

1. **Tap the network you want to use.** If the network is protected by a password, your iPad prompts you to enter the password, as shown in Figure 1.2.

Enter Password | Cancel

Password |

1.2 If the Wi-Fi network is secured with a password, use this screen to enter it.

Caution

Because the password box shows dots instead of the actual text for added security, this is no place to demonstrate your iPad speed-typing prowess. Slow and steady wins the password typing race (or something).

2. **Use the keyboard to enter the password.**

3. **Tap Join.** The iPad connects to the network and adds the Wi-Fi network signal strength icon to the status bar.

To connect to a commercial Wi-Fi operation — such as those you find in airports, hotels, and convention centers — you almost always have to take one more step. In most cases, the network prompts you for your name and credit card data so you can be charged for accessing the network. If you're not prompted right away, you will be as soon as you try to access a Web site or check your e-mail. Enter your information and then enjoy the Internet in all its Wi-Fi glory.

Connecting to known networks

If the Wi-Fi network is one that you use all the time — for example, your home or office network — the good news is your iPad remembers any network you connect to. As soon as a known network comes within range, your iPad makes the connection without so much as a peep. Thanks!

Stopping the incessant Wi-Fi network prompts

The Select a Wi-Fi Network dialog is a handy convenience if you're not sure whether a Wi-Fi network is available. However, as you move around town, you may find that dialog popping up all over the place as new Wi-Fi networks come within range. One solution is to wear your finger down to the bone with all the constant tapping of the Cancel button, but there's a better way: Just tell your iPad to shut up already with the Wi-Fi prompting. Here's how:

1. **On the Home screen, tap Settings.** The Settings screen appears.

2. **Tap Wi-Fi.** iPad opens the Wi-Fi Networks screen.

3. **Tap the Ask to Join Networks switch to the Off position, as shown in Figure 1.3.** Your iPad no longer prompts you with nearby networks. Whew!

11

| iPad | 9:59 AM | 100% |

Settings | **Wi-Fi Networks**

Wi-Fi   Not Connected

Wi-Fi   ON

Brightness & Wallpaper

Choose a Network...

Picture Frame

Logophilia   🔒 📶 ➤

General

Wireless429   📶 ➤

Mail, Contacts, Calendars

Safari   Other...   ›

iPod

Ask to Join Networks   OFF

Video   Known networks will be joined automatically. If no
                        known networks are available, you will have to
Photos   manually select a network.

Store

1.3 Toggle the Ask to Join Networks switch to Off to put a gag in the network prompts.

Okay, I hear you ask, if I'm no longer seeing the prompts, how do I connect to a Wi-Fi network if I don't even know it's there? That's a good question, and here's a good answer:

1. **On the Home screen, tap Settings.** Your iPad displays the Settings screen.

2. **Tap Wi-Fi.** The Wi-Fi Networks screen appears, and the Choose a Network list shows you the available Wi-Fi networks.

3. **Tap the network you want to use.** If the network is protected by a password, your iPad prompts you to enter the password.

4. **Use the keyboard to tap the password.**

5. **Tap Join.** The iPad connects to the network and adds the Wi-Fi network signal strength icon to the status bar.

Connecting to a hidden Wi-Fi network

Each Wi-Fi network has a network name — often called the Service Set Identifier, or SSID — that identifies the network to Wi-Fi-friendly devices such as your iPad. By default, most Wi-Fi networks broadcast the network name so you can see the network and connect to it. However, some Wi-Fi networks disable network name broadcasting as a security precaution. The idea here is that if an unauthorized user can't see the network, he or she can't attempt to connect to it. (However, some devices can pick up the network name when authorized computers connect to the network, so this is not a foolproof security measure.)

You can still connect to a hidden Wi-Fi network by entering the connection settings by hand. You need to know the network name, the network's security type and encryption type, and the network's password. Here are the steps to follow:

1. **On the Home screen, tap Settings to open the Settings screen.**

2. **Tap Wi-Fi.** You see the Wi-Fi Networks screen.

3. **Tap Other.** Your iPad displays the Other Network screen, as shown in Figure 1.4.

4. **Use the Name text box to enter the network name.**

5. **Tap Security to open the Security screen.**

6. **Tap the type of security used by the Wi-Fi network: WEP, WPA, WPA2, WPA Enterprise, WPA2 Enterprise, or None.**

7. **Tap Other Network to return to the Other Network screen.** If you chose WEP, WPA, WPA2, WPA Enterprise, or WPA2 Enterprise, your iPad prompts you to enter the password.

1.4 Use the Other Network screen to connect to a hidden Wi-Fi network.

8. **Use the keyboard to enter the password.**

9. **Tap Join.** The iPad connects to the network and adds the Wi-Fi network signal strength icon to the status bar.

Turning off the Wi-Fi antenna to save power

Your iPad's Wi-Fi antenna is constantly on the lookout for nearby Wi-Fi networks. That's useful because it means you always have an up-to-date list of networks to check out, but it takes its toll on the iPad battery. If you know you won't be using Wi-Fi for a while, you can save some battery juice for more important pursuits by turning off your iPad's Wi-Fi antenna. Here's how:

1. **On the Home screen, tap Settings.** The Settings screen appears.

2. **Tap Wi-Fi.** The Wi-Fi Networks screen appears.

3. **Tap the Wi-Fi switch to the Off position.** Your iPad disconnects from your current Wi-Fi network and hides the Choose a Networks list, as shown in Figure 1.5.

1.5 If you don't need Wi-Fi for now, turn off the antenna to save battery power.

When you're ready to resume your Wi-Fi duties, return to the Wi-Fi Networks screen and tap the Wi-Fi switch to the On position.

Working with Cellular Network Connections

Connections to the cellular network are automatic and occur behind the scenes. As soon as you switch on your 3G-enabled iPad, it checks for a 3G signal and if it finds one, it connects to the network and displays the 3G icon in the status bar, as well as the connection strength (the more bars, the better). If your current location doesn't do the 3G thing, your iPad tries to connect to an EDGE network instead. If that works, you see the E icon in the status bar (plus the usual signal strength bars). If none of that works, you see No Signal, so you might as well go home.

Tracking cellular data usage

Having a data plan with a cellular provider means never having to worry about getting access to the network. However, unless you're paying for unlimited access (lucky you!), you *should* be worrying about going over whatever maximum amount of data usage your plan provides per month. That's because going over your data max means you start paying through the nose for each megabyte, and you can run up a hefty bill in no time.

To avoid that, keep track of your cellular data usage by following these steps:

1. **On the Home screen, tap Settings.** The Settings screen appears.

2. **Tap General.** Your iPad displays the General options screen.

3. **Tap Usage.** Your iPad displays the Usage screen.

4. **Examine the Sent and Received values in the Cellular Network Data section.**

Genius

Your iPad's cellular usage values are meaningful only if they correspond to your monthly data cycle with your provider. Check with your cellular provider to see which day of the month your data resets. On that day, follow the steps above to open the Usage screen, and then tap Reset Statistics. When the iPad asks you to confirm, tap Reset.

Disabling data roaming

Data roaming is an often convenient cellular plan feature that enables you to surf the Web, check and send e-mail, and exchange text messages when you're outside your provider's normal coverage area. The down side is that roaming charges are almost always eye-poppingly expensive, and you're often talking several dollars per *minute*, depending on where you are and what type of service you're using. Not good!

Unfortunately, if you have your iPad's Data Roaming feature turned on, you may incur massive roaming charges even if you never use the device! That's because your iPad still performs background checks for things like incoming e-mail messages and text messages, so a week in some far-off land could cost you hundreds of dollars without even using the device. Again, not good!

To avoid this insanity, turn off your iPad's Data Roaming feature when you don't need it. Follow these steps:

1. **On the Home screen, tap Settings.** The Settings screen appears.
2. **Tap General.** The General screen appears.
3. **Tap Network.** The Network screen appears.
4. **Tap the Data Roaming On/Off button to change this setting to Off.**

Turning off the 3G antenna to save power

Your iPad's 3G antenna is constantly on the lookout for a 3G cellular connection. That's handy because it means you always have access whenever you're in a 3G network coverage area. However, this constant 3G searching uses up your iPad battery like crazy. If you're on a Wi-Fi network, or you don't need a 3G network connection for a while, you can preserve precious battery life by turning off your iPad's 3G antenna:

1. **On the Home screen, tap Settings.** The Settings screen appears.
2. **Tap General.** The General screen appears.
2. **Tap Network.** The Network screen appears.
3. **Tap the Enable 3G switch to the Off position.** Your iPad disconnects from your 3G cellular connection and connects to the EDGE network, if you're in an EDGE coverage area.

When you're ready to get back on the 3G highway, return to the Network screen and tap the 3G switch to the On position.

Tethering a Computer to Your iPad's Internet Connection

Here's a scenario you've probably tripped over a time or two when you've been roaming around with both your 3G-enabled iPad and your notebook computer along for the ride. You end up somewhere that you have access to just the cellular network, with no Wi-Fi in sight. This means your iPad can access the Internet (using the cellular network), but your notebook can't. That's a real pain if you want to do some work on the computer that involves Internet access.

Fortunately, there's a solution: *Internet tethering*. This means you use your iPad as a kind of Internet gateway device. That is, you connect your iPad to your notebook (either directly via a USB cable or wirelessly via Bluetooth), and your notebook can then use the iPad's cellular Internet connection to get online.

This sounds too good to be true, and to a certain extent it is. That is, your cellular provider will probably charge you extra (anywhere from $20 to $50 per month!) to use tethering, and that's *if* your provider even supports tethering. So before you get too excited about this interesting technology, check with your cellular provider and get the details.

Note If you have an Wi-Fi only iPad and an iPhone 3G or 3GS, you may be wondering if you can tether your iPad to your iPhone's 3G internet connection. That would be sweet, indeed, but alas, it's not to be. The iPad can't tether to an iPhone.

If you're ready to check it out, your first chore is to turn on Internet tethering on your iPad. Follow these steps:

1. **On the Home screen, tap Settings.** The Settings screen appears.

2. **Tap General.** The General screen opens.

3. **Tap Network.** The Network screen opens.

4. **Tap Internet Tethering to display the Internet Tethering screen.**

5. **Tap the Internet Tethering switch to the On position.** If you have Bluetooth turned off on your iPad, you see a warning dialog, and you need to tap either Turn on Bluetooth to use it or tap USB Only if you plan on making a USB connection to the notebook.

Note Remember that you won't see the Internet Tethering option if your cellular provider doesn't support Internet tethering.

Connect your iPad to the computer. On a Mac, you see a dialog telling you a new network interface has been detected. Click Network Preferences and then click Apply to create the tethering connection. You know you were successful when you see two things:

● In the Network preferences window, the iPad network interface (for example, iPad USB, if you're using a USB connection) shows connected, as shown in Figure 1.6.

1.6 When you successfully set up Internet tethering, the iPad network interface shows Connected.

● On your iPad, you see a blue Internet Tethering bar just below the status bar.

How Do I Keep My iPad in Sync?

Your iPad weighs a mere pound and a half (a tiny bit more if it's got a 3G chip shoehorned inside), so it's about as portable as a portable computer can get. This inherent packability means you'll often have your trusty iPad with you when you venture out of your home or office, but (hello?) aren't you forgetting something? That's right: You were just about to waltz outside without bringing any of your *data* with you. Your contacts, calendars, bookmarks — not to mention your music, videos, and other media — are just sitting there on your main computer, so why not take them with you? You can if you sync some or all of that data with your iPad, as you learn in this chapter.

Connecting Your iPad to Your Computer

We're all waiting for that glorious day when our computers and devices such as our iPads can just sort of *sense* each other's presence and begin a digital conversation without requiring something as inelegant as a *physical* connection. Ugh. However, despite the fact that your fancy-schmancy iPad supports *two* wireless technologies — Wi-Fi (see Chapter 1) and Bluetooth (see Chapter 3) — exchanging data between the iPad and a Mac or PC requires a wired connection.

You've got a couple of ways to make the connection:

- **USB cable.** Use the cable that comes with your iPad to attach the USB connector to a free USB port on your Mac or Windows PC, and then attach the dock connector to the 30-pin connector port on the bottom of the iPad.

- **Dock.** If you shelled out the bucks for the optional iPad dock, first plug it in to a power outlet. Using your iPad's cable, attach the USB connector to a free USB port on your Mac or Windows PC, and attach the dock connector to the 30-pin connector port on the back of the dock. Now insert your iPad into the dock's cradle.

Syncing Your iPad Automatically

Depending on the storage capacity of your iPad — 16GB, 32GB, or 64GB — you may be able to cram all your computer's iPad-friendly digital content onto the iPad hard drive. If that sounds like the way you want to go, then you can take advantage of the easiest of the iPad syncing scenarios, in which you don't have to pay any attention in the least: automatic syncing. (If that does *not* sound like the way you want to go, no worries: See the section on syncing your iPad manually a bit later in this chapter). Because you know all the iPad-able content on your Mac or Windows PC is going to fit, all you have to do is turn on your iPad and connect it to your computer.

Genius I've found that syncing can sometimes fail if your iPad is open to an app's settings screen when you launch the sync. Press the Home button to ensure that no settings or apps are open before trying to sync.

Yup, that's all there is to it! iTunes opens automatically, connects to your iPad, and begins syncing. (As an added bonus, the USB port also begins charging your iPad's battery.) Note these three things while this is happening, as shown in Figure 2.1:

- You see your iPad in the iTunes Devices list.
- You see Syncing "iPad" in the iTunes status area.
- Your iPad displays the Sync in Progress screen while the sync runs.

Eject

2.1 When you connect your iPad, iTunes springs into action and starts syncing.

Giving Your iPad a Snappy Name

This isn't necessarily a syncing topic, but I thought that while you're in iTunes, you might want to give your iPad a proper name, one that's a tad more interesting than the boring "iPad" that passes for the default name. Here's what you do:

1. **Double-click your iPad in the Devices list.** iTunes forms a text box around the name.

2. **Type the name you want to use.** You can use any characters you want, and the name can be as long as you want, although you might want to use no more than about 15 or 16 characters to ensure the name doesn't get cut off in the Devices list.

3. **Press Return or Enter to save the new name.**

As soon as you press Return or Enter, iTunes connects to your iPad and saves the name on the iPad. This way, even if you connect your iPad to another computer, that machine's version of iTunes shows your custom iPad name.

Note that you can't use your iPad while the sync is running. However, one of the iPad's nicest features is its willingness to be rudely interrupted in midsync. When the Sync in Progress screen appears, you see the Slide to Cancel slider at the bottom of the screen. If you ever need to bail out of the sync to perform some other duty, drag the slider to the right. iTunes dutifully cancels the sync so you can go about your business. When you're ready to restart the sync, click the Sync button in iTunes.

When the sync is done, you need to do two things:

1. **In iTunes, click the Eject icon beside your iPad in the Devices list.** I pointed out this icon in Figure 2.1.

2. **Remove the dock connector from the iPad's 30-pin connector port.**

Bypassing the automatic sync

Sometimes, you may want to connect your iPad to your computer, but you don't want it to sync automatically. I'm not talking here about switching to manual syncing full time; I get to that in a second. Instead, I'm talking about bypassing the sync one time only. For example, you may want to connect your iPad to your computer just to charge it (assuming you either don't have the optional dock or you don't have it with you). Or perhaps you just want to use iTunes to eyeball how much free space is left on your iPad or to check for updates to the iPad software.

Whatever the reason, you can tell iTunes to hold off the syncing this time only by using one of the following techniques:

- **Mac.** Connect the iPad to the Mac, and then quickly press and hold the Option and ⌘ keys.

- **Windows.** Connect the iPad to the Windows PC, and then quickly press and hold the Ctrl and Shift keys.

When you see that iTunes has added your iPad to the Devices list, you can release the keys.

Genius

You don't need to use iTunes to see how much free space is left on your iPad. On the Home screen, tap Settings, tap General, and then tap About. In the About screen that slides in, the Available value tells you how many gigabytes (or megabytes) of free space you have to play with.

Troubleshooting automatic syncing

Okay, so you connect your iPad to your computer and then nothing. If iTunes isn't already running, it refuses to wake up from its digital slumbers. What's up with that?

A couple of things could be the problem. First, connect your iPad, switch to iTunes on your computer, and then click your iPad in the Devices list. On the Summary tab, as shown in Figure 2.2, make sure the Open iTunes when this iPad is connected check box is selected.

2.2 Select the Open iTunes when this iPad is connected check box.

If that check box was already selected, you need to delve a bit deeper to solve the mystery. Follow these steps:

1. **Open the iTunes preferences:**
   - **Mac.** Choose iTunes ➪ Preferences, or press ⌘ +. (period).
   - **Windows.** Choose Edit ➪ Preferences, or press Ctrl ⊦ (period).

2. **Click the Devices tab.**

3. **Deselect the Prevent iPods, iPhones, and iPads from Syncing Automatically check box.**

4. **Click OK to put the new setting into effect and enable automatic syncing again.**

Syncing Your iPad Manually

When you first connected your iPad to iTunes, the brief setup routine included a screen that asked if you wanted to automatically sync certain content, such as music and photos. If you activated a check box for a particular type of content, iTunes configured the iPad to sync *all* of that content. That's fine, but depending on how much content you have, you might end of throwing a lot of stuff at your iPad.

One fine day, you'll be minding your own business and performing what you believe to be a routine sync operation when a dialog like the one shown in Figure 2.3 rears its nasty head.

Groan! This most unwelcome dialog means just what it says: You don't have enough free space on your iPad to sync all the content from your computer. You can handle this in a couple of ways:

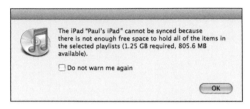

The iPad "Paul's iPad" cannot be synced because there is not enough free space to hold all of the items in the selected playlists (1.25 GB required, 805.6 MB available).

☐ Do not warn me again

OK

2.3 You see this dialog if iTunes can't fit all your stuff on your iPad.

- **Remove some of the content from your computer.** This is a good way to go if your iPad is really close to having enough space. For example, the dialog says your computer wants to send 100MB of data, but your iPad has only 98MB of free space. Get rid of a few megabytes of stuff on your computer, and you're back in the sync business.

- **Synchronize your iPad manually.** This means that you no longer sync everything on your computer. Instead, you handpick which playlists, podcasts, audiobooks, and so on are sent to your iPad. It's a bit more work, but it's the way to go if there's a big difference between the amount of content on your computer and the amount of space left on your iPad.

Syncing manually means that you handle the syncing yourself for the various content types: contacts, calendars, e-mail, bookmarks, music, podcasts, audiobooks, photos, videos, and apps. You do this using the other tabs in the iPad window: Info, Music, Photos, and so on. To learn the specifics for each type of data, see the following sections of the book:

- **Safari bookmarks.** In Chapter 4, see the section on syncing your bookmarks.
- **E-mail account info.** In Chapter 5, see the section on syncing your e-mail accounts.
- **Mail application notes.** In Chapter 5, see the section on syncing your notes.
- **Photos.** In Chapter 6, see the section on syncing photos.
- **eBooks.** In Chapter 7, see the section on syncing eBooks.
- **Music, podcasts, and audiobooks.** In Chapter 8, see the section on syncing music and other audio content.
- **Movies and TV shows.** In Chapter 9, see the section on syncing videos.
- **Contacts.** In Chapter 10, see the section on syncing your contacts.
- **Calendars.** In Chapter 11, see the section on syncing your calendar.
- **Apps.** In Chapter 13, see the section on syncing your apps.

When your sync settings are straight, you click the iTunes Sync button to perform the synchronization.

Genius

After you've decided which content you want synced, you may find that you rarely change those settings. In that case, you can reset automatic syncing by connecting your iPad, clicking your iPad in the iTunes Devices list, selecting the Automatically Sync when this iPad is Connected check box in the Summary tab, and then clicking Apply. This way, each time you connect your iPad, iTunes automatically syncs just the content you selected.

Taking Syncing to a Higher Level

Syncing data between your iPad and your Mac or PC isn't complicated, and most of the time it's a straight connect and sync task. I'm loath to add complexity to such an admirably simple procedure, but you need to know how to handle the main sync challenges that might come your way. The next few sections show you how to handle sync conflicts, deal with large sync changes, replace and refresh iPad data, and merge and sync data from two or more computers.

Handling conflicting sync changes

When you sync information between your iPad and a computer, you might think it's exclusively new data that's being transferred: new songs, new contacts, new calendar appointments, and so on. However, the sync also includes edited or changed data. For example, if you change someone's e-mail address on your iPad, the next time you sync, iTunes updates the e-mail address on the computer, which is exactly what you want.

However, what if you already changed that person's address on the computer? If you made the same edit, it's no big deal because there's nothing to sync. But what if you made a different edit? Ah, that's a problem, because

2.4 If you make different edits to the same bit of information on your iPad and your computer, the Conflict Resolver springs into action.

now iTunes doesn't know which version has the correct information. In that case, it shrugs its digital shoulders and passes off the problem to a program called Conflict Resolver, which displays the dialog shown in Figure 2.4.

If you want to deal with the problem now, click Review Now. Conflict Resolver offers you the details of the conflict. For example, in Figure 2.5 you can see that a contact's work e-mail address is different in Address Book and on the iPad. To settle the issue once and for all (you hope), click the correct version of the information, and then click Done. When Conflict Resolver tells you it will fix the problem during the next sync, click Sync Now to make it happen right away.

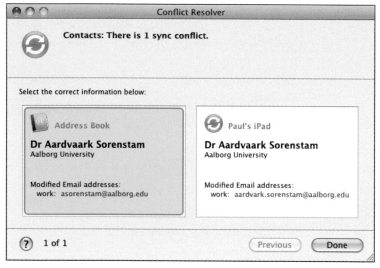

2.5 Review Now shows you the details of any conflicts.

Handling large iPad-to-computer sync changes

Syncing works both ways: Not only does your iPad receive content from your computer, but your computer also receives content from your iPad. For example, if you create any bookmarks, contacts, or appointments on your iPad, those items get sent to your computer during the sync.

However, it's implied that the bulk of the content flows from your computer to your iPad, which makes sense because for most things it's a bit easier to add, edit, and delete stuff on the computer. So that's why if you make lots of changes to your iPad content, iTunes displays a warning that the sync is going to make lots of changes to your computer content. The threshold is five percent, which means that if the sync changes more than five percent of a particular type of content on your computer — such as bookmarks or calendars — the warning appears. For example, Figure 2.6 shows the Sync Alert dialog you see if the sync will change more than five percent of your computer's bookmarks.

Information	Add	Modify	Delete
Contacts	117	2	0

Sync Alert: Syncing with Paul's iPad will change more than 25% of your contacts or groups on this computer.

2.6 iTunes warns you if the sync will mess with more than five percent of your computer's content.

If you're expecting this (because you *did* change lots of stuff on your iPad), click the Sync *Whatever* button, where *Whatever* is the type of data: Bookmarks, Contacts, and so on. If you're not sure, click Show Details to see what the changes are. If you're still scratching your head, click Sync Later to skip that part of the sync.

If you're running iTunes for Windows, you can either turn off this warning or adjust the threshold. (For some unfathomable reason, iTunes for the Mac doesn't offer this handy option.) Follow these steps:

1. **Choose Edit ⇨ Preferences, or press Ctrl+, (comma).** The iTunes dialog comes aboard.

2. **Click the Devices tab.**

3. **If you want to disable the sync alerts altogether, deselect the Warn When check box.** Otherwise, leave that check box selected and move to Step 4.

4. **Use the Warn When *Percent* of the Data on the Computer will be Changed list to set the alert threshold, where *percent* is one of the following:**

- **any.** Select this option to see the sync alert whenever syncing with the iPad will change data on your computer. iPad syncs routinely modify data on the computer, so be prepared to see the alerts every time you sync. (Of course, that may be exactly what you want.)

- **more than X%.** Select one of these options — your choices are 5% (the default), 25%, and 50% — to see the alert only when the sync will change more than X percent of some data type on the computer.

5. **Click OK to put the new settings into effect.**

Removing data from your iPad and replacing it with fresh info

After you know what you're doing, syncing contacts, calendars, e-mail accounts, and bookmarks to your iPad is a relatively bulletproof procedure that should happen without a hitch each time. Of course, this is technology we're dealing with here, so hitches do happen every now and then, and as a result you might end up with corrupt or repeated information on your iPad.

Or perhaps you've been syncing your iPad with a couple of different computers (see the section on syncing media with two or more computers later in this chapter), and you decide to cut one of the computers out of the loop and revert to just a single machine for all your syncs.

In both these scenarios, you need to replace the existing information on your iPad with a freshly baked batch of data. Fortunately, iTunes has a feature that lets you do exactly that. Here's how it works:

1. **Connect your iPad to your computer.**

2. **In the iTunes Devices list, click the iPad.**

3. **Click the Info tab.**

4. **Select the Sync check boxes for each type of information you want to work with (contacts, calendars, e-mail accounts, bookmarks, or notes).** If you don't select a check box, iTunes won't replace that information on your iPad. For example, if you like your iPad bookmarks just the way they are, don't select the Sync Bookmarks check box.

5. **In the Advanced section, select the check box beside each type of information you want to replace.** Figure 2.7 shows five check boxes: Contacts, Calendars, Bookmarks, Notes, and Mail Accounts.

6. **Click Apply.** iTunes replaces the selected information on your iPad.

| Summary | Info | Apps | Music | Movies | TV Shows | Podcasts | iTunes U | Books | Photos |

Syncing Mail accounts syncs your account settings, but not your messages. To add accounts or make other changes, tap Settings then Mail, Contacts, Calendars on this iPad.

Other

☑ Sync Safari bookmarks
☐ Sync notes

Advanced

Replace information on this iPad:
☑ Contacts
☑ Calendars
☐ Mail Accounts
☑ Bookmarks
☐ Notes

During the next sync only, iTunes will replace the selected information on this iPad with information from this computer.

2.7 Use the check boxes in the Advanced section to decide which information to replace on your iPad.

Note

If a check box in the Advanced section is disabled, it's because you didn't select the corresponding Sync check box. For example, in Figure 2.7 you see that the Sync Notes check box is deselected, so in the Advanced section, the Notes check box is disabled.

Merging data from two or more computers

Long gone are the days when our information resided on a single computer. Now it's common to have a desktop computer (or two) at home, a work computer, a smartphone (such as an iPhone), and of course your iPad. It's nice to have all that digital firepower, but it creates a big problem: You end up with contacts, calendars, and other information scattered over several machines. How are you supposed to keep track of it all?

Apple's latest solution is MobileMe, which provides seamless information integration across multiple computers (Mac and Windows), and I talk about it later in this chapter (see the section on syncing your iPad with MobileMe).

If you don't have a MobileMe account, you can still achieve a bit of data harmony. That's because iTunes offers the welcome ability to *merge* information from two or more computers on the IPad. For example, if you have contacts on your home computer, you can sync them with your IPad. If you have a separate collection of contacts on your notebook, you can also sync them with your iPad, but iTunes gives you two choices:

- **Merge Info.** With this option, your iPad keeps the information synced from the first computer and merges it with the information synced from the second computer.

- **Replace Info.** With this option, your iPad deletes the information synced from the first computer and replaces it with the information synced from the second computer.

Follow these general steps to set up your merged information:

1. **Sync your iPad with information from one computer.** This technique works with contacts, calendars, e-mail accounts, and bookmarks.

2. **Connect your iPad to the second computer.**

3. **In iTunes, click your iPad in the Devices list.**

4. **Click the Info tab.**

5. **Select the Sync check boxes that correspond to information already synced on the first computer.** For example, if you synced contacts on the first computer, select the Sync Contacts check box.

6. **Click Apply.** iTunes displays a dialog like the one shown in Figure 2.8.

2.8 You can merge contacts, calendars, e-mail accounts, and bookmarks from two or more computers.

7. **Click Merge Info.** iTunes syncs your iPad and merges the computer's information with the existing information from the first computer.

Syncing media with two or more computers

It's a major drag, but you can't sync the same type of content to your iPad from more than one computer. For example, suppose you're syncing photos from your desktop computer. If you then connect your iPad to another computer (your notebook, for example), crank up iTunes, and select the Sync Photos from check box, iTunes coughs up the dialog in Figure 2.9. As you can see, iTunes is telling you that if you go ahead with the photo sync on this computer, it will blow away all your existing iPad photos and albums!

So there's no chance of syncing the same iPad with two different computers, right? Not so fast, my friend. Let's try another thought experiment. Suppose you're syncing your iPad with your desktop computer, but you're not syncing Movies. Again, you connect your iPad to your notebook computer (or whatever), crank up iTunes, and select the Sync Movies check box. Hey, no ominous warning dialog! What gives?

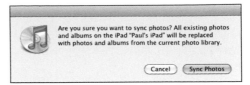

Are you sure you want to sync photos? All existing photos and albums on the iPad "Paul's iPad" will be replaced with photos and albums from the current photo library.

Cancel   Sync Photos

2.9 Syncing the same type of content from two different computers is a no-no in the iTunes world.

The deal here is that if iTunes sees that you don't have any examples of a particular type of content (such as movies) on your iPad, it lets you sync that type of content, no questions asked.

In other words, you *can* sync your iPad with multiple computers, although in a roundabout kind of way. The secret is to have no overlapping content types on the various computers you use for the syncing. For example, let's say you have a home desktop computer, a notebook computer, and a work desktop computer. Here's a sample scenario for syncing your iPad with all three machines:

- **Home desktop (music and video only).** Select the Sync music check box in the Music tab, and select all the Sync check boxes in the Video tab. Deselect the Sync check boxes on the Photos and Podcasts tabs.

- **Notebook (photos only).** Select the Sync photos from check box on the Photos tab. Deselect all the Sync check boxes in the Music, Podcasts, and Video tabs.

- **Work desktop (podcasts only).** Select the Sync box in the Podcasts tab. Deselect the Sync check boxes in the Music, Photos, and Video tabs.

Syncing Your iPad with MobileMe

When you go online, you take your life along with you, of course, so your online world becomes a natural extension of your real world. However, just because it's online doesn't mean the digital version of your life is any less busy, chaotic, or complex than the rest of your life. Apple's MobileMe service is designed to ease some of that chaos and complexity by automatically syncing your most important data — your e-mail, contacts, calendars, and bookmarks. Although the syncing itself may be automatic, setting it up is not, unfortunately. The rest of this chapter shows you what to do.

MobileMe works particularly well with the iPad, because when you're on the town or on the road, you need data pushed to you. To ensure your iPad works seamlessly with your MobileMe data, you need to add your MobileMe account and configure the iPad's MobileMe sync settings.

Setting up your MobileMe account on your iPad

Start by setting up your MobileMe account on your iPad:

1. **On the Home screen, tap Settings.** Your iPad opens the Settings screen.

2. **Tap Mail, Contacts, Calendars.** The Mail, Contacts, Calendars screen appears.

3. **Tap Add Account.** The Add Account screen appears.

4. **Tap the MobileMe logo.** Your iPad displays the MobileMe screen, as shown in Figure 2.10.

5. **Tap the Name text box, and enter your name.**

6. **Tap the Address text box, and enter your MobileMe e-mail address.**

7. **Tap the Password text box, and enter your MobileMe password.** You also can tap the Description text box and enter a short description of the account.

8. **Tap Next.** Your iPad verifies the account info and displays the MobileMe screen, as shown in Figure 2.11.

2.10 Use the MobileMe screen to configure your MobileMe account on your iPad.

2.11 Use this MobileMe screen to activate push e-mail, contacts, calendars, and bookmarks.

9. **If you want to use push e-mail, leave the Mail switch set to On.**

10. **If you want to use push contacts, tap the Contacts switch to On and then tap Sync.**

11. **If you want to use push calendars, tap the Calendars switch to On and then tap Sync.**

12. **If you want to use push bookmarks, tap the Bookmarks switch to On and then tap Sync.**

13. **Tap Save.** Your iPad returns you to the Mail settings screen with your MobileMe account added to the Accounts list.

Setting up MobileMe synchronization on your iPad

The "mobile" part of MobileMe means that no matter where you are, your e-mail messages, contacts, and calendars get pushed to your iPad and remain fully synced with all your other devices. Your iPad comes with this push feature turned on, but if you want to double-check this, or if you want to turn off push in order to concentrate on something else, you can configure the setting by following these steps:

1. **In the Home Screen, tap Settings.** The Settings screen appears.

2. **Tap Mail, Contacts, Calendars.** The Mail, Contacts, Calendars screen appears.

3. **Tap Fetch New Data.** Your iPad displays the Fetch New Data screen, as shown in Figure 2.12.

2.12 You use the Fetch New Data screen to configure MobileMe synchronization on your iPad.

4. **If you want MobileMe data sent to you automatically, tap the Push switch to the On position.** Otherwise, tap Push to the Off position.

5. **If you turned push off, or if your iPad includes applications that don't support push, tap the frequency with which your iPad should fetch new data: Every 15 Minutes, Every 30 Minutes, Hourly, or Manually.**

If you want to keep your Mac in sync with MobileMe's push services, you need to add your MobileMe account to the Mail application and configure your Mac's MobileMe synchronization feature.

Setting up your MobileMe account on your Mac

Follow these steps to get your MobileMe account into the Mail application:

1. **In the Dock, click the Mail icon.** The Mail application appears.

2. **Choose Mail ⇨ Preferences to open the Mail preferences.**

3. **Click the Accounts tab.**

4. **Click +.** Mail displays the Add Account dialog.

5. **Type your name in the Full Name text box.**

6. **Type your MobileMe e-mail address in the Email Address text box.**

7. **Type your MobileMe password in the Password text box.**

8. **Leave the Automatically set up account check box selected.**

9. **Click Create.** Mail verifies the account info and returns you to the Accounts tab with the MobileMe account added to the Accounts list.

Setting up MobileMe synchronization on your Mac

Macs were made to sync with MobileMe, so syncing should be a no-brainer. To ensure that's the case, you need to configure your Mac to make sure MobileMe sync is activated and that your e-mail accounts, contacts, and calendars are part of the sync process. Follow these steps to set your preferences:

1. **Click the System Preferences icon in the Dock.** Your Mac opens the System Preferences window.

2. **In the Internet & Wireless section, click the MobileMe icon.** The MobileMe preferences appear.

3. **Click the Sync tab.**

4. **Select the Synchronize with MobileMe check box.** Your Mac enables the check boxes beside the various items you can sync, as shown in Figure 2.13.

5. **In the Synchronize with MobileMe list, choose Automatically.**

6. **Select the check box beside each data item you want to sync with your MobileMe account, particularly the following push-related items:**

   - **Bookmarks**
   - **Calendars**
   - **Contacts**
   - **Mail Accounts**

7. **Click the Close button.** Your Mac is now ready for MobileMe syncing.

2.13 Select the Synchronize with MobileMe check box, and then select the items you want to sync.

Configuring your MobileMe account on your Windows PC

MobileMe is happy to push data to your Windows PC. However, unlike with a Mac, your Windows machine wouldn't know MobileMe if it tripped over it. To get Windows hip to the MobileMe thing, you need to do two things:

- **Download and install the latest version of iTunes (at least version 9).**
- **Download and install the MobileMe Control Panel for Windows, which you can find here:** http://support.apple.com/downloads/MobileMe_Control_Panel_for_Windows.

With that done, you now configure MobileMe to work with your Windows PC by following these steps:

1. **On the Windows PC that you want to configure to work with MobileMe, choose Start ⇨ Control Panel to open the Control Panel window.**

2. **Double-click the MobileMe icon.** If you don't see this icon, first open the Network and Internet category. The MobileMe Preferences window appears.

3. **Use the Member Name text box to type your MobileMe member name.**

4. **Use the Password text box to type your MobileMe password.**

5. **Click Sign In.** Windows signs in to your account.

6. **Click the Sync tab.**

7. **Select the Sync with MobileMe check box, and then choose Automatically in the Sync with MobileMe list, as shown in Figure 2.14.**

8. **Select the Contacts check box, and then use the Contacts list to select the address book you want to sync.**

9. **Select the Calendars check box, and then use the Calendars list to select the calendar you want to sync.**

10. **Select the Bookmarks check box, and then use the Bookmarks list to select the Web browser you want to sync.**

11. **If you want to run a sync immediately, click Sync Now.**

12. **If you see the First Sync Alert dialog, choose Merge Data and click Allow.**

13. **Click OK.**

2.14 Use the MobileMe Preferences dialog to set up your Windows PC to work with MobileMe.

How Do I Configure My iPad?

If you've made your way through the first two chapters of the book, then you're connected to a network and you have all your desktop data synced to your iPad. This book should end there, right? What else could anyone need? Ah, you'd be surprised. Although the iPad works like a champ right out of the box, even champs can improve their game. In particular, you may find that your iPad's default settings make sense for the average user, but you and I both know you're far from average (because, of course, you bought this book!). This chapter helps you fix that by showing you how to configure your iPad to work the way you do.

Creating a Custom Home Screen

When you first start your iPad, and each time you press the Home button, the Home screen appears, and you use this screen as the launching pad (so to speak) for all your iPad adventures. Using the Home screen requires almost no training: Just tap the icon you want, and the app loads lickety-split. It's perfection itself.

Oh, but things are never as perfect as they appear, are they? In fact, you'll find several hairs in the Home screen soup:

- The icons in the top row are a bit easier to find and a bit easier to tap.

- If you have more than 20 icons, they extend onto a second (or third or fourth) Home screen. If the app you want isn't on the main Home screen, you must first flick to the screen that has the app's icon (or tap the dot for the screen you want) and then tap the icon.

- If your icons extend onto multiple Home screens, the four icons in the iPad's Dock area appear on every Home screen, so they're always available.

Note

How do you end up with more than 20 icons? Easy: the App Store. This is an online retailer solely devoted to apps designed to work with the iPad's technologies: multi-touch, GPS, the accelerometer, wireless, and more. You can download apps via your cellular network or your Wi-Fi connection, so you can always get apps when you need them. On the Home screen, tap the App Store icon to see what's available.

All this means that you can make the Home screen more efficient by doing three things: moving your four most-used icons to iPad's Dock, moving four other commonly used icons to the top row of the main Home screen, and making sure any icon you tap frequently appears somewhere on the main Home screen.

You can do all this by rearranging the Home screen icons as follows:

1. **Display the Home screen.**

2. **Tap and hold any Home screen icon.** When you see the icons wiggling, release your finger.

3. **Tap and drag the icons into the positions you prefer.** To move an icon to a different screen, tap and drag the icon to the left edge of the current screen (if you want to move it to a previous screen) or to the right edge of the current screen (if you want to move it to a later screen), wait for the new screen to appear, and then drop the icon where you want it. You can include a maximum of six icons on the Dock. So if you have room, you can drop the icon on the Dock.

4. **Rearrange the existing Dock icons by dragging them left or right to change the order.**

5. **To replace a Dock icon, first tap and drag the icon off the Dock to create some space, then tap and drag any Home screen icon into the Dock.**

6. **Press the Home button.** iPad saves the new icon arrangement.

Moving unused icons off the main Home screen

The best way to make the main Home screen more manageable is to get rid of any icons you don't use. No need for note-taking? Get rid of the Notes icon! No time to watch talking cats and other online videos? Say so long to the YouTube icon! Installed a bunch of apps you use only rarely? Get rid of them, too!

Unfortunately, you can't delete the default iPad icons, and although you can uninstall any third-party apps, you probably don't want to go that far for any app you still use once in a while. The solution to both problems is to create a new Home screen and move your seldom-used icons to that screen. That way, your main Home screen holds just your favorite icons, and the ones you use once in a blue moon (or never) are out of the way.

Follow these steps to clean up your Home screen:

1. **On the Home screen, tap and hold any Home screen icon until you see all the icons wiggling.**

2. **For each icon you want off the main Home screen, tap and drag the icon to the right until the new Home screen appears, and then release the icon.**

3. **Press the Home button.** iPad saves your new icon arrangement.

Adding a Safari Web Clip to the Home screen

Do you visit a certain Web page all the time? You can set up a bookmark to that page in iPad's Safari browser, but an even faster way to access the page is to add it to the Home screen as a Web Clip icon. A *Web Clip* is a link to a page that preserves the page's scroll position and zoom level. For example, suppose a page has a form at the bottom. To use that form, you have to navigate to the page, scroll to the bottom, and then zoom into the form to see it better. However, you can perform all three actions — navigate, scroll, and zoom — automatically with a Web Clip.

Follow these steps to save a page as a Web Clip icon on the Home screen:

1. **Use your iPad's Safari browser to navigate to the page you want to save.**

2. **Scroll to the portion of the page you want to see.**

3. **Pinch and spread your fingers over the area you want to zoom in on until you can comfortably read the text.**

4. **Press + at the top of the screen.** iPad displays a list of options.

5. **Tap Add to Home Screen.** iPad prompts you to edit the Web Clip name, as shown in Figure 3.1.

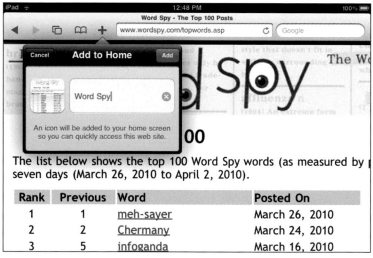

3.1 You can edit the Web Clip name before adding the icon to the Home screen.

6. **Edit the name as needed.** Names up to about 10-14 characters can be displayed on the Home screen without being broken. (The fewer uppercase letters you use, the longer the

name can be.) For longer names, iPad displays the first few and last few characters (depending on the locations of spaces in the name), separated by an ellipsis (...). For example, if the name is My Home Page, it appears in the Home screen as My Ho...Page.

7. **Tap Add.** iPad adds the Web Clip to the Home screen and displays the Home screen. (If your main Home screen is already full to the brim with icons, iPad adds the Web Clip to the first screen that has space available.) Figure 3.2 shows a Home screen with a Web Clip added.

3.2 The Web Clip has been added to the Home screen.

Genius

To delete a Web Clip from the Home screen, tap and hold any Home screen icon until the icon dance begins. Each Web Clip icon displays an X in the upper-left corner. Tap the X of the Web Clip you want to remove. When iPad asks you to confirm, tap Delete and press the Home button to save the configuration.

Resetting the default Home screen layout

If you make a bit of a mess of your Home screen, or if someone else is going to be using your iPad, you can reset the Home screen icons to their default layout. Follow these steps:

1. **On the Home screen, tap Settings.** The Settings screen appears.

2. **Tap General.** The General screen appears.

3. **Tap Reset.** The Reset screen appears.

4. **Tap Reset Home Screen Layout.** iPad warns you that the Home screen will be reset to the factory default layout.

5. **Tap Reset.** iPad resets the home screen to the default layout, but it doesn't delete the icons for any apps you've added.

Protecting iPad with a Passcode

When your iPad is asleep, the device is locked in the sense that tapping the touchscreen or pressing the volume controls does nothing. This sensible arrangement prevents accidental taps when the device is in your pocket or rattling around in your backpack or handbag. To unlock the device, you press either the Home button or the Sleep/Wake button and then drag the Slide to Unlock slider, and you're back in business.

Unfortunately, this simple technique means that anyone else who gets his or her mitts on your iPad also can be quickly back in business — *your* business! If you have sensitive or confidential information on your device, or if you want to avoid digital joyrides that run up massive roaming or data charges, you need to truly lock your iPad.

You do that by specifying a four-digit passcode that must be entered before anyone can use the iPad. Follow these steps to set up your passcode:

1. **On the Home screen, tap Settings.** The Settings screen appears.

2. **Tap General.** The General screen appears.

3. **Tap Passcode Lock.** The Passcode Lock screen appears.

4. **Tap Turn Passcode On.** The Set Passcode screen appears as shown in Figure 3.3.

5. **Tap your four-digit passcode.** For security, the numbers appear in the Enter a passcode box as dots. When you finish, iPad prompts you to reenter the passcode.

6. **Tap your four-digit passcode again.**

Caution You really, really need to remember your iPad passcode! If you forget it, you're locked out of your own device and the only way to get back in is to completely reset the iPad (as described later in this chapter).

3.3 Use the Set Passcode screen to lock your iPad with a four-digit passcode.

With your passcode now active, iPad displays the Passcode Lock screen. (You also can get to this screen by tapping Settings in the Home screen, then General, then Passcode Lock.) This screen offers five buttons:

- **Turn Passcode Off.** If you want to stop using your passcode, tap this button and enter the passcode (for security; otherwise an interloper could just shut off the passcode).

- **Change Passcode.** Tap this button to enter a new passcode. (Note that you first need to enter your old passcode and then enter the new passcode.)

- **Require Passcode.** This setting determines how much time elapses before the iPad locks the device and requests the passcode. The default setting is Immediately, which means you see the Enter Passcode screen (see Figure 3.4) as soon as you finish dragging Slide to Unlock. The other options are After 1 minute, After 5 minutes, After 15 minutes, After 1 hour, and After 4 hours. Use one of these settings if you want to be able to work with your iPad for a bit before getting locked out. For example, the After 1 minute option is good if you need to quickly check e-mail without having to enter your passcode.

- **Picture Frame.** Tap this setting to Off if you don't want your iPad used as a picture frame while it's locked.

● **Erase Data.** When this setting in On, your iPad will self-destruct, er, I mean erase all its data when it detects ten incorrect passcode attempts. Ten failed passcode attempts almost always means that some nasty person has your device and is trying to guess the passcode. If you have sensitive or private data on your device, having the data erased automatically is a good idea.

With the passcode activated, when you bring the iPad out of standby, you drag the Slide to Unlock slider as usual, and then the Enter Passcode screen appears, as shown in Figure 3.4. Type your passcode to unlock the iPad.

3.4 To unlock your iPad, you need to enter your four-digit passcode.

Configuring When iPad Goes to Sleep

You can put your iPad into Standby mode at any time by pressing the Sleep/Wake button once. This drops the power consumption considerably (mostly because it shuts off the screen), but you can still receive incoming notifications, and if you have the iPod app running, it continues to play.

However, if your iPad is on but you're not using it, the device automatically goes into standby mode after five minutes. This is called Auto-Lock, and it's a handy feature because it saves battery power (and prevents accidental taps) when your iPad is just sitting there.

If you're not comfortable with the default five-minute Auto-Lock interval, you can make it shorter or longer, or you can disable it altogether. Follow these steps:

1. **On the Home screen, tap Settings.** The Settings screen appears.

2. **Tap General.** The General screen appears.

3. **Tap Auto-Lock.** The Auto-Lock screen appears, as shown in Figure 3.5.

4. **Tap the interval you want to use.** You have five choices: 2 minutes, 5 minutes, 10 minutes, 15 minutes, or Never.

3.5 Use the Auto-Lock screen to set the Auto-Lock interval or to turn it off.

Turning Sounds On and Off

Your iPad is often a noisy little thing that makes all manner of rings, beeps, and boops, seemingly at the slightest provocation. Consider a short list of the events that can give the iPad's lungs a workout:

- Incoming e-mail messages
- Outgoing e-mail messages
- Calendar alerts
- Locking and unlocking the device
- Tapping the keys on the on-screen keyboard

What a racket! None of this may bother you when you're on your own, but if you're in a meeting, a movie, or anywhere else where extraneous sounds are unwelcome, you may want to turn off some or all of the iPad's sound effects.

To prevent this faux pas, you can switch your iPad into silent mode, which means it doesn't play any alerts or sound effects.

You switch the iPad between regular and silent modes using the Volume rocker. Use the following techniques to switch between silent and regular modes:

- To put the device in silent mode, tap the bottom part of the Volume rocker (or, if you're in landscape mode, the right side of the Volume rocker) until the Volume icon goes dark.

- To resume the regular mode, tap the top part of the Volume rocker (or if you're in landscape mode, the left side of the Volume rocker) until the Volume icon shows the sound level you want.

If silent mode is a bit too drastic, you can control exactly which sounds your iPad utters by following these steps:

1. **On the Home screen, tap Settings.** The Settings screen appears.

2. **Tap Sounds.** The Sounds screen appears, as shown in Figure 3.6.

3. **Drag the volume slider to set the overall volume of the iPad.**

4. **For the rest of the settings, such as New Mail and Calendar Alerts, tap the On/Off switch to turn each sound on or off.**

iPad 📶	1:06 PM	100% 🔋

Settings | ◀ General **Sounds**

📶 **Wi-Fi**	Wireless429
🖼 **Brightness & Wallpaper**	
🖼 **Picture Frame**	
⚙ **General**	
✉ **Mail, Contacts, Calendars**	
🧭 **Safari**	
♫ **iPod**	
🎬 **Video**	
🌼 **Photos**	
🛍 **Store**	

◀ ———●——————— 🔊

New Mail	ON
Sent Mail	ON
Calendar Alerts	ON
Lock Sounds	ON
Keyboard Clicks	ON

3.6 Use the Sounds screen to turn the iPad's sounds on and off.

Adjusting the Brightness of the Screen

Your iPad's touchscreen offers a crisp, bright display that's easy to read in most situations. Unfortunately, keeping the screen bright enough to read comfortably extracts a heavy cost in battery power. To help balance screen brightness and battery life, your iPad comes with a built-in ambient light sensor. That sensor checks the surrounding light levels and adjusts the brightness of the iPad screen accordingly:

- If the ambient light is dim, the iPad screen is easier to read, so the sensor dims the screen brightness to save battery power.

- If the ambient light is bright, the iPad screen is harder to see, so the sensor brightens the screen to improve readability.

This feature is called Auto-Brightness, and it's sensible to let your iPad handle this stuff for you. However, if you're not happy with how Auto-Brightness works, or if you simply have an uncontrollable urge to tweak things, you can follow these steps to adjust the screen brightness by hand:

1. **On the Home screen, tap Settings.** The Settings screen appears.

2. **Tap Brightness & Wallpaper.** The Brightness & Wallpaper screen appears, as shown in Figure 3.7.

3. **Drag the Brightness slider left for a dimmer screen or right for a brighter screen.**

4. **To prevent your iPad from controlling the brightness automatically, turn the Auto-Brightness setting to Off.**

iPad 🛜	1:15 PM	99% 🔋
Settings	**Brightness & Wallpaper**	
🛜 **Wi-Fi** Wireless429		
Brightness & Wallpaper	☀ ━━━━━◯━━━━━ ☀	
📷 **Picture Frame**	**Auto-Brightness** `ON`	
⚙ **General**	**Wallpaper**	
✉ **Mail, Contacts, Calendars**		

3.7 Use the Brightness & Wallpaper screen to control the iPad's screen brightness by hand.

Note

Even if you leave Auto-Brightness turned on, you still may want to adjust the Brightness slider because this affects the relative brightness of the screen. For example, suppose you adjust the slider to increase brightness by 50 percent and you leave Auto-Brightness turned on. In this case, Auto-Brightness still adjusts the screen automatically, but any brightness level it chooses is 50 percent brighter than it would be otherwise.

Setting the iPad Wallpaper

The iPad wallpaper is the background image you see when you unlock the device. That is, it's the image you see when the Slide to Unlock screen appears, and also when the Enter Passcode screen appears if you're protecting your iPad with a passcode (as described earlier in this chapter). The default wallpaper is a pretty lake view at sunset with low hills in the background, and as nice as that photo is, you might just be getting a bit tired of looking at it. No worries! Your iPad comes with 19 other wallpapers you can choose, and you can even use one of your own photos as the wallpaper.

Using a predefined wallpaper

Follow these steps to use one of iPad's predefined wallpapers:

1. **On the Home screen, tap Settings.** The Settings screen appears.

2. **Tap Brightness & Wallpaper.** The Brightness & Wallpaper screen appears.

3. **Tap Wallpaper.** Your iPad prompts you to choose a photo source.

4. **Tap Wallpaper.** iPad displays its collection of wallpaper images, as shown in Figure 3.8.

5. **Tap the image you want to use.** The Wallpaper Preview screen appears.

6. **Tap Set Home Screen.** If you want to use the wallpaper for the lock screen, tap Set Lock Screen instead.

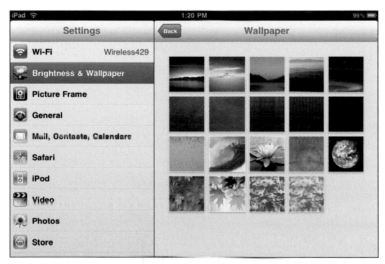

3.8 Your iPad comes with a number of predefined wallpaper images.

Using an existing photo as the wallpaper

If your iPad contains images in a photo album synced from your computer, you can use one of those images as your wallpaper by following these steps:

1. **On the Home screen, tap Settings.** The Settings screen appears.

2. **Tap Brightness & Wallpaper.** The Brightness & Wallpaper screen appears.

3. **Tap Wallpaper.** Your iPad prompts you to choose a photo source.

4. **Tap the photo album that contains the image you want to use.** iPad displays the images in the album you choose.

5. **Tap the image you want to use.** The Wallpaper Preview screen appears, as shown in Figure 3.9.

53

6. **Select where you want the wallpaper to appear.**

- **Set Lock Screen.** Tap this button to apply the wallpaper only to the Lock screen.

- **Set Home Screen.** Tap this button to apply the wallpaper only to the Home screen.

- **Set Both.** Tap this button to apply the wallpaper to the Lock screen and the Home screen.

7. **Tap and drag the image so it's positioned on the screen the way you want.**

8. **Pinch and spread your fingers over the image to set the zoom level you want.**

9. **Tap Set.** iPad sets the image as the wallpaper.

3.9 Use the Move and Scale screen to set the position and zoom level for the new wallpaper.

Connecting Your iPad with a Bluetooth Headset

Your iPad is configured to use a wireless technology called Bluetooth, which enables you to make wireless connections to other Bluetooth-friendly devices. Most Macs come with Bluetooth built in, and they can use it to connect to a wide range of Bluetooth devices, including a mouse, keyboard, cell phone, PDA, printer, digital camera, and even another Mac. Your iPad can at least connect to a Bluetooth headset, which lets you listen to music and movies without wires and without disturbing your neighbors.

In theory, connecting Bluetooth devices should be criminally easy: You turn on each device's Bluetooth feature — in Bluetooth jargon, you make the device *discoverable* — bring them within 33 feet of each other, and they connect without further ado. In practice, however, there's usually at least a bit of further ado (and sometimes plenty of it). This usually takes one or both of the following forms:

- **Making your device discoverable.** Unlike Wi-Fi devices that broadcast their signals constantly, most Bluetooth devices only broadcast their availability when you say so. This makes sense in many cases because you usually only want to connect a Bluetooth component such as a headset with a single device. By controlling when the device is discoverable, you ensure that it works only with the device you want it to.

- **Pairing the iPad and the device.** As a security precaution, many Bluetooth devices need to be *paired* with another device before the connection is established. In most cases, the pairing is accomplished by entering a multidigit *passkey* — your iPad calls it a PIN — that you must then enter into the Bluetooth device (assuming, of course, that it has some kind of keypad). In the case of a headset, the device comes with a default passkey that you must enter into your iPad to set up the pairing.

Making your iPad discoverable

So your first order of Bluetooth business is to ensure that your iPad is discoverable by activating the Bluetooth feature. First, check to see if Bluetooth is already on: In the status bar, look for the Bluetooth logo to the left of the battery status icon, as shown in Figure 3.10.

Bluetooth Icon

3.10 If your iPad is discoverable, you see the Bluetooth icon in the status bar.

If you don't see the Bluetooth icon, follow these steps to turn on Bluetooth and make your iPad discoverable:

1. **On the Home screen, tap Settings.** The Settings screen appears.

2. **Tap General.** The General screen appears.

3. **Tap Bluetooth.** The Bluetooth screen appears.

4. **Tap the Bluetooth On/Off button to change the setting to On, as shown in Figure 3.11.**

3.11 Use the Bluetooth screen to make your iPad discoverable.

Pairing your iPad with a Bluetooth headset

If you want to listen to music, headphones are a great way to go because the sound is often better than with the built-in iPad speakers, and no one else around is subjected to Weezer at top volume. Add Bluetooth into the mix, and you have an easy and wireless audio solution for your iPad.

Follow these general steps to pair your iPad with a Bluetooth headset:

1. **On the Home screen, tap Settings.** The Settings screen appears.

2. **Tap General.** The General screen appears.

3. **Tap Bluetooth.** The Bluetooth screen appears.

4. **If the headset has a separate switch or button that makes the device discoverable, turn on that switch or press that button.** Wait until you see the correct headset name appear in the Bluetooth screen, as shown in Figure 3.12.

3.12 When you make your Bluetooth headset discoverable, the device appears in the Bluetooth screen.

5. **Tap the name of the Bluetooth headset.** Your iPad should pair with the headset automatically, and you see Connected in the Bluetooth screen, as shown in Figure 3.13; you can skip the rest of these steps. Otherwise, you see the Enter PIN screen.

6. **Enter the headset's passkey in the PIN box.** See the headset documentation to get the passkey; it's often 0000.

7. **Tap Connect.** Your iPad pairs with the headset and returns you to the Bluetooth screen, where you now see Connected beside the headset name.

8. **Tap Quit, and the headset is ready to use.**

3.13 When you have paired your iPad with the Bluetooth headset, you see Connected beside the device in the Bluetooth screen.

Selecting a paired headset as the audio output device

After you've paired a Bluetooth headset, your iPad usually starts using the headset as the output device right away. If it doesn't, follow these steps to make it do so:

1. **On the Home screen, tap iPod.** The iPod app loads. At the top left of the screen, the iPod app shows the current output device. If you see a speaker icon (see Figure 3.14), it means your iPad is using the built-in speaker as the audio output device.

Speaker Icon

3.14 A speaker icon shows that your iPad is using the built in speaker for audio output.

2. **Tap the Bluetooth icon that appears in the status bar at the bottom of the screen.** The Audio Device dialog appears, as shown in Figure 3.15.

3. **Tap your paired Bluetooth headset.** Your iPad starts playing the song through the headset.

3.15 Use the Audio Device dialog to select your paired Bluetooth headset.

Unpairing your iPad from a Bluetooth headset

When you no longer plan to use a Bluetooth headset for a long period of time, you should unpair it from your iPad. Follow these steps:

1. **On the Home screen, tap Settings.** The Settings screen appears.

2. **Tap General.** The General screen appears.

3. **Tap Bluetooth.** The Bluetooth screen appears.

4. **Tap the name of the Bluetooth headset.**

5. **Tap Forget this Device.** Your iPad unpairs the headset.

More Useful iPad Configuration Techniques

You've seen quite a few handy iPad customization tricks so far, but you're not done yet, not by a long shot. The next few sections take you through a few more heart-warmingly useful iPad customization techniques.

Switching your iPad to Airplane mode

When you board a flight, aviation regulations in most countries are superstrict: no wireless signals of *any* kind, which means your iPad is a real hazard to sensitive airline equipment because it also transmits Wi-Fi and Bluetooth signals, even if no Wi-Fi receivers or Bluetooth devices are within 30,000 feet of your current position.

Your pilot or friendly flight attendant will suggest that everyone simply turn off their devices. Sure, that does the job, but darn it you have an iPad, which means you can do plenty of things outside of its wireless capabilities: listen to music or an audiobook, watch a show, view photos, and much more.

So how do you reconcile the no-wireless-and-that-means-*you* regulations with the iPad's multitude of wireless-free apps? You put your iPad into a special state called *Airplane mode*. This mode turns off the transceivers — the internal components that transmit and receive wireless signals — for the iPad's Wi-Fi and Bluetooth features. With your iPad now safely in compliance with federal aviation regulations, you're free to use any app that doesn't rely on wireless transmissions.

Follow these steps to activate Airplane mode in your iPad Wi-Fi + 3G:

1. **On the Home screen, tap Settings.** The Settings screen appears.

2. **Tap the Airplane Mode On/Off switch to turn this setting On.** Your iPad disconnects your cellular network and your wireless network (if you have a current connection). Notice, as well, that while Airplane mode is on, an Airplane icon appears in the status bar in place of the signal strength and network icons.

Note If a flight attendant sees you playing around with your iPad, he or she may ask you to confirm that the device is off. (One obviously iPad-savvy attendant even asked me if my device was in Airplane mode.) Showing the Airplane icon should be sufficient.

Configuring parental controls

If your children have access to your iPad, or if they have iPads of their own, you may be a bit worried about some of the content they might be exposed to on the Web, on YouTube, or in iTunes. Similarly, you may not want them installing apps or giving away their current location.

For all those and similar parental worries, you can sleep better at night by activating the iPad's parental controls. These controls restrict the content and activities kids can see and do. Here's how to set them up:

1. **On the Home screen, tap Settings.** The Settings screen appears.

2. **Tap General.** The General screen appears.

3. **Tap Restrictions.** The Restrictions screen appears.

4. **Tap Enable Restrictions.** iPad displays the Set Passcode screen, which you use to specify a four-digit code that you can use to override the parental controls. (Note that this passcode is not the same as the passcode lock code you learned about earlier in the chapter in the section covering how to protect your iPad with a passcode.)

5. **Tap the four-digit restrictions passcode, and then retype the code.** iPad returns you to the Restrictions screen and enables all the controls, as shown in Figure 3.16.

6. **In the Allow section, for each app or task, tap the On/Off switch to enable or disable the restriction.**

7. **If you don't want your children to be able to make purchases within apps, tap the In-App Purchases switch to Off.**

8. **Tap Ratings For, and then tap the country whose ratings you want to use.**

9. **For each of the content controls — Music & Podcasts, Movies, TV Shows, and Apps — tap the control, and then tap the highest rating you want your children to use.**

10. **Tap General.** iPad puts the new settings into effect.

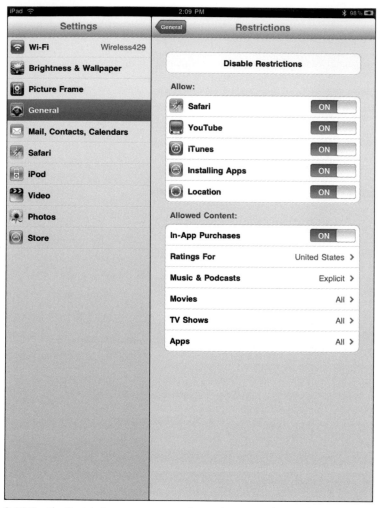

3.16 Use the Restrictions screen to configure the parental controls you want to use.

Customizing the Home button

The Home button is the starting point for most of your iPad excursions, and it seems like the simplest of the iPad knickknacks:

- If your iPad is in Standby mode, press the Home button to display the Slide to Unlock screen.

- If your iPad is already on, press the Home button to return to the Home screen.

- If your iPad is already on and showing the Home screen, press the Home button to display the Search screen.

That's it, right? Not so fast! You can actually customize the Home button to do some useful things. No, you can't change any of the built-in behaviors that your iPad performs when you press the Home button. However, you can customize what your iPad does when you "double-press" the Home button. Apple actually calls this "double-clicking" the Home button, which is at least more familiar terminology, so I'll switch to that for the rest of this section.

By default, your iPad performs one of the following actions when you double-click the Home button:

- If the iPod is playing, your iPad displays the iPod Playback controls.
- If the iPod is not playing, your iPad returns you to the Home page.

These are useful shortcuts to know, for sure, but you can customize this behavior by following these steps:

1. **On the Home screen, tap Settings.** The Settings screen appears.

2. **Tap General.** The General screen appears.

3. **Tap Home.** The Home screen appears, as shown in Figure 3.17.

4. **Tap the screen you want to appear when you double-click the Home button: Home, Search, or iPod.**

5. **If you always want to see the screen you chose in Step 4 when you double-click Home, tap the iPod Controls switch to Off.**

3.17 Use the Home screen to customize Home button double-clicks.

Customizing the keyboard

If you've never been a big fan of onscreen keyboards, particularly the stylus-activated keyboards on most tablet devices, or the iPhone keyboard, which is a bit too small for rapid and accurate typing, then I think you'll love the iPad keyboard. In landscape mode, the keyboard runs along the long edge of the iPad, meaning that it takes up the full eight inches of available screen width. To put this into perspective, the iPad's landscape keyboard is actually *wider* than the Apple Wireless Keyboard (if you measure just the letter keys, such as Q to P on the top row). In other words, your days of typing with a stylus or thumb are over. Unless you have basketball-player-size hands, with the iPad keyboard you can type normally. Yes!

The iPad keyboard even changes depending on the app you use. For example, the regular keyboard features a spacebar at the bottom. However, if you're surfing the Web with your iPad's Safari browser, the keyboard that appears when you type in the address bar does away with the spacebar. In its place you find a period (.), a slash (/), and a button that enters the characters *.com*. Web addresses don't use spaces so Apple replaced the spacebar with three things that commonly appear in a Web address. Nice!

Another nice innovation you get with the iPad keyboard is a feature called Auto-Capitalization. If you type a punctuation mark that indicates the end of a sentence — for example, a period (.), a question mark (?), or an exclamation mark (!) — or if you press Return to start a new paragraph, the iPad automatically activates the Shift key, because it assumes you're starting a new sentence.

On a related note, double-tapping the spacebar activates a keyboard shortcut: Instead of entering two spaces, the iPad automatically enters a period (.) followed by a space. This is a welcome bit of efficiency because otherwise you'd have to tap the Number key (.?123) to display the numbers and punctuation marks, tap the period (.), and then tap the spacebar.

Genius

Typing a number or punctuation mark normally requires three taps: tapping Number (.?123), tapping the number or symbol, and then tapping ABC. Here's a faster way: Tap and hold the Number key to open the numeric keyboard, slide the *same* finger to the number or punctuation symbol you want, and then release the key. This types the number or symbol and redisplays the regular keyboard all in one touch.

One thing the iPad keyboard doesn't seem to have is a Caps Lock feature that, when activated, enables you to type all-uppercase letters. To do this, you need to tap and hold the Shift key and then use a different finger to tap the uppercase letters. However, the iPad keyboard actually *does* have a Caps Lock feature; it's just that it's turned off by default.

To turn on Caps Lock, and to control the Auto-Capitalization and the spacebar double-tap short-cut, follow these steps:

1. **On the Home screen, tap Settings.** The Settings screen appears.

2. **Tap General.** The General screen appears.

3. **Tap Keyboard.** The Keyboard screen appears, as shown in Figure 3.18.

iPad	2:17 PM	∗ 99%
Settings	General	**Keyboard**

Wi-Fi — Wireless429
Brightness & Wallpaper
Picture Frame
General
Mail, Contacts, Calendars
Safari
iPod
Video
Photos
Store

Auto-Correction — ON
Auto-Capitalization — ON
Enable Caps Lock — OFF
"." Shortcut — ON

Double tapping the space bar will insert a period followed by a space.

International Keyboards — 1 >

3.18 Use the Keyboard screen to customize a few keyboard settings.

4. **If you no longer want your iPad to suggest spelling corrections as you type, tap Auto-Correction to Off.**

5. **Use the Auto-Capitalization setting to turn this feature On or Off.**

6. **Use the Enable Caps Lock setting to turn this feature On or Off.**

7. **Use the "." Shortcut setting to turn this feature On or Off.**

8. **To add an international keyboard layout, tap International Keyboards to open the Keyboards screen, and then set the keyboard layout you want to add to On.**

Note

When you're using two or more keyboard layouts, the keyboard sprouts a new key to the left of the spacebar (it looks like a stylized globe). Tap that key to run through the layouts, the names of which appear briefly in the spacebar.

Resetting the iPad

If you've spent quite a bit of time in the iPad's Settings screen, your device probably doesn't look much like it did fresh out of the box. That's okay, though, because your iPad should be as individual as you are. However, if you've gone a bit *too* far with your customizations, your iPad might feel a bit alien and uncomfortable. That's okay, too, because I know an easy solution to the problem: You can erase all your customizations and revert the iPad to its default settings.

A similar problem comes up when you want to sell or give your iPad to someone else. Chances are good that you don't want the new owner to see your data — contacts, appointments, e-mail, favorite Web sites, music, and so on — and it's unlikely the other person wants to wade through all that stuff anyway (no offense). To solve this problem, you can erase not only your custom settings, but also all the content you stored on the iPad.

The iPad's Reset app handles these scenarios and a few more to boot. Here's how it works:

1. **On the Home screen, tap Settings.** The Settings screen appears.

2. **Tap General.** The General screen appears.

3. **Tap Reset.** The Reset screen appears, as shown in Figure 3.19.

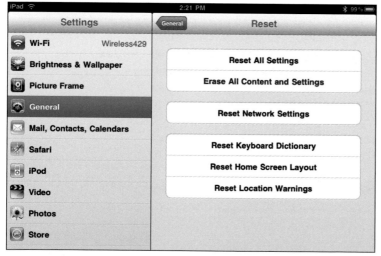

3.19 Use the Reset screen to reset various aspects of your iPad.

Caution

If you have any content on your iPad that isn't synced with iTunes — for example, iTunes music you've recently downloaded or an Apps Store program you've recently installed — you lose that content if you choose Reset All Content and Settings. First sync your iPad with your computer to save your content, and then run the reset.

4. **Tap one of the following reset options:**

   - **Reset All Settings.** Tap this option to reset your custom settings to the factory default settings.

   - **Erase All Content and Settings.** Tap this option to reset your custom settings and remove any data you stored on the iPad.

   - **Reset Network Settings.** Tap this option to delete your Wi-Fi network settings, which is often an effective way to solve Wi-Fi problems.

   - **Reset Keyboard Dictionary.** Tap this option to reset your keyboard dictionary. This dictionary contains a list of the keyboard suggestions that you've rejected. Tap this option to clear the dictionary and start fresh.

   - **Reset Home Screen Layout.** Tap this option to reset your Home screen icons to their default layout.

   - **Reset Location Warnings.** Tap this option to wipe out the location preferences for your apps. A location warning is the dialog you see when you start a GPS-aware app for the first time, and your iPad asks if the app can use your current location. You tap either OK or Don't Allow, and these are the preferences you're resetting here.

5. **When the iPad asks you to confirm, tap Reset.**

Note

Remember that the keyboard dictionary contains rejected suggestions. For example, if you type "Viv", iPad suggests "Big" instead. If you tap the "Big" suggestion to reject it and keep "Viv", the word "Big" is added to the keyboard dictionary.

Cutting, Copying, and Pasting Data

What do you do if, for example, you come across a snappy quotation in a Web page that you want to share with your friends? You *could* memorize the quote and then enter it by hand in, say, an e-mail message. Fortunately, your iPad offers an alternative that lets you avoid such drudgery: You can cut or copy text or photos, and then paste the data wherever you need it. Sweet! The next few sections provide the details.

Cutting, copying, and pasting text

How you select and then either cut or copy text depends on whether that text is editable or non-editable. The next two sections provide you with the details.

Selecting and copying non-editable text

The simplest case is non-editable text, such as you get on a Web page. In that scenario, when the text you want to use is on the screen, tap and hold anywhere within the text. After a second or two, your iPad selects the text and displays blue selection handles around it, as shown in Figure 3.20. If necessary, tap and drag the selection handles to select more or less of the text, and then tap Copy.

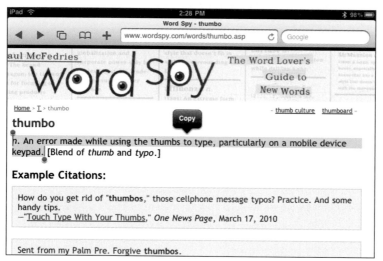

3.20 For text you can't edit, tap and hold within the text to select it, and then tap Copy to copy it.

Selecting and then cutting or copying editable text

If the text is editable, such as the text in a note, an e-mail message you're composing, or any text box, the process is more involved, but only ever so slightly:

1. **Tap and hold anywhere within the text.** After a short pause for effect, your iPad displays several buttons above the text, as shown in Figure 3.21.

3.21 For editable text, tap and hold within the text to see these options.

2. **Tap one of the following options:**

   - **Select.** Tap this button if you want to select only some of the text. Your iPad displays blue selection handles around the word you tapped.

   - **Select All.** Tap this button if you prefer to select all the text. The iPad displays the buttons shown in Figure 3.22; if you don't need to adjust the selection, skip to Step 4.

3. **Tap and drag the selection handles to select the text you want to work with.** The iPad displays a new set of buttons above the text, as shown in Figure 3.22.

3.22 Select your text, and choose what you want to do with it.

4. **Tap the action you want iPad to take with the text:**

   - **Cut.** Tap this button to remove the text and store it in the iPad's memory.

   - **Copy.** Tap this button to store a copy of the text in the iPad's memory.

Pasting text

With your text cut or copied and residing snugly in the iPad's memory, you're ready to paste the text. If you want to paste the text into a different app, open that app. Position the cursor where you want the text to appear, tap the cursor, and then tap Paste, as shown in Figure 3.23. Your iPad dutifully adds the cut or copied text.

3.23 Tap the cursor, and then tap Paste to place your cut or copied text in the app.

Copying and pasting a photo

If you want to make a copy of a photo, such as an image shown on a Web page, the process is more or less the same as copying non-editable text:

1. **Tap and hold the photo.** After a second or two, your iPad displays a pop-up menu of image options.
2. **Tap Copy.** The iPad copies the photo into its memory.
3. **Open the app where you want the copy of the photo to appear.**
4. **Position the cursor where you want the photo to appear, and then tap the cursor.**
5. **Tap Paste.** The iPad pastes the photo.

Undoing a paste

The Cut, Copy, and Paste commands make the iPad feel like a full computer. That's good, but it also means you can make the same pasting errors that you can with your regular computer. For example, you might paste the text or photo in the wrong spot, or after you've performed the paste, you might realize that you selected the wrong data.

Frustrating? Yes. A big problem? Nope! Slap your forehead lightly in exasperation, and then perform one of the iPad's coolest tricks: shake it. Your iPad displays the options shown in Figure 3.24. Tap Undo Paste to reverse your most recent paste, and then move on with your life.

3.24 Reverse an imprudent paste by shaking the iPad and tapping Undo Paste.

Searching Your iPad

Parkinson's Law of Data pithily encapsulates an inescapable fact of digital life: "Data expands to fill the space available for storage." So it doesn't matter whether you have a 16GB, 32GB, or 64GB iPad, you'll keep adding more data — music, photos, contacts, e-mail messages, Safari bookmarks, and on and on — and your iPad hard drive will inexorably fill up.

That's cool because it means you can bring more of your digital world with you wherever you go, but another law quickly comes into play; call it McFedries' Law of Digital Needles in Electronic Haystacks: "The more data you have, the harder it is to find what you need."

Fortunately, the iPad rides to the rescue here, too, by offering search features. As explained in the next couple of sections, you can search within some of the iPad apps, or you can search across the entire iPad.

Searching within an app

If you know the app that contains the data you're desperately searching for, you may be able to run your search directly within that app. Your iPad adds the search function to Mail, Contacts, Calendar, Notes, and iPod. Here's how it works:

1. **In the app, tap the status bar at the top of the screen.** This scrolls to the top of the app, where you see a Search box.
2. **Tap inside the Search box.** iPad displays the on-screen keyboard.

3. **Type your search text.**

4. **If the app supports field-specific searching, tap the button that corresponds to the field you want to search.** For example, in Mail, as shown in Figure 3.25, you can tap From, To, or Subject, or you can tap All to search the entire list of messages.

5. **Tap Search.** The app instantly displays the items that match your text.

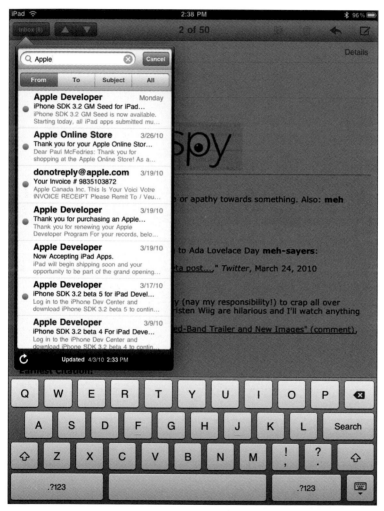

3.25 In an app that supports searching, tap the Search box, type your search text, and then tap Search.

Genius

When you search Mail, you may not find the message you're looking for. However, if you're using a service such as MobileMe or Gmail where the messages are stored on the server, you may not be out of luck. At the bottom of the Mail search results, if you see the Continue Search on Server command, tap it to perform your search on whatever remaining messages are stored on the server.

Searching across apps with Spotlight

If you use a Mac, then you probably know how indispensable the Spotlight search feature is. It's just a humble text box, but Spotlight enables you to find *anything* on your Mac in just a blink or two of an eye. It's an essential tool in this era of massive hard drives. (Windows 7 and Windows Vista users get much the same functionality with Start menu searches.)

The size of your iPad's hard drive might pale in comparison to your desktop's drive, but you can still pack an amazing amount of stuff into that tiny package, so you really need a way to search your *entire* iPad, not just an app or two. Your iPad comes through for you big time by offering a Spotlight search feature that enables you to search a variety of iPad data: e-mail, contacts, calendars, bookmarks, apps, and much more. And, best of all, Spotlight on the iPad is just as easy to use as Spotlight on the Mac:

1. **Tap the Home button to return to the Home screen.**

2. **Flick to the right, or press the Home button again.** The iPad displays the Spotlight screen, which is located just to the left of the main Home screen.

3. **Enter your search text.** Your iPad immediately begins displaying items that match your text as you type, as shown in Figure 3.26.

4. **Tap Search to see the complete results.** If you see the item you're looking for, tap it to open it.

Genius

If you find yourself using Spotlight searches all the time, it can be a bit of a pain to always have to return to the Home screen and then flick to get to the Spotlight screen. To save time, configure the Home button so that double-clicking it takes you directly to the Spotlight screen. See the section explaining how to customize the Home button earlier in this chapter for the details.

3.26 As you type, your iPad instantly begins displaying items that match your text.

Configuring Spotlight search settings

Spotlight looks for a variety of items within your iPad's hard drive. If you find you're getting too many results, you can configure Spotlight to search only selected sources, and you can change the order in which Spotlight returns the results. Here's how:

1. **On the Home screen, tap Settings.** The Settings screen appears.

2. **Tap General.** The General screen appears.

3. **Tap Home.** The Home screen appears.

4. **Tap Search Results.** The Search Results screen appears, as shown in Figure 3.27.

5. **For each item you want to rearrange in the results order, tap and drag the move handle on the right to position the item in the list.**

6. **For each item you don't want included in Spotlight search results, tap it to remove the check mark.**

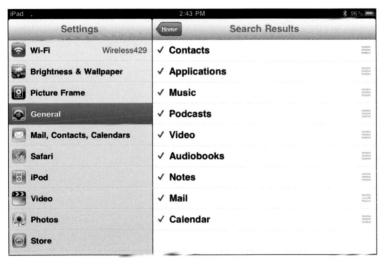

3.27 Use the Search Results screen to configure the items that Spotlight searches.

How Can I Get More Out of iPad Web Surfing?

When Apple announced the iPad in January 2010, one of the presenters was demonstrating the iPad's Safari Web browser and summarized the experience with a terrific line: "It just feels right to hold the Internet in your hands." That's about as succinct a description of Web surfing on the iPad as you're ever going to come across, not just because it's perfect in its pithiness, but also because the iPad just might be the ultimate Web surfing tool. It's portable, fast, intuitive, and offers *no* compromises — it shows actual, full-size Web pages, rendered as each site designer intended. However, that doesn't mean you can't make browsing on your iPad even better. This chapter takes you through my favorite tools and techniques for getting even more out of Web surfing on your iPad.

Touchscreen Tips for Web Surfing

The case in favor of crowning the iPad the best Web surfing appliance ever isn't hard to make: It's blazingly fast, it renders most sites perfectly, and the large screen means you almost always see a complete (horizontally, at least) view of the regular version of each page (rather than a partial view of the page or some ugly and dumbed-down mobile-only version of the page).

But what really sets the iPad's Web surfing apart not only from other tablet devices, but also from desktop, notebook, and netbook computers, is the touchscreen. With other devices, although you can click links and fill in forms, the page is really a static entity that just sits there. However, with the iPad (as well as its smaller touchscreen cousin, the iPhone), you can zoom into and out of the page by spreading and pinching your fingers, and you can pan the page by flicking a finger in the direction you want to go. You really feel as though you're not just interacting with the Web page, but *manipulating* the Web page with your bare hands!

The touchscreen is the key to efficient and fun Web surfing on the iPad, so here's a little collection of touchscreen tips that ought to make your Web excursions even easier and more pleasurable:

- **Double-tap.** A quick way to zoom in on a page that has various sections is to double-tap on the specific section — be it an image, a paragraph, a table, or a column of text — that you want magnified. Your iPad zooms the section to fill the width of the screen. Double-tap again to return the page to the regular view.

Note

The double-tap-to-zoom trick works only on pages that have identifiable sections. If a page is just a wall of text, you can double-tap until the cows come home (that's a long time) and nothing much happens.

- **Precision zooming.** Zooming on the iPad is straightforward: To zoom in, spread two fingers apart; to zoom out, pinch two fingers together. However, when you zoom in on a Web page, it's almost always because you want to zoom *in on* something. It may be an image, a link, a text box, or just a section of text. To ensure that your target ends up in the middle of the zoomed page, pinch your thumb and forefinger together on the screen as if you are pinching the target you want to zoom in on. Spread your thumb and forefinger apart to zoom in.

● **The old pan-and-zoom.** Another useful technique for getting a target in the middle of a zoomed page is to zoom and pan at the same time. That is, as you spread (or pinch) your fingers, you also move them up, down, left, or right to pan the page at the same time. This takes a bit of practice, and often the iPad allows you to pan either horizontally or vertically (not both), but it's still a useful trick.

● **One tap to the top.** If you're reading a particularly long-winded Web page and you're near the bottom, you may have quite a long way to scroll if you need to head back to the top to get at the address bar or tap the Search icon. Save the wear and tear on your flicking finger! Instead, tap the status bar; Safari immediately transports you to the top of the page.

● **Tap and hold to see where a link takes you.** You "click" a link in a Web page by tapping it with your finger. In a regular Web browser, you can see where a link takes you by hovering the mouse pointer over the link and checking out the link address in the status bar. That doesn't work in your iPad, of course, but you can still find out the address of a link before tapping it. Hold your finger on the link for a few seconds and Safari displays a pop-up screen that shows the link address, as shown in Figure 4.1. If the link looks legit, either tap Open to surf there in the current browser page, or tap Open in New Page to start a fresh page. (See the section about opening and managing multiple browser pages later in this chapter for more info on browser pages.) If you decide not to go there, click Cancel.

4.1 Hold your finger on a link to see the link address and several link options.

- **Tap and hold to make a copy of a link address.** If you want to include a link address in another app, such as a note or an email message, you can copy it. Tap and hold your finger on the link for a few seconds, and Safari displays the pop-up screen (refer to Figure 4.1). Click Copy to place the link address into memory, switch to the other app, tap the cursor, and then tap Paste.

- **Use the portrait view to navigate a long page.** When you rotate your iPad 90 degrees, the touchscreen switches to landscape view, which gives you a wider view of the page. Return the iPad to its upright position, and you return to portrait view. If you have a long way to scroll in a page, first use the portrait view to scroll down and then switch to the landscape view to increase the text size. Scrolling in the portrait view goes much faster than in landscape.

- **Two-fingered frame scrolling.** Some Web sites are organized using a technique called *frames*, where the overall site takes up the browser window, but some of the site's pages appear in a separate rectangular area — called a *frame* — usually with its own scroll bar. In such sites, you may find that the usual one-fingered scroll technique scrolls only the entire browser window, not the content within the frame. To scroll the frame stuff, you must use *two* fingers to do the scrolling. Weird!

- **Getting a larger keyboard.** The on-screen keyboard appears when you tap into a box that allows typing. I've noticed, however, that the keyboard you get in landscape view uses noticeably larger keys than the one you see in portrait view. For the fumble-fingered among us, larger keys are a must, so always rotate the iPad into landscape mode to enter text.

Note

Remember that rotating the iPad changes the view only if your iPad is upright. The iPad uses gravity to sense the change in orientation, so if it's lying flat on a table, rotating the iPad won't do anything. So rotate it first before you put it on the table.

- **Save typing with standard Web addresses.** Most Web sites have addresses that start with http://www. and end with .com/. Safari on your iPad knows this, and it uses this otherwise unremarkable fact to save you tons of typing. If you enter just a single block of text into the address bar — it could be a single word such as *wiley* or two or more words combined into one, such as *wordspy* — and then tap Go, Safari automatically adds http://www. to the front and .com/ at the end. So wiley becomes http://www.wiley.com/ and wordspy becomes http://www.wordspy.com/.

Juggling Multiple Web Pages

These days, it's a rare Web surfer who marches sequentially through a series of Web pages. In your own surfing sessions, you probably leave a few Web pages open full-time (for things like Google searches and RSS feed monitoring), and you likely come across lots of links that you want to check out while still leaving the original page open in the browser. In your computer's Web browser, you probably handle these and similar surfing situations by launching a tab for each page you want to leave open in the browser window. It's an essential Web browsing technique, but can it be done with your iPad's Safari browser?

Yes, indeed, although not with tabs. Instead, Safari offers the next best thing: *pages*. A page is a kind of browser "window," and when you create a new page, you can use it to display a different Web site. Then it's a quick tap and flick to switch between them. (The next couple of sections fill in all these details.) And you're not restricted to a meager two pages, no sir. Your iPad lets you open up to nine — count 'em, *nine* — pages, so you can throw some wild Web page parties.

Opening and managing multiple browser pages

Follow these steps to open and load multiple pages:

1. **In Safari, tap the Pages icon in the status bar, as shown in Figure 4.2.** Safari displays a thumbnail version of the current page.

Pages icon

4.2 Tap the Pages icon to create a new page.

2. **Tap New Page.** Safari opens a blank page using the full screen.

3. **Load a Web site into the new page.** You can do this by selecting a bookmark, entering an address, searching for a site, or whatever.

4. **Repeat Steps 1 to 3 to load as many pages as you need.** As you add pages, Safari keeps track of how many are open and displays the number in the Pages icon, as shown in Figure 4.3.

iPad 🛜	2:41 PM	100% 🔋
	Paul McFedries' Tech Tonic	

◀ ▶ 🗔 📖 ✚ | mcfedries.com/cs/ | ⟳ | Google

Sign in | Join | Help
Search

Paul McFedries' Tech Tonic
Making the world a better place, one computer book at a time

Home   **Lingua Techna**   **Books**   **Forums**   **Downloads**

Tags, Tags, Tags

4.3 The Pages icon tells you how many pages you have on the go.

Note Some Web-based apps and Web page links are configured to automatically open the page in a new window, so you may see a new page being created when you tap a link. Also, if you add a Web Clip to your Home screen (as I described in Chapter 3), tapping the icon opens the Web Clip in a new Safari page.

Caution Be careful if you have the full complement of nine browser pages opened. If you click a link that automatically opens in a new browser page, Safari automatically shuts down the first browser page, which could be a bit of a problem if you had some important info in that window. To avoid this problem, consider opening a maximum of eight Safari pages so you always have an extra page available if you need it.

Navigating open pages using page thumbnails

When you have two or more pages fired up, you can use these techniques to impress your friends:

- **Switch to another page.** Tap the Pages icon to get to the thumbnail view, shown in Figure 4.4, and then tap the page.

- **Close a page.** Tap the Pages icon, and then tap the X in the upper-left corner. Safari trashes the page without a whimper of protest.

Genius If you're in portrait mode and you're having trouble reading the text or viewing the images in a thumbnail, turn your iPad to landscape mode. This gives you wider thumbnails that are slightly more magnified for easier reading.

4.4 Tap the Pages icon to see thumbnail versions of your open pages.

Filling in Online Forms

Many Web pages include forms where you fill in some data and then submit the form, which sends the data off to some server for processing. Filling in these forms in your iPad's Safari browser is mostly straightforward:

- **Text box.** Tap inside the text box to display the touchscreen keyboard, tap out your text, and then tap Done.

83

- **Text area.** Tap inside the text area, and then use the keyboard to tap your text. Most text areas allow multiline entries, so you can tap Return to start a new line. When you finish, tap Done.

- **Check box.** Tap the check box to toggle the check mark on and off.

- **Radio button.** Tap a radio button to activate it.

- **Command button.** Tap the button to make it do its thing (usually submit the form).

Many online forms consist of a bunch of text boxes or text areas. If the idea of performing the tap-type-Done cycle over and over isn't appealing to you, fear not. Your iPad's Safari browser offers an easier method:

1. **Tap inside the first text box or text area.** The keyboard appears.

2. **Tap to type the text you want to enter.** Above the keyboard, notice the Previous and Next buttons, as shown in Figure 4.5.

4.5 If the form contains multiple text boxes or text areas, you can use the Previous and Next buttons to navigate them.

3. **Tap Next to move to the next text box or text area.** If you need to return to a text box, tap Previous instead.

4. **Repeat Steps 2 and 3 to fill in the text boxes.**

5. **Tap Done.** Safari returns you to the page.

I haven't yet talked about selection lists, and that's because your iPad's browser handles them in an interesting way. When you tap a list, Safari displays the list items in a separate box, as shown in Figure 4.6. In the list of items, the currently selected item appears with a check mark to its right. Tap the item you want to select.

4.6 Tap a list to see its items in a separate box for easier selecting.

Turning on AutoFill for faster forms

The iPad's Safari browser makes it relatively easy to fill in online forms, but it can still be slow going, particularly if you have to do lots of text box or text area typing. To help make forms less of a chore, your iPad's Safari browser supports a welcome feature called AutoFill. Just as with the desktop version of Safari (or just about any other mainstream browser), AutoFill remembers the data you enter into forms and then enables you to fill in similar forms with a simple tap of a button. You also can configure AutoFill to remember usernames and passwords.

To take advantage of this nifty new feature, you first have to turn it on by following these steps:

1. **On the Home screen, tap Settings.** Your iPad opens the Settings screen.

2. **Tap Safari.** The Safari screen appears.

3. **Tap AutoFill to open the AutoFill screen.**

4. **Tap the Use Contact Info switch to the On position.** This tells Safari to use your item in the Contacts app to grab data for a form. For example, if a form requires your name, Safari uses your contact name.

5. **The My Info field should show your name; if it doesn't, tap the field and then tap your item in the Contacts list.**

6. **If you want Safari to remember the usernames and passwords you use to log into sites, tap the Names & Passwords switch to the On position.** A completed AutoFill screen appears in Figure 4.7.

4.7 Fill in the AutoFill screen to make online forms less of a chore.

Now when you visit an online form and access any text field in the form, the AutoFill button becomes enabled. Tap AutoFill to fill in those portions of the form that correspond to your contact data, as shown in Figure 4.8. Notice that the fields Safari was able to automatically fill in display with a colored background.

4.8 Tap the AutoFill button to fill in form fields with your contact data.

Saving Web site login passwords

If you enabled the Names & Passwords option in the AutoFill screen, each time you fill in a username and password to log into a site, Safari displays the dialog shown in Figure 4.9 that asks if you want to remember the login data, and it gives you three choices:

- **Yes.** Tap this button to have Safari remember your username and password.

- **Never for this Website.** Tap this button to tell Safari not to remember the username and password, and to never again prompt you to save the login data.

- **Not Now.** Tap this button to tell Safari not to remember the username and password this time, but to prompt you again next time you log into this site.

87

4.9 If you configured Safari to remember usernames and passwords, you see this dialog when you log into a site.

Note Your iPad is a cautious beast, so it doesn't offer to save all the passwords you enter. In particular, if the login form is part of a secure site, then your iPad doesn't ask if you want to save the password. This means you won't be tempted to store the password for your online bank, corporate Web site, or any site where you saved your credit card data (such as Amazon and similar online shopping sites).

Using Bookmarks for Faster Surfing

The Web era is into its third decade now, so you certainly don't need me to tell you that the Web is a manifestly awesome resource that redefines the phrase *treasure trove*. No, at this stage of your Web career, you're probably most concerned with finding great Web treasures and with returning to the best or most useful of those treasures in subsequent surfing sessions. Safari's History list can help here (I talk about it later in this chapter), but the best way to ensure that you can easily return to a site a week, a month, or even a year from now is to save that site as a bookmark.

Syncing your bookmarks

By far, the easiest way to get bookmarks for your favorite sites into your iPad is to take advantage of your best bookmark resource: the Safari browser on your Mac (or your Windows PC), or the Internet Explorer browser on your PC (which calls them *favorites*). You've probably used those browsers for a while and have all kinds of useful and fun bookmarked sites at your metaphorical fingertips. To get those bookmarks at your literal fingertips — that is, on your iPad — you need to include bookmarks as part of the synchronization process between the iPad and iTunes (which I talked about in general terms in Chapter 2).

Caution

Having used Safari or Internet Explorer for a while means having lots of great sites bookmarked, but it likely also means that you have lots of digital dreck — sites you no longer visit or that have gone belly-up. Before synchronizing your bookmarks with the iPad, consider taking some time to clean up your existing bookmarks. You'll thank yourself in the end.

Genius

What's that? You've already synced your bookmarks to your iPad, and you now have a bunch of useless sites clogging up iPad Safari's bookmark arteries? Not a problem! Return to your desktop Safari (or Internet Explorer), purge the bogus bookmarks, and then resync your iPad. Any bookmarks you blew away also get trashed from your iPad.

Bookmark syncing is turned on by default, but you should follow these steps to make sure:

1. **Connect your iPad to your computer.**

2. **In the iTunes sources list, click the iPad.**

3. **Click the Info tab.**

4. **Scroll down to the Web Browser section, and use one of the following techniques:**

   - **Mac.** Select the Sync Safari Bookmarks check box, as shown in Figure 4.10.

4.10 Make sure the Sync Safari bookmarks check box is selected.

● **Windows.** Select the Sync Bookmarks With check box, and then select your Web browser from the drop-down list.

5. **Click Apply.** iTunes begins syncing the bookmarks from your computer to your iPad.

Adding bookmarks by hand

Even if you have your iPad bookmarks off to a flying start by copying a bunch of existing bookmarks from your Mac or Windows PC and now have a large collection of bookmarks at your beck and call, it doesn't mean your iPad bookmark collection is complete. After all, you might (heck, you *will*) find some interesting sites while you're surfing with the iPad. If you think you'll want to pay those sites another visit down the road, you can create new bookmarks right on the iPad. Here are the steps to follow:

1. **On the iPad, use Safari to navigate to the site you want to save.**

2. **Tap the + button in the status bar.**

3. **Tap Add Bookmark.** This opens the Add Bookmark screen, as shown in Figure 4.11.

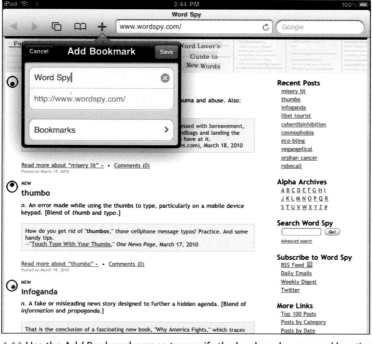

4.11 Use the Add Bookmark screen to specify the bookmark name and location.

4. **Tap into the top box, and enter a name for the site that helps you remember it.** This name is what you see when you scroll through your bookmarks.

5. **Tap Bookmarks.** This displays a list of your bookmark folders.

6. **Tap the folder you want to use to store the bookmark.** Safari returns you to the Add Bookmark screen.

7. **Tap Save.** Safari saves the bookmark.

Note

Syncing bookmarks is a two-way street, which means that any site you bookmark in your iPad is added to your desktop Safari (or Internet Explorer) the next time you sync.

Getting Firefox bookmarks into your iPad

iTunes bookmark syncing works only with Safari and Internet Explorer. So are you out of luck if your entire Web life is bookmarked in Firefox? Nope. Fortunately Firefox has a feature that lets you export your bookmarks to a file. You can then import those bookmarks to Safari or Internet Explorer and then sync with your iPad. It's a bit of a winding road, I know, but it's better than starting from scratch. Here are the details:

1. **Crank up Firefox, and start the export procedure like so:**

   - **Firefox 3 (Mac).** Choose Bookmarks ⇨ Organize Bookmarks (or press Shift+⌘+B) to open the Library. Click the Import and Backup button, and then click Export HTML.

   - **Firefox 3 (Windows).** Choose Bookmarks ⇨ Organize Bookmarks (or press Ctrl+Shift+B) to open the Library. Click the Import and Backup button, and then click Export HTML.

   - **Firefox 2 (Windows).** Choose Bookmarks ⇨ Organize Bookmarks to open the Bookmarks Manager, and then choose File ⇨ Export.

2. **In the Export Bookmarks File dialog, choose a location for the file and click Save.** Firefox saves its bookmarks to a file named bookmarks.html.

3. **Import the Firefox bookmarks file to your browser of choice:**

   - **Safari.** Choose File ⇨ Import Bookmarks, locate and click the bookmarks.html file, and then click Import.

   - **Internet Explorer.** In versions 8 and 7, press Alt+Z and then click Import and Export; in version 6, choose File ⇨ Import and Export. In the Import/Export Wizard, click Next, click Import Favorites, and then follow the wizard's instructions to import the bookmarks.html file.

4. **Connect your iPad to your computer.** iTunes opens, connects to the iPad, and syncs the bookmarks, which now include your Firebox bookmarks.

Managing your bookmarks

After you have a few bookmarks stashed away in the bookmarks list, you may need to perform a few housekeeping chores from time to time, including changing a bookmark's name, address, or folder; reordering bookmarks or folders; or getting rid of bookmarks that have worn out their welcome.

Before you can do any of this, you need to get the Bookmarks list into Edit mode by following these steps:

1. **In Safari, tap the Bookmarks icon in the status bar, as shown in Figure 4.12.** Safari opens the Bookmarks list.

Bookmarks icon

4.12 Tap the Bookmarks icon to display the Bookmarks list.

2. **If the bookmark you want to mess with is located in a particular folder, tap to open that folder.** For example, if you've synced with Safari, you should have a folder named Bookmarks Bar, which includes all the bookmarks and folders that you've added to the Bookmarks Bar in your desktop version of Safari.

3. **Tap Edit.** Your iPad switches the Bookmarks list to Edit mode, as shown in Figure 4.13. With Edit mode on the go, you're free to toil away at your bookmarks. Here are the techniques to master:

   - **Edit bookmark info.** Tap the bookmark to fire up the Edit Bookmark screen. From here, you can edit the bookmark name, change the bookmark address, and change the bookmark folder. When you're finished, tap the name of the current bookmark folder in the top-left corner of the screen.

   - **Change the bookmark order.** Use the drag icon on the right to tap-and-drag a bookmark to a new position in the list. Ideally, you should move your favorite bookmarks near the top of the list for easiest access.

- **Add a bookmark folder.** Tap New Folder to launch the Edit Folder screen, and then tap a folder title and select a location. Feel free to use bookmark folders at will, because they're a great way to keep your bookmarks neat and tidy (if you're into that kind of thing).

- **Delete a bookmark.** No use for a particular bookmark? No problem. Tap the Delete icon to the left of the bookmark, and then tap the Delete button that appears.

When the dust settles and your bookmark chores are finished for the day, tap Done to get out of Edit mode.

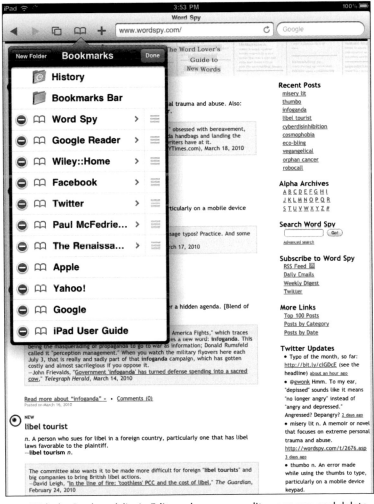

4.13 With the Bookmark list in Edit mode, you can edit, rearrange, and delete bookmarks to your heart's content.

Getting Even More Out of Safari on Your iPad

You've seen lots of great Safari tips and techniques so far in this chapter, but I hope you're up for even more, because you've got a ways to go. In the rest of this chapter, you learn such useful techniques as using the History list, changing the default search engine, viewing RSS feeds, and configuring Safari's security options.

Retracing your steps with the handy History list

Bookmarking a Web site (as I described earlier in this chapter) is a good idea if that site contains interesting or fun content that you want to revisit. Sometimes, however, you may not realize that a site had useful data until a day or two later. Similarly, you may like a site's stuff, but decide against bookmarking it, only to regret that decision down the road. You could waste a big chunk of your day trying to track down the site, but then you may run into Murphy's Web Browsing Law: A cool site that you forget to bookmark is never found again.

Fortunately, your iPad has your back. As you navigate the nooks and crannies of the Web, iPad keeps track of where you go and stores the name and address of each page in the History list. The iPad's limited memory means that it can't store tons of sites, but it might have what you're looking for. Here's how to use it:

1. **In Safari, tap the Bookmarks icon (refer to Figure 4.12) in the status bar.** Safari opens the Bookmarks list.

2. **If you see the Bookmarks screen (refer to Figure 4.13), skip to Step 3.** Otherwise, tap the folder names that appear in the upper-left corner of the screen until you get to the Bookmarks screen.

3. **Tap History.** Safari opens the History screen, as shown in Figure 4.14. The screen shows the sites you've visited today at the top, followed by a list of previous surfing dates.

4. **If you visited the site you're looking for on a previous day, tap the day.** Safari displays a list of the sites you visited on that day.

5. **Tap the site you want to revisit.** Safari loads the site.

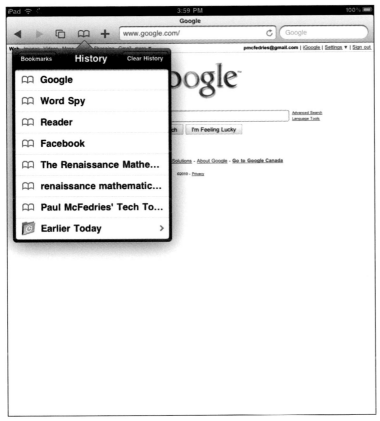

4.14 Safari stores your recent browsing past in the HIstory list.

Maintaining your privacy by deleting the History list

Your iPad's History list of sites you've recently surfed is a great feature when you need it, and it's an innocuous feature when you don't. However, at times the History list is just plain uncool. For example, suppose you shop online to get a nice gift for your spouse's birthday. If he or she also uses your iPad, your surprise might get ruined if the purchase page accidentally shows up in the History list. Similarly, if you visit a private corporate site, a financial site, or any other site you wouldn't want others to see, the History list might betray you.

And sometimes unsavory sites can end up in your History list by accident. For example, you might tap a legitimate-looking link in a Web page or email message, only to end up in some dark, dank Net neighborhood. Of course, you high-tailed it out of there right away with a quick tap of Safari's Back button, but that nasty site is now lurking in your History.

Whether you have sites on the History list that you wouldn't want anyone to see, or if you just find the idea of your iPad tracking your movements on the Web to be a bit sinister, follow these steps to wipe out the History list:

1. **In Safari, tap the Bookmarks icon in the status bar.** Safari opens the Bookmarks list.

2. **Tap the folder names that appear in the upper-left corner of the screen until you get to the Bookmarks screen.**

3. **Tap History.** Safari opens the History screen.

4. **Tap Clear History.** Safari prompts you to confirm.

5. **Tap Clear History.** Safari deletes every site from the History list.

Note Here's another way to clear the History, and it may be faster if you're not currently working in Safari. In the Home screen, tap Settings, tap Safari, and then tap Clear History. When your iPad asks you to confirm, tap Clear History.

Changing the default search engine

When you tap the Search box at the top of the Safari screen, your iPad loads the Google screen, places the cursor inside the Search box, and displays the keyboard so you can enter your search text and then run the search. The screen is named Google because Google is the iPad's default search engine. We all love Google, of course, but if you have something against it, for some reason, you can switch to using Yahoo! as your search engine of choice. Here's how:

1. **In the Home screen, tap Settings.** Your iPad opens the Settings screen.

2. **Tap Safari.** The Safari screen appears.

3. **Tap Search Engine.** Your iPad opens the Search Engine screen.

4. **Tap Yahoo!.** Your iPad now uses Yahoo! as the default search engine. In the Search screen, you can now enter your search text and tap the Yahoo! button.

Viewing an RSS feed

Some Web sites remain relatively static over time, so you only need to check in every once in a while to see if anything's new. Other sites change content regularly, such as once a day or once a week, so you know in advance when to check for new material. However, on the more verbose sites — particularly blogs — the content changes frequently, although not regularly. For these sites, keeping up with new content can be time-consuming, and it's criminally easy to miss new information. (Murphy's Blog Reading Law: You always miss the post that everyone's talking about.)

To solve this problem, tons of Web sites now maintain RSS feeds; RSS stands for Real Simple Syndication. A *feed* is a special file that contains the most recent information added to the site. The bad news is that your iPad's Safari browser doesn't give you any way to subscribe to a site's feed like you can with desktop Safari or Internet Explorer. The good news is that your iPad can use a Web-based RSS reader application (http://reader.mac.com/) that can interpret a site's RSS feed and display the feed in the comfy confines of Safari.

Here's how it works:

1. **In Safari, navigate to a Web page that you know has an RSS feed.**

2. **Pan and zoom the page until you find the link to the RSS feed.** The link is often accompanied by (or consists entirely of) an icon that indentifies it as leading to a feed. Look for an XML icon, an RSS icon, or an orange feed icon, as shown in Figure 4.15.

Subscribe to Word Spy
RSS Feed
Daily Emails
Weekly Digest
Twitter

en agenda. [Blend of

More Links
Top 100 Posts

4.15 Most feed links are identified by a standard feed icon.

3. **Tap the link.** Safari loads the RSS file into the reader.mac.com feed reader application, as shown in Figure 4.16.

Note Like other links, such as Web pages, you can bookmark RSS feed links and save them to the Home screen.

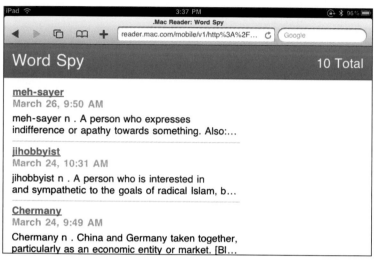

4.16 When you tap an RSS feed link, Safari loads the RSS file into the reader.mac.com feed reader application.

Setting the Web browser security options

It's a jungle out there in cyberspace, with nasty things lurking in the digital weeds. The folks at Apple are well aware of these dangers, of course, so they've clothed your iPad in protective gear to help keep the bad guys at bay. Safari, in particular, has five layers of security:

- **Phishing protection.** A *phishing* site is a Web site that on the surface appears to belong to a reputable company, such as an online bank or major corporation. In reality, some dark-side hackers have cobbled the site together to fool you into providing your precious login data, credit card data, social security number, or other private information. Many of these sites either are well-known or sport tell-tale signs that mark them as fraudulent. iPad Safari comes with a Fraud Warning setting that, when activated, displays a warning about such sites.

- **JavaScript.** This is a programming language that Web site developers commonly use to add features to their pages. However, programmers who have succumbed to the dark side of The Force can use JavaScript for nefarious ends. Your iPad comes with JavaScript support turned on, but you can turn it off if you're heading into an area of the Web where you don't feel safe. However, many sites won't work without JavaScript, so we don't recommend turning it off full time.

- **Pop-up blocking.** Pop-up ads (and their sneakier cousins, the pop-under ads) are annoying at the best of times, but they really get in the way on the iPad because the pop-up not only creates a new Safari page, but it immediately switches to that page. So now you have to tap the Pages icon, delete the pop-up page, and then (if you already had two or more pages running) tap the page that generated the pop-up. Boo! So you can thank your preferred deity that not only does your iPad come with a pop-up blocker that stops these pop-up pests, but it's turned on by default, to boot. However, some sites use pop-ups for legitimate reasons: media players, login pages, important site announcements, and so on. For those sites to work properly, you may need to turn off the pop-up blocker temporarily.

- **Cookies.** These are small text files that many sites store on the iPad, and they use those files to store information about your browsing session. The most common example is a shopping cart, where your selections and amounts are stored in a cookie. However, for every benign cookie, at least one not-so-nice cookie is used by a third-party advertiser to track your movements and display ads supposedly targeted to your tastes. Yuck. By default, your iPad doesn't accept third-party cookies, so that's a good thing. However, you can configure Safari to accept every cookie that comes its way or no cookies at all (neither of which we recommend).

Follow these steps to customize your iPad's Web security options:

1. **On the Home screen, tap Settings.** The Settings screen slides in.

2. **Tap Safari.** Your iPad displays the Safari screen, as shown in Figure 4.17.

iPad	3:17 PM	97%

Settings

Wi-Fi Wireless429
Brightness & Wallpaper
Picture Frame
General
Mail, Contacts, Calendars
Safari
iPod
Video
Photos
Store

Safari

General

Search Engine .... Google >

AutoFill .... On >

Always Show Bookmarks Bar .... OFF

Security

Fraud Warning .... ON

Warn when visiting fraudulent websites.

JavaScript .... ON

Block Pop-ups .... ON

Accept Cookies .... From visited >

Clear History

Clear Cookies

Clear Cache

Developer .... >

4.17 Use the Safari screen to set your iPad's Web security settings.

3. **Tap the Fraud Warning setting to toggle phishing protection On and Off.**

4. **Tap the JavaScript setting to toggle JavaScript support On and Off.**

5. **Tap the Block Pop-ups setting to toggle pop-up blocking On and Off.**

6. **To configure the cookies that Safari allows, tap Accept Cookies, tap the setting you want — None, From visited, or Always — and then tap Safari.** The From visited setting (the default) means that Safari accepts cookies directly from the sites you surf to; it spits out any cookies from third-party sites such as advertisers.

7. **If you want to get rid of all the cookies that have been stored on your iPad, tap Clear Cookies and, when you're asked to confirm, tap Clear Cookies.** It's a good idea to clear cookies if you're having trouble accessing a site or if you suspect some unwanted cookies have been stored on your iPad (for example, if you surfed for a while with Accept Cookies set to Always.)

How Do I Make the Most of E-mail on My iPad?

The more time people spend sending status updates on social networking sites, and the more they text, tweet, and Skype, the more old-fashioned e-mail seems. Updating your Facebook status and posting a tweet about some great new site you've found are cool things to do; reading incoming messages and composing new messages and responses are mundane things to do. Yes, e-mail is dishwater-dull, but you know what else it is? It's *universal*. Almost everyone who's online has an e-mail account, and it remains the best way to get in touch and exchange information, at least digitally. Your iPad comes with a decent e-mail app that's easy to use, but there are still plenty of tricks and techniques you should know to help you get the most out of Mail on your iPad.

Managing Your iPad E-mail Accounts

The Mail app that comes with your iPad is a nice e-mail program that makes the most of the iPad's two orientations: In portrait mode, you see a big version of the current message, complete with embedded photos and other media; in landscape mode, you get a two-pane view that shows your Inbox messages in one pane and the current message in the other pane. (Landscape mode is great for composing messages because you get the huge keyboard and nice, big compose window.)

The Mail app also has a few features and settings that make it ideal for doing e-mail away from your desk. First, however, you have to set up your iPad with one or more e-mail accounts.

Syncing your e-mail accounts

The Mail app on your iPad is most useful when it's set up to use an e-mail account that you also use on your computer. That way, when you're on the road or out on the town, you can check your messages and rest assured that you won't miss anything important (or even anything unimportant, for that matter). This is most easily done by syncing an existing e-mail account between your computer and your iPad. That is, if you've got an existing account already up and running — whether it's a Mail account on your Mac, or an Outlook or Windows Mail account on your Windows PC — you can convince iTunes to gather all the account details and pass them along to your iPad.

Note For some accounts, you need to be careful that your iPad doesn't delete incoming messages from the server before you have a chance to download them to your computer. I show you how to set that up later in this chapter.

Here's how it works:

1. **Connect your iPad to your computer.**

2. **In the iTunes sources list, click the iPad.**

3. **Click the Info tab.**

4. **In the Mail Accounts section, use one of the following techniques:**

   - **Mac.** Select the Sync Mail Accounts check box, and then select the check box beside each account you want to add to iPad, as shown in Figure 5.1.

   - **Windows.** Select the Sync Mail Accounts From check box, select your e-mail program from the drop-down list, and then select the check box beside each account you want to add to iPad.

5.1 Make sure you select the Sync selected Mail account check box and at least one account in the list.

5. **Click Apply.** You may see a message asking if AppleMobileSync can be allowed access to your keychain (your Mac's master password list).

6. **If you see that message, click Allow.** iTunes begins syncing the selected e-mail account settings from your computer to your iPad.

Note

Remember that iPad syncs only your e-mail account *settings* (username, password, mail servers, and so on), not your e-mail account *messages*.

Adding an account by hand

Syncing e-mail accounts as I described in the previous section is useful when you want to do the e-mail thing on multiple devices. However, you may also prefer to have an e-mail account that's iPad-only. For example, if you join an iPad mailing list, you may prefer to have those message sent to just your iPad. That's a darn good idea, but it means that you have to set up the account on the iPad itself, which, as you soon see, requires a fair amount of tapping.

Caution

You may think you can avoid the often excessive tapping required to enter a new e-mail account into your iPad by creating the account in your computer's e-mail program and then syncing with your iPad. That works, but there's a hitch: You *must* leave the new account in your e-mail program. If you delete it or disable it, iTunes also deletes the account from the iPad.

How you create an account on your iPad with the sweat of your own brow depends on the type of account you have. First, there are the five e-mail services that your iPad recognizes:

- **Microsoft Exchange.** Your iPad supports accounts on Exchange servers, which are common in large organizations like corporations or schools. Exchange uses a central server to store messages, and you usually work with your messages on the server, not your iPad. However, one of the great features in iPad is support for Exchange ActiveSync, which automatically keeps your iPad and your account on the server synchronized. I discuss the ActiveSync settings later in this chapter.

- **MobileMe.** This is Apple's Web-based e-mail service (that also comes with applications for calendars, contacts, storage, and more).

- **Google Gmail.** This is a Web-based e-mail service run by Google.

- **Yahoo! Mail.** This is a Web-based e-mail service run by Yahoo!.

- **AOL.** This is a Web-based e-mail service run by AOL.

Your iPad knows how to connect with these services, so to set up any of these e-mail accounts, you only need to know the address and the account password.

Otherwise, your iPad Mail app supports the following e-mail account types:

- **POP.** Short for Post Office Protocol, this is the most popular type of account. Its main characteristic for our purposes is that incoming messages are stored only temporarily on the provider's mail server. When you connect to the server, the messages are downloaded to iPad and removed from the server. In other words, your messages (including copies of messages you send) are stored locally on your iPad. The advantage here is that you don't need to be online to read your e-mail. After it's downloaded to your iPad, you can read it (or delete it or whatever) at your leisure.

- **IMAP.** Short for Internet Message Access Protocol, this type of account is most often used with Web-based e-mail services. It's the opposite of POP (sort of) because all your incoming messages, as well as copies of messages you send, remain on the server. In this case, when Mail works with an IMAP account, it connects to the server and works with the messages on the server itself, not on your iPad (although it *looks* like you're working with the messages locally). The advantage here is that you can access the messages from multiple devices and multiple locations, but you must be connected to the Internet to work with your messages.

Your network administrator or your e-mail service provider can let you know what type of e-mail account you have. Your administrator or provider also can give you the information you need to set up the account. This includes your e-mail address, the username and password you use to check for new messages (and perhaps also the security information you need to specify to send messages), the host name of the incoming mail server (typically something like mail.*provider*.com, where *provider*.com is the domain name of the provider), and the host name of the outgoing mail server (typically either mail.*provider*.com or smtp.*provider*.com).

With your account information clutched in your fist, follow these steps to forge a brand-new account on your iPad:

1. **On the Home screen, tap Settings.** Your iPad opens the Settings screen.

2. **Tap Mail, Contacts, Calendars.** The Mail, Contacts, Calendars screen appears.

3. **Tap Add Account.** This opens the Add Account screen, as shown in Figure 5.2.

5.2 Use the Add Account screen to choose the type of e-mail account you want to add.

4. **You have two ways to proceed:**

   - If you're adding an account for Microsoft Exchange, MobileMe, Google Gmail, Yahoo! Mail, or AOL, tap the corresponding logo. In the account information screen that appears, enter your name, e-mail address, password, and an account description. Tap Save, and you're done!

   - If you're adding another account type, tap Other and continue with Step 5.

5. **Tap Add Mail Account to open the New Account screen.**

6. **Use the Name, Address, Password and Description text boxes to enter the corresponding account information, and then tap Save.**

7. **Tap the type of account you're adding: IMAP or POP.**

8. **In the Incoming Mail Server section, use the Host Name text box to enter the host name of your provider's incoming mail server, as well as your username and password.**

9. **In the Outgoing Mail Server (SMTP) section, use the Host Name text box to enter the host name of your provider's outgoing (SMTP) mail server.** If your provider requires a username and password to send messages, enter those as well.

10. **Tap Save.** Your iPad verifies the account info and then returns you to the Mail settings screen with the account added to the Accounts list.

Specifying the default account

If you've added two or more e-mail accounts to your iPad, Mail specifies one of them as the default account. This means that Mail uses this account when you send a new message, when you reply to a message, and when you forward a message. The default account is usually the first account you add to your iPad. However, you can change this by following these steps:

1. **On the Home screen, tap Settings.** The Settings screen appears.

2. **Tap Mail, Contacts, Calendars.** Your iPad displays the Mail, Contacts, Calendars screen.

3. **In the Mail section of the screen, tap Default Account.** This opens the Default Account screen, which displays a list of your accounts. The current default account is shown with a check mark beside it, as shown in Figure 5.3.

iPad 🔋	4:21 PM	@ ⚡ 95% 🔋

Settings	Mail, Contacts...	Default Account

📶 Wi-Fi Wireless429	My MobileMe Account ✓
🖼 Brightness & Wallpaper	My Gmail Account
🖼 Picture Frame	My POP account
⚙ General	
✉ Mail, Contacts, Calendars	
🧭 Safari	
🎵 iPod	
📹 Video	
🌼 Photos	
⚫ Store	

5.3 Use the Default Account screen to set the default account you want Mail to use when sending messages.

4. **Tap the account you want to use as the default.** Your iPad places a check mark beside the account.

5. **Tap Mail to return to the Mail settings screen.**

Switching to another account

When you open the Mail app (by tapping Mail in the Dock in your iPad's Home screen), you usually see the Inbox folder of your default account. If you have multiple accounts set up on your iPad and you want to see what's going on with a different account, follow these steps to make the switch:

1. **On the Home screen, tap Mail to open the Mail app.**

2. **In landscape mode, tap the mailbox button in the top-left corner of the screen (but below the status bar).** If you're in portrait mode, tap Inbox and then tap the mailbox button. The Mail app displays the Mailboxes screen.

3. **Tap Accounts.** The Accounts screen appears, as shown in Figure 5.4.

4. **Tap the account you want to work with.** Mail displays a list of the account's folders.

5.4 Use the Accounts screen to choose the e-mail account you want to play with.

Temporarily disabling an account

The Mail app checks for new messages at a regular interval. (I show you how to configure this interval a bit later in this chapter.) If you have several accounts configured in Mail, this incessant checking can put quite a strain on your iPad battery. To ease up on the juice, you can disable an account temporarily to prevent Mail from checking it for new messages. Here's how:

1. **On the Home screen, tap Settings.** Your iPad displays the Settings screen.

2. **Tap Mail, Contacts, Calendars to see the Mail settings.**

3. **Tap the account you want to disable.** Your iPad displays the account's settings.

4. **Tap the Account switch to Off, as shown in Figure 5.5.**

5. **Tap Done to return to the Mail settings screen.**

When you're ready to work with the account again, repeat these steps to turn the Account switch back to On.

Syncing your notes

If you use the Notes app on your iPad to jot down quick thoughts, ideas, and other mental tidbits, you may want to transfer those notes to your computer so you can incorporate them into another document, add them to a to-do list, or whatever.

5.5 In the account's settings screen, tap the Account switch to Off.

> **Note**
>
> To sync notes on your Mac, you must be running Mac OS X 10.5.7 or later.

Notes syncing is turned off by default, so you need to follow these steps to activate it:

1. **Connect your iPad to your computer.**
2. **In the iTunes sources list, click the iPad.**
3. **Click the Info tab.**
4. **Scroll down to the Other section (refer to Figure 5.1), and then use one of the following techniques:**
   - **Mac.** Select the Sync Notes check box.
   - **Windows.** Select the Sync Notes With check box, and then select an application from the drop-down list (such as Outlook).
5. **Click Apply.** iTunes begins syncing the notes from your computer to your iPad.

Deleting an account

If an e-mail account has grown tiresome and boring (or you just don't use it anymore), you should delete it to save storage space, speed up sync times, and save battery power. Follow these steps:

1. **On the Home screen, tap Settings.** The Settings screen appears.

2. **Tap Mail, Contacts, Calendars to get to the Mail settings.**

3. **Tap the account you want to delete.** This opens the account's settings.

4. **Tap Delete Account.** Your iPad asks you to confirm.

5. **Tap Delete.** Your iPad returns you to the Mail settings screen, and the account no longer graces the Accounts list.

Configuring E-mail Accounts

Setting up an e-mail account on your iPad is one thing, but making that account do useful things — or sometimes, anything at all! — is quite another. The next few sections take you through a few useful settings that help you get more out of e-mail and troubleshoot e-mail problems.

Managing multiple devices by leaving messages on the server

In today's increasingly mobile world, it's not unusual to find you need to check the same e-mail account from multiple devices. For example, you may want to check your business account using not only your work computer but also your home computer, or your iPad while commuting or traveling.

If you need to check e-mail on multiple devices, you can take advantage of how POP e-mail messages are delivered over the Internet. When someone sends you a message, it doesn't come directly to your computer. Instead, it goes to the server that your ISP (or your company) has set up to handle incoming messages. When you ask your e-mail client to check for new messages, it communicates with the POP server to see if any messages are waiting in your account. If so, the client downloads those messages to your computer and then instructs the server to delete the copies of the messages that are stored on the server.

The trick, then, is to configure the e-mail program so it leaves a copy of the messages on the POP server after you download them. That way, the messages are still available when you check messages using another device. Fortunately, the intuitive folks who designed the version of Mail on your iPad must have understood this, because the program automatically sets up POP accounts to do just that. Specifically, after you download any messages from the POP server to your iPad, the Mail app leaves the messages on the server.

Here's a good overall strategy that ensures you can download messages on all your devices, but prevents messages from piling up on the server:

- **Let your main computer be the computer that controls deleting the messages from the server.** In Mac OS X, Mail's default setting is to delete messages from the server after one week, and that's fine.

- **Set up all your other devices — particularly your iPad — to not delete messages from the server.**

Note
Outlook, Outlook Express, and Windows Live Mail always configure POP accounts to delete messages from the server as soon as you retrieve them. You need to fix that. In Outlook, choose Tools ⇨ Account Settings, click the account, click Change, and then click More Settings. Click the Advanced tab, and select the Leave a Copy of Messages on the Server check box. In Outlook Express or Windows Live Mail, choose Tools ⇨ Accounts, click your e-mail account, and click Properties. Click the Advanced tab, and then select the Leave a Copy of Messages on Server check box.

It's a good idea to check your iPad POP accounts to ensure they're not deleting messages from the server. To do that, or to use a different setting — (such as deleting messages after a week or when you delete them from your Inbox), — follow these steps:

1. **On the Home screen, tap Settings.** The Settings screen appears.

2. **Tap Mail, Contacts, Calendars.** Your iPad opens the Mail, Contacts, Calendars settings screen.

3. **Tap the POP account you want to work with.** The account's settings screen appears.

4. **Tap Advanced.** Your iPad displays the Advanced screen.

5. **Tap Remove.** The Remove screen appears, as shown in Figure 5.6.

6. **Tap Never.** If you prefer that your iPad delete messages from the server after a set period of time, tap After One Day, After One Week, or After One Month.

5.6 Use the Remove screen to ensure your iPad is leaving messages on your POP server.

Fixing outgoing e-mail problems by using a different server port

For security reasons, some Internet service providers (ISPs) insist on routing all their customers' outgoing mail through the ISP's Simple Mail Transfer Protocol (SMTP) server. This usually isn't a big deal if you're using an e-mail account maintained by the ISP, but it can lead to the following problems if you're using an account provided by a third party (such as your Web site host):

- Your ISP might block messages sent using the third-party account because it thinks you're trying to relay the message through the ISP's server (a technique often used by spammers).

- You might incur extra charges if your ISP allows only a certain amount of SMTP bandwidth per month or a certain number of sent messages, whereas the third-party account offers higher limits or no restrictions at all.

- You might have performance problems, with the ISP's server taking much longer to route messages than the third-party host.

You may think that you can solve the problem by specifying the third-party host's SMTP server in the account settings. However, this usually doesn't work because outgoing e-mail is sent by default through port 25; when you use this port, the outgoing mail goes through the ISP's SMTP server.

To work around this problem, many third-party hosts offer access to their SMTP server via a port other than the standard port 25. For example, the MobileMe SMTP server (smtp.me.com) also accepts connections on ports 465 and 587.

Here's how to configure an e-mail account to use a nonstandard SMTP port:

1. **On the Home screen, tap Settings.** You see the Settings screen.

2. **Tap Mail, Contacts, Calendars.** The Mail, Contacts, Calendars settings screen appears.

3. **Tap the POP account you want to work with.** The account's settings screen appears.

4. **Tap SMTP.** Your iPad displays the SMTP screen.

5. **In the Primary Server section, tap the name of your server.** Your iPad displays the server settings.

6. **Tap Server Port.** Your iPad displays a keypad so you can enter the port number, as shown in Figure 5.7.

5.7 In the server's settings screen, tap Server Port to enter the new port number to use for outgoing messages.

Configuring authentication for outgoing mail

Because spam is such a big problem these days, many ISPs now require SMTP authentication for outgoing mail, which means that you must log onto the SMTP server to confirm that you're the person sending the mail (as opposed to some spammer spoofing your address). If your ISP requires authentication on outgoing messages, you need to configure your e-mail account to provide the proper credentials.

If you're not sure about any of this, check with your ISP. If that doesn't work out, by far the most common type of authentication is to specify a username and password (this happens behind the scenes when you send messages). Follow these steps to configure your iPad e-mail account with this kind of authentication:

1. **On the Home screen, tap Settings.** Your iPad displays the Settings screen.

2. **Tap Mail, Contacts, Calendars.** The Mail, Contacts, Calendars settings screen appears.

3. **Tap the POP account you want to work with.** The account's settings screen appears.

4. **Tap SMTP.** Your iPad displays the SMTP screen.

5. **In the Primary Server section, tap the server name.** Your iPad displays the server's settings.

6. **In the Outgoing Mail Server section, tap Authentication.** Your iPad displays the Authentication screen.

7. **Tap Password.**

8. **Tap the server address to return to the server settings screen.**

9. **In the Outgoing Mail Server section, enter your account username in the User Name box and the account password in the Password box.**

Configuring E-mail Messages

The rest of this chapter takes you through a few useful and timesaving techniques for handling e-mail messages on your iPad.

Configuring iPad to automatically check for new messages

By default, your iPad checks for new messages only when you tell it to, like so:

1. **On the Home screen, tap Mail to open the Mail app.**

2. **In landscape mode, tap the mailbox button in the top-left corner of the screen (but below the status bar).** If you're in portrait mode, tap Inbox and then tap the mailbox button. The Mail app displays the Mailboxes screen.

3. **Tap Accounts.** The Accounts screen appears.

4. **Tap the account you want to work with.** Mail displays a list of the account's folders.

5. **Tap the Inbox folder.** Mail opens the folder and checks for messages.

Genius

While you have an account's Inbox mailbox open, you can check for messages again by tapping the Refresh icon on the left side of the Inbox menu bar.

This is usually the behavior you want, because it limits bandwidth if you're using the cellular network, and it saves battery life. However, if you're busy with something else and you're expecting an important message, you may prefer to have your iPad check for new messages automatically. Easy money! The Auto-Check feature is happy to handle everything for you. Here's how you set it up:

1. **On the Home screen, tap Settings to display the Settings screen.**

2. **Tap Mail, Contacts, Calendars.** The Mail, Contacts, Calendars settings screen appears.

3. **Tap Fetch New Data.** Your iPad opens the Fetch New Data screen.

4. **In the Fetch section, tap the interval you want to use.** For example, if you tap Every 15 minutes, as shown in Figure 5.8, your iPad checks all your accounts for new messages every 15 minutes.

5. **Click Advanced to open the Advanced screen.**

6. **For each account you want your iPad to check automatically, tap the account and then tap Fetch.** If you don't want your iPad to check a particular account for messages automatically, tap the account and then tap Manual.

When you're ready to return to checking for new messages on your own time, repeat these steps, and when you get to the Fetch New Data screen, tap Manual.

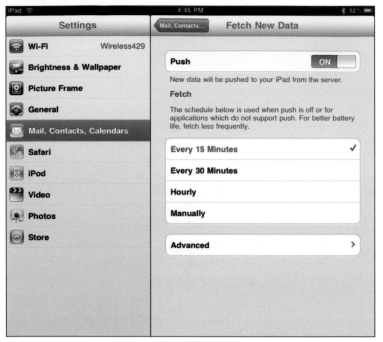

5.8 Use the Fetch New Data screen to configure your iPad to check for new messages automatically.

Displaying more messages in your Inbox message list

When you display an account's Inbox message list, the number of messages you see depends on the orientation of your iPad:

- In landscape mode (which displays the Inbox list automatically), you see about eight messages, as shown in Figure 5.9.

- In portrait mode (where you have to tap Inbox to see the message list), you see about ten messages.

5.9 In landscape mode, the Inbox message list displays about eight messages at a time.

The reason you see so few messages in either mode is that Mail displays for each message the sender, the subject line, and a two-line preview of the message. Of course, it's not a big whoop to flick through the rest of your messages (it's kind of fun, actually), but if you're looking for (or waiting for) a particular message, it would be nice to see more messages on the screen at once.

Can this be done? Of course, it's the iPad! The secret is to reduce the number of lines that Mail uses for the message preview. Reduce the preview to a single line, and you now see 10 messages in landscape mode and 13 messages in portrait; get rid of the preview altogether, and you see 14 messages in landscape mode and a whopping 18 messages per portrait screen.

Follow these steps to reduce the preview size:

1. **On the Home screen, tap Settings.** The Settings screen appears.

2. **Tap Mail, Contacts, Calendars to open the Mail screen.**

3. **In the Mail section, tap Preview.** Your iPad displays the Preview screen, as shown in Figure 5.10.

4. **Tap the number of lines you want to use.** To reduce the preview to a single line, tap 1 Line; to see no preview at all, tap None.

5.10 Use the Preview screen to set the number of lines that Mail uses to preview the Inbox messages.

Processing e-mail faster by identifying messages sent to you

In your iPad's Mail app, the Inbox folder tells you who sent you each message, but it doesn't tell you to whom the message was sent (that is, which addresses appeared on the To line or the Cc line). No big deal, right? Maybe, maybe not. You see, bulk mailers — I'm talking newsletters, mailing lists, and, notoriously, spammers — often don't send messages directly to each person on their subscriber lists. Instead, they use a generic bulk address, which means, significantly, that your e-mail address doesn't appear on the To or Cc lines. That's significant because most newsletters and mailing lists — and all spam — are low-priority messages that you can ignore when you're processing a stuffed Inbox.

Okay, great, but what good does all this do you if Mail doesn't show the To and Cc lines? You can configure Mail to show a little icon for messages that were sent directly to you:

- If the message includes your address in the To field, you see a "To" icon beside the message.

- If the message includes your address in the Cc field, you see a "Cc" icon beside the message.

Neat! Here's how to make this happen:

1. **On the Home screen, tap Settings.** The Settings screen appears.

2. **Tap Mail, Contacts, Calendars.** The Mail, Contacts, Calendars screen appears.

3. **In the Mail section, tap the Show To/Cc Label switch to the On position.**

When you examine your Inbox, you see the To and Cc icons on messages addressed to you, and you don't see either icon on bulk messages, as shown in Figure 5.11.

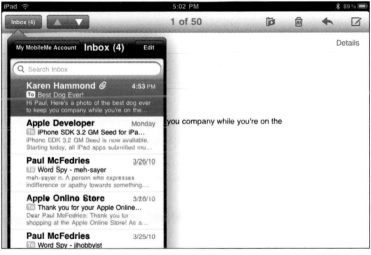

5.11 With the Show To/Cc Label switch turned on, Mail shows you which messages were addressed directly to you.

E-mailing a link to a Web page

The Web is all about finding content that's interesting, educational, and, of course, fun. And if you stumble across a site that meets one or more of these criteria, then the only sensible thing to do is share your good fortune with someone else, right? So, how do you do that? Some sites are kind enough to include an Email This Page link (or something similar), but you can't count on having one of those around. Instead, the usual method is to copy the page address, switch to your e-mail program, paste the address into the message, choose a recipient, and then send the message.

And, yes, with your iPad's copy-and-paste feature, you can do all that on your iPad, but boy, that sure seems like a ton of work. So are you stuck using this unwieldy method? Not a chance (you probably knew that). Your iPad includes a great little feature that enables you to plop the address of the current Safari page into an e-mail message with just a couple of taps. You then ship out the message, and you've made the world a better place.

Here's how it works:

1. **Use Safari to navigate to the site you want to share.**

2. **Tap the + button in the status bar.** Safari displays a dialog with several options.

3. **Tap Mail Link to this Page.** This opens a new e-mail message. As you can see in Figure 5.12, the new message already includes the page title as the Subject and the page address in the message body.

5.12 When you tap the Mail Link to this Page option, your iPad creates a new e-mail message with the page title and address already inserted.

4. **Choose a recipient for the message.**

5. **Edit the message text as you see fit.**

6. **Tap Send.** Your iPad fires off the message and returns you to Safari.

Setting a minimum message font size

Some people who send e-mails must have terrific eyesight because the font they use for the message text is positively microscopic. Such text is tough to read even on a big screen, but when it's crammed into the iPad's touchscreen, you'll be reaching for the nearest magnifying glass. Of course, that same touchscreen can also solve this problem: a quick finger spread magnifies the text accordingly.

That's easy enough if you just get the occasional message with nanoscale text, but if a regular correspondent does this, or if your eyesight isn't quite what it used to be (so *all* your messages appear ridiculously teensy), then a more permanent solution might be in order. Your iPad rides to the rescue once again by letting you configure a minimum font size for your messages. This means that if the message font size is larger than what you specify, your iPad displays the message as is; however, if the font size is smaller than your specification, your iPad scales up the text to your minimum size. Your tired eyes will be forever grateful.

Follow these steps to set your minimum font size:

1. **On the Home screen, tap Settings.** The Settings screen appears.

2. **Tap Mail, Contacts, Calendars.** Your iPad displays the Mail, Contacts, Calendars settings screen.

3. **In the Mail section, tap Minimum Font Size.** The Minimum Font Size screen appears, as shown in Figure 5.13.

4. **Tap the minimum font size you want to use: Small, Medium, Large, Extra Large, or Giant.** Mail uses the font size you select (or larger) when displaying your messages.

5.13 Use the Minimum Font Size screen to set the smallest text size that you want Mail to use when it displays a message.

Creating a custom iPad signature

E-mail signatures can range from the simple — a signoff such as "Cheers," or "All the best," followed by the sender's name — to baroque masterpieces filled with contact information, snappy quotations, even text-based artwork! On your iPad, the Mail app takes the simple route by adding the following signature to all your outgoing messages (new messages, replies, and forwards):

```
Sent from my iPad
```

I really like this signature because it's short, simple, and kinda cool (I, of course, *want* my recipients to know that I'm using my iPad!). If that default signature doesn't rock your world, you can create a custom one that does. Follow these steps:

1. **On the Home screen, tap Settings.** Your iPad opens the Settings screen.

2. **Tap Mail, Contacts, Calendars.** You see the Mail, Contacts, Calendars settings screen.

3. **In the Mail section, tap Signature.** The Signature screen appears, as shown in Figure 5.14.

iPad 📶		5:07 PM		⚡ 89% 🔋

Settings		Mail, Contacts...	Signature	Clear

Settings

- 📶 **Wi-Fi**   Wireless429
- 🖼 **Brightness & Wallpaper**
- 🖼 **Picture Frame**
- ⚙️ **General**
- ✉️ **Mail, Contacts, Calendars**
- 🧭 **Safari**
- 🎵 **iPod**
- 🎬 **Video**
- 🌼 **Photos**
- 🛒 **Store**

Sent from my iPad|

5.14 Use the Signature screen to create your custom iPad e-mail signature.

4. **Enter the signature you want to use.**

5. **Tap Mail, Contacts, Calendars.** Mail saves your new signature and uses it on all outgoing messages.

Caution   Mail doesn't give any way to cancel your edits and return to the original signature, so enter your text carefully. If you make a real hash of things, tap Clear to get a fresh start.

Disabling remote images in messages

Lots of messages nowadays come not just as plain text, but also with fonts, colors, images, and other flourishes. This fancy formatting, called either *rich text* or *HTML*, makes for a more pleasant e-mail experience, particularly when using images in messages, because who doesn't like a bit of eye candy to brighten their day?

Note

HTML stands for Hypertext Markup Language and is a set of codes that folks use to put together Web pages.

Unfortunately, however, getting images in your e-mail messages can sometimes be problematic:

- **A cellular connection may cause trouble.** For example, it may take a long time to load the images, or if your data plan has an upper limit, you may not want a bunch of e-mail images taking a big bite out of that limit.

- **Not all e-mail images are benign.** A *Web bug* is an image that resides on a remote server and is added to an HTML-formatted e-mail message by referencing an address on the remote server. When you open the message, Mail uses the address to download the image for display within the message. That sounds harmless enough, but if the message is junk e-mail, it's likely that the address also contains either your e-mail address or a code that points to your e-mail address. So when the remote server gets a request to load the image, it knows not only that you've opened the message, but also that your e-mail address is legitimate. So, not surprisingly, spammers use Web bugs all the time because, for them, valid e-mail addresses are a form of gold.

The iPad Mail app displays remote images by default. To disable remote images, follow these steps:

1. **On the Home screen, tap Settings.** Your iPad opens the Settings screen.
2. **Tap Mail, Contacts, Calendars.** You see the Mail, Contacts, Calendars settings screen.
3. **In the Mail section, tap the Load Remote Images switch to the Off position.** Mail saves the setting and no longer displays remote images in your e-mail messages.

Configuring your Exchange ActiveSync settings

If you have an account on a Microsoft Exchange Server 2003 or 2007 network, and that server has deployed Exchange ActiveSync, you're all set to have your iPad and Exchange account synchronized automatically. That's because ActiveSync supports wireless push technology, which means that if anything changes on your Exchange server account, that change is immediately synced with your iPad:

- **E-mail.** If you receive a new message on your Exchange account, ActiveSync immediately displays that message in your iPad's Mail app.

- **Contacts.** If someone at work adds or edits data in the server address book, those changes are immediately synced to your iPad Contacts list.

- **Calendar.** If someone at work adds or edits an appointment in your calendar, or if someone requests a meeting with you, that data is immediately synced with your iPad's Calendar application.

ActiveSync works both ways, too, so if you send e-mail messages, add contacts or appointments, or accept meeting requests, your server account is immediately updated with the changes. And all this data whizzing back and forth is safe, because it's sent over a secure connection.

Your iPad also gives you a few options for controlling ActiveSync, and the following steps show you how to set them:

1. **On the Home screen, tap Settings.** Your iPad opens the Settings screen.

2. **Tap Mail, Contacts, Calendars to open the Mail, Contacts, Calendars settings.**

3. **Tap your Exchange account.** The Exchange ActiveSync screen appears, as shown in Figure 5.15.

4. **To sync your Exchange e-mail account, tap the Mail On/Off switch to the On position.**

5. **To sync your Exchange address book, tap the Contacts On/Off switch to the On position, and then click Sync.**

My Exchange Account   Done

Exchange Account

Account Info   >

Mail   ON

Contacts   ON

Calendars   ON

Mail Days to Sync   3 Days >

Delete Account

5.15 Use the Exchange ActiveSync screen to customize your iPad's ActiveSync support.

6. **To sync your Exchange calendar, tap the Calendars On/Off switch to the On position, and then click Sync.**

7. **To control the amount of time that gets synced on your e-mail account, tap Mail Days to Sync and then tap the number of days, weeks, or months you want to sync.**

How Can I Have Fun with My iPad's Photos?

The iPad's large, high-resolution display makes it the perfect portable photo album. No more whipping out wallet shots of your kids: Just show people your iPad photo albums! The iPad also comes with some great features that make it a breeze to browse photos and run slide shows. However, your iPad is capable of more than just viewing photos. It's actually loaded with cool features that enable you to manipulate photos and use those photos to enhance other parts of your digital life. This chapter is your guide to these features.

Getting Photos Ready for Your iPad

I mentioned in this chapter's introduction that your iPad comes with features that make it almost ridiculously easy to browse photos, no matter how large your collection. That's true as far as it goes, but I should really have added a caveat: The iPad makes it easy to browse your photos *if* your photos have at least some semblance of organization.

To understand what I mean, and to get a sense of how much (or how little) prep work you have to do, here's a quick look at the five viewing modes offered by your iPad's Photos app:

- **Photos.** Tap this button at the top of the Photos app screen to see a list of all the photos stored on your iPad. The good news here is that the Photos app does *not* show the name of each photo, so you don't have to spend time fixing all those oddball names that your digital camera supplies to your images.

- **Albums.** Tap this button to see your photos organized by album, where an *album* is a collection of photos that are related in some way. On a Windows PC, the Photos app uses your photo folders as albums, so be sure to organize your photos into their proper folders and give the folders descriptive names. On a Mac, you also can use folders to organize your photos, but if you have iPhoto, you can create your own albums right in the program, as I describe in the next section.

- **Events.** Tap this button to see stacks of your photos organized by event. In iPhoto on a Mac, an *event* is a collection of photos taken during a particular time period, such as an afternoon outing or a day trip. To get the most out of the Events view, make sure your iPhoto events have descriptive names (click the current name, type the new name, and then press Return). If iPhoto created multiple events for the same time period, hold down ⌘, click each event, and then choose Events ➪ Merge Events.

- **Faces.** Tap this button to see stacks of your photos organized by the people in each photo. To take advantage of this cool feature, you need to have iPhoto '09 (or later) on a Mac, and you need to use the program to add names to the faces in your photos, as described later in this chapter.

- **Places.** Tap this button to see a world map that shows pushpins for each location where you took at least one photo. To map your photos, you need to have iPhoto '09 (or later) on a Mac, and you need to use the program to add locations to your photos, as described later in this chapter.

Using iPhoto to organize your photos into albums

As I mentioned earlier, an album is a collection of photos that are related in some way. If you have iPhoto on your Mac, you can create customized albums that include only the photos you want to view. Follow these steps:

1. **Choose File ⇨ New Album (or press ⌘+N).** iPhoto prompts you for an album name.

2. **Type a name for the new album.**

3. **Click Create.** iPhoto adds a new album to the Albums section of the sidebar.

4. **Click Photos.**

5. **For each photo you want to add to the new album, click and drag the photo and drop it on the album.**

Genius

For a faster way to create and populate an album, first open the Photos section of the iPhoto library or open an event you want to work with. Press and hold the ⌘ key, and click each photo you want to include in your album. When you're finished, choose File ⇨ New Album from Selection (you also can press Shift+⌘+N). Type the new album name, and click Create.

Using iPhoto to add names to faces in your photos

One of the awesome features in iPhoto '09 is that you can annotate your photos by adding names to the faces that appear in them. This enables you to navigate your photos by name in iPhoto. Even better, your iPad's Photos app picks up these names and enables you to view all the photos in which a certain person appears.

Follow these steps to add names to the faces in your photos:

1. **Click the photo that you want to annotate.**

2. **Click Name.** iPhoto displays its naming tools, adds boxes around each face in the photo, and displays Unnamed for each unrecognized face.

Note

To add names to the faces in your photos, you must be using iPhoto '09 or later. To check this, click iPhoto in the menu bar and then click About iPhoto.

3. **For the face you want to name, click Unnamed.** iPhoto opens a text box below the face.

4. **Type the person's name, or select it from the list of contacts that appears as you type, as shown in Figure 6.1, and press Return.**

6.1 Type the person's name or select the name from your Address Book contacts.

5. **Repeat Steps 3 and 4 to name each person in the photo.** If iPhoto didn't mark a face in the photo, click Add Missing Face, size and position the box over the face, click Done, and then follow Steps 3 and 4.

6. **Click Done.** iPhoto exits naming mode.

Using iPhoto to map your photos

You can tell iPhoto the locations where your photos were taken. When you sync your photos to your iPad, this location data goes along with the photos, and you can use the Photos app to display a map that shows those locations. This enables you to view all your photos taken in a particular place.

Note To map your photos, you must be using iPhoto '09 or later. To check this, click iPhoto in the menu bar and then click About iPhoto.

Follow these steps to add a location to a photo:

1. **Position the mouse pointer over the event that you want to map.** If you want to map a single photo, instead, open the event and position the pointer over the photo.

2. **Click the Information icon (the *i* in the lower-right corner of the photo).** iPhoto displays the Information window.

3. **Click Event Place.** If you're working with a single photo, click Photo Place instead. iPhoto displays a list of places you've previously defined, if any.

4. **Click Find on Map.** The Add New Place window appears.

5. **Use the Search box to type the location, and press Return.** iPhoto opens a Google map and adds a pushpin to mark the location, as shown in Figure 6.2.

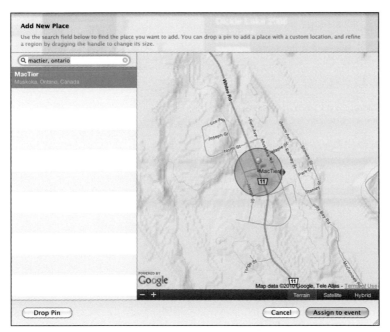

6.2 Use the Add New Place window to position the pushpin and assign the location to your event or photo.

6. **Click and drag the pin to the correct location, if necessary.**

7. **Click Assign to Event.** If you're working with a single photo, click Assign to Photo instead.

8. **Click Done.** iPhoto closes the information window.

Genius If you have a GPS-enabled camera phone — such as an iPhone — iPhoto automatically picks up location data from the photos. However, for this to work, you must activate this feature. Choose iPhoto ⇨ Preferences to open the iPhoto preferences, and click the Advanced tab. In the Look up Places list, choose Automatically. Note that you may still have to add or edit location names for your photos.

Syncing Photos

No iPad's media collection is complete without a few choice photos to show off around the water cooler. If you have some good pics on your computer, you can use iTunes to send those images to the iPad. Note that Apple supports a number of image file types — the usual TIFF and JPEG formats that you normally use for your photos as well as BMP, GIF, JPG2000 or JP2, PICT, PNG, PSD, and SGI.

Syncing computer photos to your iPad

If you use your computer to process lots of photos and you want to take copies of some or all of those photos with you on your iPad, then follow these steps to get synced:

1. **Connect your iPad to your computer.**

2. **In iTunes, click your iPad in the Devices list.**

3. **Click the Photos tab.**

4. **Select the Sync Photos From check box.**

5. **Choose an option from the drop-down menu:**

   - **iPhoto (Mac only).** Choose this item to sync the photos, albums, and events you've set up in iPhoto.

   - **Choose Folder.** Choose this command to sync the images contained in a folder you specify.

   - **My Pictures (or Pictures on Windows Vista).** Choose this item to sync the images in the My Pictures (or Pictures) folder.

Note

If you have another photo-editing application installed on your computer, chances are good that it also appears in the Sync photos from list.

6. **Select the photos you want to sync.** The controls you see depend on what you chose in Step 5:

- **If you chose either My Pictures or Choose folder.** In this case, select either the All photos option or the Selected Folders option. If you select the latter, select the check box beside each subfolder you want to sync.

- **If you chose iPhoto.** In this case, you get two further options: Select the All Photos, Albums, and Events option to sync your entire iPhoto library; select the Selected Albums and Events option, and then select the check box beside each album and event you want to sync, as shown in Figure 6.3.

LIBRARY	
♫ Music	
📺 Movies	
📺 TV Shows	
🎙 Podcasts	
📖 Books	
Apps	
STORE	
iTunes Store	
Downloads	
▼ DEVICES	
▶ Paul's...	
▶ SHARED	
▶ GENIUS	
▶ PLAYLISTS	

Summary | Info | Apps | Music | Movies | TV Shows | Podcasts | iTunes U | Books | **Photos**

☑ Sync Photos from: 📷 iPhoto ⬍

○ All photos, albums, and events
◉ Selected albums and events, and automatically include [no events ⬍]
☐ Include videos

Albums:

☐ Last 12 Months	
☐ Last Import	
☑ iPhonography	36
☑ Dogs, Dogs, Dogs	30
☑ Vacation Pics	166

Events: 🔍

☑ Gypsy	36
☑ Florence	5
☑ Wedding Pics	66
☐ Flowers	
☑ Bahamas	166
☑ Dickie Lake 2006	79
☐ Brickworks Pics	
☑ St. Maarten	43

Capacity
14.02 GB

☐ Audio   ☐ Photos   ☐ Other   ☐ Free
565.6 MB   58.8 MB   215.9 MB   13.20 GB

[Cancel]
[Apply]

6.3 If you have iPhoto '09 on your Mac, you can sync specific albums and events to your iPad.

7. **Click Apply.** iTunes syncs the iPad using your new settings.

Note iTunes doesn't sync exact copies of your photos to the iPad. Instead, it creates what Apple calls TV-quality versions of each image. These are copies of the images that have been reduced in size to match the iPad's screen size. This makes the sync go faster, and the photos take up much less room on your iPad.

Syncing iPad photos to your computer

If you create a Safari bookmark on your iPad and then sync with your computer, that bookmark is transferred from the iPad to the default Web browser on your computer. That's a sweet deal that also applies to contacts and appointments, but unfortunately it doesn't apply to media files, which, with one exception, travel along a one-way street from your computer to your iPad.

Ah, but then there's that one exception, and it's a good one. If you receive any photos on your iPad (via, say, an e-mail message or text message), the sync process reverses itself and enables you to send some or all of those images to your computer. Sign me up!

Note Actually, there's a second exception. If you use the iTunes application on your iPad to purchase or download music, those files are transferred to your computer during the next sync. iTunes creates a Store category called Purchased on *iPad*, where *iPad* is the name of your iPad. When the sync is complete, you can find your music there, as well as in the Music Library.

The iPad-to-computer sync process bypasses iTunes entirely. Instead, your computer deals directly with iPad and treats it just as though it's some garden-variety media storage device. How this works depends on whether your computer is a Mac or a Windows PC, so I'll use separate sets of steps.

To sync your iPad photos to your Mac, follow these steps:

1. **Connect your iPad to your Mac.** iPhoto opens, adds your iPad to the Devices list, and displays the photos from your iPad's Camera Roll album, as shown in Figure 6.4.

Note If you've imported some of your iPad photos in the past, you probably don't want to import them again. That's very sensible of you, and you can prevent that by hiding those photos. Select the Hide Photos Already Imported check box.

6.4 When you connect your iPad to your Mac, iPhoto shows up to handle the import of the photos.

2. **Use the Event Name text box to name the event that these photos represent.**

3. **Choose how you want to import the photos:**

   - If you want to import every photo, click Import All.

   - If you want to import only some of the photos, select the ones you want to import and click Import Selected.

4. **If you want to leave the photos on your iPad, click Keep Originals.** Otherwise, click Delete Originals to clear the photos from your iPad.

Here's how things work if you're syncing with a Windows 7 or Windows Vista PC:

1. **Connect your iPad to your Vista PC.** The AutoPlay dialog appears.

2. **Click Import Pictures Using Windows.** The rest of these steps assume you selected this option. However, if you have another photo management application installed, it should appear in the AutoPlay list, and you can click it to import the photos using that program.

3. **Type a tag for the photos.** A tag is a word or short phrase that identifies the photos.

4. **Click Import.** Windows imports the photos and opens Windows Photo Gallery to display them.

Preventing your iPad from sending photos to your computer

Each and every time you connect your iPad to your computer, you see iPhoto (on your Mac) or the AutoPlay dialog (in Windows 7 or Windows Vista without iTunes installed). This is certainly convenient if you actually want to send photos to your computer, but you may find that you do that only once in a blue moon. In that case, having to deal with iPhoto or a dialog every time could cause even the most mild-mannered among us to start pulling out our hair. If you prefer to keep your hair, you can configure your computer to not pester you about getting photos from your iPad.

Note Configuring your computer to not download photos from your iPad means that in the future you either need to reverse the setting or manually import your photos.

Here's how you set this up on your Mac:

1. **Connect your iPad to your Mac.**

2. **Choose Finder ⇨ Applications to open the Applications folder.**

3. **Double-click Image Capture.** The Image Capture application opens.

4. **Click your iPad in the Devices list.**

5. **Click the Connecting This iPad Opens menu, and then click No Application, as shown in Figure 6.5.**

6. **Choose Image Capture ⇨ Quit Image Capture.** Image Capture saves the new setting and shuts down. The next time you connect your iPad, iPhoto ignores it.

> Paul's iPad
>
> **Connecting this iPad opens:**
>
> No application
>
> ☐ Share iPad
>
> ☐ Delete after import

6.5 In the Image Capture window, choose No Application to prevent iPhoto from starting when you connect your iPad.

Follow these steps to convince Windows 7 and Windows Vista not to open the AutoPlay dialog each time you connect your iPad:

1. **Choose Start ⇨ Default Programs to open the Default Programs window.**

2. **Click Change AutoPlay Settings.** The AutoPlay dialog appears.

3. **In the Devices section, open the Apple iPad list and choose Take No Action.**

4. **Click Save.** Windows saves the new setting.

Importing photos directly from a camera

If you have a stack of photos on a digital camera or iPhone, you may think the only way to get them onto your iPad is to first sync the camera's photos to your Mac or PC and then sync the photos from your computer to your iPad. And you'd be right, *most* of the time. However, Apple offers a way to avoid this time-consuming route: the Camera Connection Kit. This is an iPad accessory designed to get photos directly from a camera to an iPad. The kit comes with two adapters:

- **Camera Connector.** Connect this adapter's 30-pin connector to the 30-pin port on the iPad, and then connect the USB cable to the digital camera's USB port.

- **SD Card Reader.** Connect this adapter's 30-pin connector to the 30-pin port on the iPad, and then insert the digital camera's SD (Secure Digital) card (or, in fact, *any* SD card).

The Photos app recognizes the connection, and you can then import some or all of the photos to the iPad.

Getting More Out of Your iPad's Photos

After you've dumped a bucketful of photos onto your iPad, you can start messing around with those photos by tapping the Photos icon on the Home screen. In the Photos app, you use the five tabs at the top of the screen — Photos, Albums, Events, Faces, and Places, described earlier — to view your photos from different angles, so to speak. The next few sections take you through a few of the more interesting features of the Photos app.

Sneaking a peek at a stack of photos

The most straightforward way to browse your photos is to tap the Photos tab to see a complete list of all your iPad photos, flick up (and down, if need be) to scroll the images, and then tap the picture you want to check out. When you're finished, tap All Photos to return to the list.

Three of the tabs in the Photos app screen — Albums, Events, and Faces — display your photos grouped into related categories called *stacks*. For example, in the Albums tab, each stack is based on a photo album name (where each album is either a folder from your PC or Mac, or a photo album defined in iPhoto); similarly, the stacks in Events and Faces are based on the event and face metadata you've defined in iPhoto.

Each stack shows a representative photo on top, and you may see the edge of a photo or two underneath, so you immediately run across a stacking problem: unless you can be certain which photos are in the stack (say, from the stack name and the photo on top), what do you do if you're not sure whether a particular stack contains the photo or photos you want to work with? Rather than opening stacks willy-nilly to find the one you want, the Photos app gives you a much more elegant solution. Place two fingers over a stack, and spread the fingers. As you move your fingers apart, the Photos app spreads out the stack's photos, as you can see in Figure 6.6. If that's not the stack you want, lift your fingers off the screen to return the photos to the stack; if it is the stack you want, keep spreading your fingers until the stack fills the screen.

6.6 Spread your fingers over a stack to sneak a peek at the stack's photos.

Scrolling, rotating, zooming, and panning photos

You can do so much with your photos after they're in your iPad, and it isn't your normal photo-browsing experience. You aren't just a passive viewer because you can actually take some control over what you see and how the pictures are presented.

You can use the following techniques to navigate and manipulate your photos:

● **Scroll.** You view your photos by flicking. If you're in landscape mode, flick left to view the next photo and right to view the previous shot; if you're in portrait mode, flick up to see the next image and down to display the previous image. Alternatively, tap the screen to display a sequence of thumbnails at the bottom of the Photos app window, and run your finger along those thumbnails to quickly peruse the photos.

● **Rotate.** When a landscape shot shows up on your iPad, it gets letterboxed at the top (that is, you see black space above and below the image). To get a better view, rotate the screen into the landscape position and the photo rotates right along with it, filling the entire screen. When you come upon a photo with a portrait orientation, rotate the iPad back to the upright position for best viewing.

● **Flip.** To show a photo to another person, flip the iPad so the back is towards you and the bottom is now the top. The iPad automatically flips the photo right side up.

● **Zoom.** Zooming magnifies the shot that's on the screen. You can use two methods to do this:

  ○ **Double-tap the area of the photo that you want to zoom in on.** The iPad doubles the size of the portion you tapped. Double-tap again to return the photo to its original size.

  ○ **Spread and pinch.** To zoom in, spread two fingers apart over the area you want magnified. To zoom back out, pinch two fingers together.

● **Pan.** After you zoom in on the photo, drag your finger across the screen to move the photo along with your finger, an action known as *panning*.

Note You can scroll to another photo if you're zoomed in, but it takes much more work to get there because the iPad thinks you're trying to pan. For faster scrolling, return the photo to its normal size and then scroll.

Adding an existing photo to a contact

You can assign a photo to a contact in two ways: the photo straight from a photo album, or through the Contacts app.

First, here's how you assign a photo from a photo album:

1. **Tap Photos in the Home screen.** The Photos app appears.

2. **Locate the image you want to use.**

3. **Tap the photo you want to use.** The Photos app opens the photo.

4. **Tap the screen to reveal the controls.**

5. **Tap the Action button.** The Action button is the arrow that appears on the right side of the menu bar. The Photos app displays a list of actions you can perform.

6. **Tap Assign to Contact.** A list of all your contacts appears.

7. **Tap the contact you want to associate with the photo.** The Move and Scale screen appears.

8. **Drag the image so it's positioned on the screen the way you want.**

9. **Pinch or spread your fingers over the image to set the zoom level you want.**

10. **Tap Use.** iPad assigns the photo to the contact and returns you to your photo album.

To assign a photo using the Contacts app, follow these steps:

1. **On the Home screen, tap the Contacts icon to open the Contacts app.**

2. **Tap the contact that you want to add a photo to.** Your iPad displays the contact's Info screen.

3. **Tap Edit to put the contact into Edit mode.**

4. **Tap Add Photo.** Your iPad displays the Photo Albums screen.

5. **Tap the album that contains the photo you want to use.**

6. **Tap the photo you want.** The Move and Scale screen appears.

7. **Drag the image so it's positioned on the screen the way you want.**

8. **Pinch or spread your fingers over the image to set the zoom level you want.**

9. **Tap Use.** iPad assigns the photo to the contact and returns you to the Info screen.

10. **Tap Done.** Your iPad exits Edit mode.

Starting a photo slide show

If flicking to scroll through your photos seems like too much work, or if you're busy baking bread or pursuing some other two-handed activity, you can get your iPad to do all the work for you. When you're viewing your Photos list, or the photos in an album, event, or stack, you can crank up a slide show that displays each photo for a few seconds and then automatically moves on to the next image.

You can get a slide show up and sliding by following these steps:

1. **On the Home screen, tap the Photos icon to open the Photos app.**

2. **Open the list of photos you want to use.** For example, if you want to show the photos from a particular event, open that event stack.

3. **Tap the screen to reveal the controls.**

4. **Tap Slideshow in the menu bar.** The Slideshow Options dialog appears, as shown in Figure 6.7.

6.7 Use the Slideshow Options to set up a basic iPad slide show.

5. **If you want to listen to some music while the slide show runs, tap the Play Music switch to On and tap Music to choose the type of music you want to hear.** If you're more of a silent movie fan, tap the Play Music switch to Off to bypass the tunes.

6. **Tap an option in the Transition section to define how the Photos app transitions from one photo to the next.** Choose one of the following: Cube, Dissolve, Ripple, Wipe, or Origami.

7. **Tap Start Slideshow.** The Photos app starts the show.

To pause the show, tap the screen; tap Play to resume the festivities.

Creating a custom photo slide show

Okay, the basic slide show is pretty cool, but your iPad also offers a few settings for creating custom slide shows. For example, you can set how long each photo lingers onscreen, and you can configure the slide show to display your photos randomly.

Here's how to customize your slide show settings:

1. **On the Home screen, tap the Settings icon.** The Settings screen opens.

2. **Tap the Photos icon.** Your iPad displays the Photos screen, as shown in Figure 6.8.

6.8 Use your iPad's Photos screen to create a custom slide show.

You get six settings to configure your custom slide show:

- **Play Each Slide For.** You use this setting to set the amount of time that each photo appears on-screen. Tap Play Each Slide For, and then tap a time: 2 Seconds, 3 Seconds (this is the default), 5 Seconds, 10 Seconds, or 20 Seconds.

- **Repeat.** This setting determines whether the slide show repeats from the beginning after the last photo is displayed. To turn on this setting, tap the Repeat switch to the On position.

- **Shuffle.** You use this setting to display the album photos in random order. To turn on this setting, tap the Shuffle switch to the On position.

Playing a slide show with your own background music

Here's a little bonus that the iPad throws your way. Yes, you can wow them back home by running a custom slide show with some prefab music, but you can positively make their jaws hit the floor when you add your *own* music soundtrack to the show! They'll be cheering in the aisles.

Here's how you do it:

1. **On your iPad's Home screen, tap the iPod icon to open the iPod app.**
2. **Tap the playlist, and then tap a song to get the playlist going.**
3. **Press the Home button to return to the Home screen.**
4. **Tap the Photos icon to open the Photos app.**
5. **Open the Photos list or a photo stack, tap Slideshow, and then tap Start Slideshow to launch the slide show.** Your iPad runs the slide show, and all the while your music plays in the background.

Setting up your iPad as a digital photo frame

Digital photo frames are devices that look like slightly bulked-up versions of regular photo frames, but they display a series of digital photos instead of just a single photo. A digital photo frame is a great idea in theory, but in practice they're a bit unwieldy, mostly because you have to somehow get your digital photos into the device (using a memory card, wireless network connection, USB cable, or whatever).

Why bother with that hassle when your iPad not only has your photos already, but sits up nice and pretty when it's moored in the optional dock accessory or propped up by Apple's iPad Case? Just insert the iPad into the dock or case, and launch your slide show as described earlier.

Before getting to all that, you may want to take a second and configure a few iPad settings related to using the device as a picture frame:

1. **On the Home screen, tap Settings.** The Settings app appears.

2. **Tap Picture Frame.** The Picture Frame screen appears, as shown in Figure 6.9.

6.9 Use the Picture Frame screen to configure your iPad's picture frame feature.

You get six settings to configure your picture frame:

- **Transition.** You use this setting to specify the type of transition that your iPad uses between each photo. Tap Transition and then tap the type of transition you prefer: Cube, Dissolve (the default), Ripple, Wipe, or Origami.

- **Zoom in on Faces.** Leave this setting on to have your iPad zoom in on a recognizable face.

- **Shuffle.** You use this setting to display the album photos in random order. To turn on this setting, tap the Shuffle switch to the On position.

- **All Photos.** Tap this option to have your iPad include all of your photos in the frame display.

- **Albums.** Tap this option to include only your album photos in the show.

- **Events.** Tap this option to include only your event photos in the show.

Deleting a photo

If your iPad contains a synced photo you don't need anymore, you can delete it to reduce clutter in the stack that holds it. Happily, you don't have to worry about this being a permanent deletion, either. The syncing process goes only from your computer to your iPad when it comes to photos that come from your computer. So even if you remove a photo from the iPad, it remains safe on your computer.

To delete a photo, follow these steps:

1. **Tap Photos in the Home screen.** The Photos app appears.

2. **Locate the image you want to blow away.** For example, if you know the photo is part of a particular event, open that event stack.

3. **Tap the doomed photo.** The Photos app opens the photo.

4. **Tap the screen to reveal the controls.**

5. **Tap the Delete button (the trash can icon).** The Photos app asks you to confirm the deletion.

6. **Tap Delete Photo.** The Photos app tosses the photo into the trash, wipes its hands, and returns you to the photos.

Sharing Photos

You'll most often use the Photos app for personal trips down Memory Lane, and there's nothing wrong with that. However, photos are for sharing, right? Of course! And with the iPad's big, bright screen, it's easy to gather a few nearby folks around and show off your digital masterpieces by flicking left and right, up and down. That's fine for nearby victims, uh, people you can cajole into huddling around your iPad, but far-flung folks are another matter. How can you share your photo goodness with people across town or across the country? Lots of ways, actually: You can send a photo via e-mail or text message; you can upload a photo to Flickr; and you can use your MobileMe account. In the rest of this chapter, I show you all these sharing techniques and more.

Sending a photo via e-mail

More often than you'd think, being able to send photos from your iPad to someone's e-mail is a handy trick. This is particularly true if it's a photo you've just received on your iPad (say, via an e-mail message), because then you can share the photo pronto, without having to trudge back to your computer. You can e-mail any existing photo from one of your iPad photo albums.

Caution

Having the technology to e-mail a photo at your fingertips is wonderful, but bear in mind that your recipient doesn't see the photo in its natural state. Instead, your iPad shrinks the photo to 640 pixels wide by 480 pixels tall, a pale shadow of its original 1600×1200-pixel glory.

Follow these steps to send a photo from your iPad via e-mail:

1. **On the Home screen, tap Photos.** The Photos app appears.
2. **Locate the image you want to use.** For example, if you know the photo is part of a particular album, open that album stack.
3. **Tap the screen to reveal the controls.**
4. **Tap the Action button.** The Action button is the arrow that appears on the right side of the menu bar. The Photos app displays the Select Photos screen.
5. **Tap the photo you want to use.** The Photos app selects the photo.
6. **Tap Email.** In the New Message screen that appears, the photo appears in the body of the message.
7. **Choose your message recipient, and enter a Subject line.**
8. **Tap Send.** Your iPad sends the message and returns you to the photo.

Note

To send a photo via e-mail, you must have a default e-mail account set on your iPad. See Chapter 5 for information about setting up a default e-mail account.

Sending a photo to your Flickr account

If you have a Flickr account, you can send photos from your iPad by e-mail. Flickr gives you an e-mail address just for doing this. When you want to upload a photo to Flickr, you simply attach it to an e mail as described earlier in the chapter and then enter the address given you by Flickr into the address field. You can find out the address to use for this by going to the following page:

www.flickr.com/account/uploadbyemail

Using Your iPad to Work with MobileMe Photos

Push e-mail, push contacts, and push calendars are the stars of the MobileMe show, and rightly so. However, the MobileMe interface at me.com also includes another Web application that shouldn't be left out of the limelight: the Gallery. You use this application to create online photo albums that you can share with other people, and you can even allow those folks to download your photos and upload their own.

You generally work with the Gallery either within the MobileMe interface on me.com or by using compatible applications on your computer, such as iPhoto on your Mac. However, your iPad also can work with the Gallery, as you see in the next few sections.

Using your iPad to send photos to the MobileMe Gallery

Your MobileMe account includes a Gallery application that you can use to create and share photo albums. You can upload photos to an album directly from the me.com site, or you can use iPhoto on your Mac to handle the upload chores.

However, what if you're cruising around town and use your iPad to snap a great photo of something? Do you really want to wait until you get back to your computer, sync the iPad, and then upload the photo? Of course not! Fortunately, you don't have to, because you can send photos directly to your MobileMe Gallery right from your iPad (assuming you've got 3G or you can find a nearby Wi-Fi hotspot).

Configuring an album to allow e-mail uploads

Before you can send those photos to your MobileMe Gallery, you have to configure the MobileMe album to allow e-mail photo uploads. Follow these steps:

1. **Use a Web browser to navigate to me.com, and log into your MobileMe account.**

2. **Click the Gallery icon to access the MobileMe Gallery.**

3. **Display the Album Settings dialog:**
   - If you're creating a new photo album, click +.
   - If you want to use an existing album, click the album and then click Adjust Settings.

4. **Select the Allow: Adding of Photos Via Email, iPhone, or iPad check box, as shown in Figure 6.10.**

5. **If you want Gallery visitors to see the e-mail address used for sending photos to this album, select the Show: Email Address for Uploading Photos check box.**

6. **If you're creating a new album, type a name and configure the other settings as needed.**

7. **Click Publish.** If you're creating a new album, click Create instead.

Album Settings

Album Name: iPhonography

Allow: ☑ Downloading of photos, movies or entire album
☐ Uploading of photos or movies via web browser
☑ Adding of photos via email, iPhone or iPad
paulmcfedries ██████@post.me.com

Show: ☑ Photo or movie titles
☐ Email address for uploading photos

Advanced: ☐ Hide album on my Gallery page

Cancel   Publish

6.10 Select the Allow: Adding of Photos Via Email, iPhone, or iPad check box to enable your friends and fans to upload pictures to your Gallery.

Caution If you configure your album so anyone can see it, be careful about showing the e-mail address; otherwise, your Gallery could be invaded by irrelevant or even improper photos.

Note If you selected the Show: Email Address for Uploading Photos check box, album visitors can see the upload address by clicking the Send to Album icon in your Web Gallery page.

Sending a photo to your own MobileMe Gallery

Now you're ready to send photos from your iPad directly to your MobileMe Gallery. Assuming you have an Internet connection on your iPad (see Chapter 1), here's how it works:

1. **On the Home screen, tap Photos to open the Photos app.**

2. **Locate the image you want to use.** For example, if you know the photo is part of a particular event, open that event stack.

3. **Tap the photo you want to use.** The Photos app opens the photo.

4. **Tap the screen to reveal the controls.**

5. **Tap the Action button.** The Action button is the arrow that appears on the right side of the menu bar. The Photos app displays a list of actions you can perform.

6. **Tap Send to MobileMe.** Your iPad displays the Publish Photo screen, as shown in Figure 6.11.

7. **Tap a title for the photo as well as an optional description.**

8. **Tap the album you want to use for the photo.**

9. **Tap Publish.** Your iPad blasts the photo to your MobileMe Gallery and then displays a list of options.

10. **Tap one of the following options:**

    - **View on MobileMe.** Tap this option to open the MobileMe Gallery and view the photo on your iPad.

    - **Tell a Friend.** Tap this option to create a new e-mail message that includes a link to the photo that you just published.

    - **Close.** Tap this option to return to your photo album.

6.11 Use the Publish Photo screen to ship a photo to your MobileMe Gallery.

Sending a photo to someone else's MobileMe Gallery

If you want to send a photo to another person's MobileMe Gallery, first check to make sure that e-mail uploads are allowed. Open the other person's Web Gallery in any desktop browser (this won't work in your iPad's Safari browser), and then click Send to Album. If you see the Send to Album dialog, note the e-mail address and click OK. (If nothing happens when you click Send to Album, it means the person doesn't want to share the address with the likes of you.)

Assuming you have the album upload address in your mitts, you can send a photo from your iPad to that person's MobileMe Gallery by following these steps:

1. **On the Home screen, tap Photos to open the Photos application.**

2. **Locate the image you want to use.** For example, if you know the photo is part of a particular album, open that album stack.

3. **Tap the screen to reveal the controls.**

4. **Tap the Action button.** The Action button is the arrow that appears on the right side of the menu bar. The Photos app displays the Select Photos screen.

5. **Tap the photo you want to use.** The Photos app selects the photo.

6. **Tap Email.** Your iPad displays the New Message screen.

7. **Tap the To field, and enter the other person's MobileMe Gallery upload e-mail address.**

8. **Tap the Subject field, and edit the subject text.** This is the title that appears under the photo in the MobileMe Gallery.

9. **Tap Send.** Your iPad fires off the photo to the other person's Gallery.

Viewing your MobileMe Gallery in your iPad

After you have an album or two lurking in your MobileMe Gallery, others can view your albums by using your special Gallery Web address, which takes the following form:

http://gallery.me.com/*username*

Here, *username* is your MobileMe username. For a specific album, the address looks like this:

http://gallery.me.com/*username/#nnnnnn*

Here, *nnnnnn* is a number that MobileMe assigns to you.

Naturally, because your Gallery is really just a fancy Web site, you can access it using your iPad's Safari browser, which also provides you with tools for navigating an album.

Follow these steps to use your iPad to access and navigate a photo album in your MobileMe Gallery:

1. **On the Home screen, tap Safari.** Your iPad opens the Safari screen.

2. **Tap the address bar to open it for editing.**

3. **Enter your MobileMe Gallery address, and tap Go.** The My Gallery page appears.

4. **Tap the album you want to view.** Safari displays thumbnail images for each photo.

5. **Tap the first photo you want to view.** Safari displays the photo as well as the controls for navigating the album, as shown in Figure 6.12. If you don't see the controls, tap the photo.

6. **Tap the Next and Previous buttons to navigate the photos.**

If you check out your MobileMe Gallery frequently, save it as a bookmark for faster access. With the My Gallery page displayed, tap +, tap Add Bookmark, and then tap Save.

6.12 Safari showing a photo from a MobileMe Gallery album.

How Do I Manage My eBook Library on My iPad?

Chances are good that you're holding a physical book in your hands right now as you read these words. Physical books are an awesome invention: They're portable, easy-to-use, and fully "show-off-able," whether being read on the subway or sitting on a bookshelf at home. Physical books aren't going away anytime soon, but the age of electronic books — eBooks — is upon us. Amazon's Kindle lit a fire under the eBook category, but it's clunky to use and tied to Amazon; the iPhone and iPod touch are actually the most popular eReaders today, but they're a bit too small. As you see in this chapter, the iPad fills in these gaps by being easy to use, by supporting an open eBook format, and by having a screen that seems tailor-made for reading books.

Installing the iBooks App

In this chapter, I concentrate on iBooks, which is Apple's new eReader app. However, it's important to stress right off the bat that you're not restricted to using iBooks for reading eBooks on your iPad. Tons of great eBook apps are available (I mention a few of them at the end of this chapter; see the section on reading other eBooks on your iPad), so feel free to use any or all of them in addition to (or even instead of) iBooks.

Unlike the other apps I've talked about in this book, iBooks isn't part of the default iPad app collection. Instead, you have to install it (it's free) from the App Store:

1. **On the Home screen, tap App Store.** Your iPad opens the App Store.

2. **Tap search to open the Search page.**

3. **Tap inside the Search box to display the keyboard, type iBooks, and then tap Search.** The search results appear.

4. **Tap the iBooks app.** The app's Info screen appears.

5. **Tap the FREE icon.** The Free icon changes to the Install icon.

6. **Tap Install.** The App Store asks for your iTunes account password.

7. **Type your password, and tap OK.** The App Store downloads and installs the app, and an iBooks icon appears on the Home screen.

8. **When the installation is complete, tap the iBooks icon to launch the app.** Figure 7.1 shows the iBooks Library, which looks like a bookcase.

Getting Your Head around eBook Formats

If there's one reason why eBooks haven't taken off (in the same way that, say, digital music now rules the planet), it's because the eBook world is hopelessly, head-achingly confusing. As I write this, at least two dozen (yes, two *dozen!*) different eBook formats are available, with new formats jumping on the eBook bandwagon with distressing frequency. That's bad enough, but it gets worse when you consider that some of these formats require a specific eReading device or program. For example, the Kindle eBook format requires either the Kindle eReader or the Kindle app; similarly, the Microsoft LIT format requires the Microsoft Reader program. Finally, things turn positively chaotic when you realize that some formats come with built-in restrictions that prevent you from reading eBooks in other devices or programs, or sharing eBooks with other people.

7.1 The iBooks Library is designed to mimic a real bookcase.

We're a long way from the simplicity and clarity that comes with having a near-universal eBook format (such as the MP3 format in music), but there are signs of hope because one format seems to be slowly emerging from the fray: EPUB. This is a free and open eBook standard created by the International Digital Publishing Forum (IDPF; see www.idpf.org/). EPUB files (which use the .epub extension) are supported by most eReader programs and by most eReader devices (with the Amazon Kindle being the very noticeable exception). EPUB is leading the way not only because it's free and non-proprietary, but also because it offers quite a few cool features:

- Text is resizable, so you can select the size that's most comfortable for you.

- The layout and formatting of the text is handled by cascading style sheets (CSS), which is an open and well-known standard that makes it easy to alter the look of the text, including changing the font.

- Text is "re-flowable," which means that when you change the text size or the font, the text wraps naturally on the screen to accommodate the new character sizes. (This is opposed to some eBook formats that simply zoom in or out of the text.)

- A single eBook can have alternative versions of the book in the same file.

- eBooks can include high-resolution images right on the page.

- Publishers can protect book content by adding *digital rights management* (DRM) support. DRM refers to any technology that restricts the usage of content to prevent piracy. (Depending on where you fall in the "information wants to be free" spectrum, DRM may not be "cool" and may not even be considered a "feature.")

So the first bit of good news is that the iBooks app supports the EPUB format, so all the features listed above are available in the iBooks app.

Note

For the record, I should also mention that you can use the iBooks app to read books in three other formats: plain text, HTML, and PDF.

The next bit of good news is iBooks' support for EPUB means that a vast universe of public domain books is available to you. On its own, Google Books (http://books.google.com/) offers over a *million* public domain eBooks. Several other excellent EPUB sites exist on the Web, and I tell you about them, as well as tell you how to get them onto your iPad, a bit later (see the section on adding other EPUB eBooks).

By definition, public-domain eBooks are DRM-free, and you can use them in any way you see fit. However, lots of the EPUB books you'll find come with DRM restrictions. In the case of iBooks, the DRM scheme-of-choice is called FairPlay. This is the DRM technology that Apple used on iTunes for many years. Apple phased out DRM on music a while ago, but still uses it for other content, such as movies, TV shows, and audiobooks.

FairPlay means that many of the eBooks you download through iBooks face the following restrictions:

- You can access your books on a maximum of five computers, each of which must be authorized with your iTunes Store account info.
- You can read your eBooks only on your iPad or on a computer that has iTunes installed.

It's crucial to note here two restrictions you'll trip over with DRM-encrusted eBooks:

- FairPlay eBooks will *not* work on other eReader devices that support the EPUB format, including the Sony Reader and the Barnes & Noble Nook.
- EPUB format books that come wrapped in some other DRM scheme will *not* work on your iPad.

However, remember that DRM is an optional add-on to the EPUB format. Although it's expected that most publishers will bolt FairPlay DRM onto books they sell in the iBookstore, it's not required, so you should be able to find DRM-free eBooks in the iBookstore (and elsewhere).

Note   If you have an Amazon Kindle, I'm afraid you won't be able to transfer any of your Kindle eBooks directly to your iPad, or vice versa. The Kindle doesn't support EPUB, so it can't load even your DRM-free EPUB books. The Kindle uses a proprietary eBook format, so Kindle eBooks won't transfer to the iPad (or any other eReader). However, Amazon does offer a Kindle app for the iPad, so you can use that app to read your Kindle books.

Managing Your iBooks Library

The iBooks app comes with a virtual wood bookcase, which is a nice bit of eye candy, for sure, but is certainly no more than that since the real point is to fill that bookcase with your favorite digital reading material. So your first task is to add a few titles to the bookcase, and the next few sections show you how to do just that.

Browsing books in the iBookstore

You'll see a bit later that you can grab eBooks via the iTunes Store, but what if you're out and about with your iPad, you've got a bit of time to kill, and you decide to start a book? That's no problem, because iBooks has a direct link to Apple's new book marketplace, the iBookstore. Your iPad can establish a wireless connection to the App Store anywhere you have Wi-Fi access or a cellular signal (ideally 3G for faster downloads, assuming you have a 3G version of the iPad). You can browse and search the books, read reviews, and purchase any book you want (or grab a title from the large collection of free books). The eBook downloads to your iPad and adds itself to the iBooks bookcase. You can start reading within seconds!

What about the selection? When Apple announced the iPad and the iBooks app, they also announced that five major publishers would be stocking the iBookstore: Hachette, HarperCollins, Macmillan, Penguin, and Simon & Schuster. Apple also promised that more publishers would be added; so along with all those free eBooks, you can rest assured the iBookstore will have an impressive selection.

To access the iBookstore, follow these steps:

1. **Display the iBooks Library.**

    - If you haven't loaded the app yet, tap the iBooks icon to open the iBooks app.

    - If you're in the iBooks app and reading a book, tap the screen to display the controls and then tap Library.

2. **Tap the Store icon.**

As you can see in Figure 7.2, your iPad organizes the iBookstore similar to the App Store. That is, you get four browse buttons in the menu bar — Featured, NY Times, Top Charts, and Publishers. You use these buttons to navigate the iBookstore.

Here's a summary of what each browse button does for you:

- **Featured.** Tap this button to display a list of books picked by the iBookstore editors. The list shows each book's cover, title, author, category, star rating, number of reviews, and price. Tap New to see the latest apps, and tap What's Hot to see the most popular items.

- **NY Times.** Tap this button to access the New York Times Bestsellers screen, which displays the top sellers in two lists: Fiction and Nonfiction.

- **Top Charts.** Tap this button to see a collection of charts, including the Top Paid books and the Top Free books.

- **Purchases.** Tap this button to see a list of the books you've downloaded.

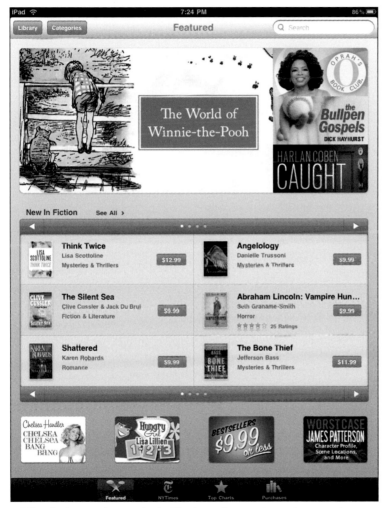

7.2 Use the browse buttons in the iBookstore's menu bar to locate and manage apps for your iPad.

The iBookstore also includes a Search box on the upper-right corner so you can search for the book you want, as well as a Categories button on the upper-left side so you can browse books by category.

Note Tap a book to get more detailed information about it. The Info screen that appears is divided into two sections: The top section shows standard book data, such as the title, author, cover, publisher, and number of pages; the bottom section is a scrollable window that gives you a description of the book, lists related books, and offers user reviews of the book.

Downloading a free eBook

Thousands upon thousands of books are in the public domain, meaning that the rights of those books are no longer owned by any publisher or author. This means anyone can publish such books, and the digital versions tend to be free for the taking. You might think these would be ancient, obscure tomes of little interest to anybody, but you'd be surprised. The iBookstore has a Classics category that offers some of the best books in history, from Bram Stoker's *Dracula* to Lewis Carroll's *Alice's Adventures in Wonderland* (a personal fave).

Note In the iBookstore, the free books say FREE on the right side of the book link. If you're looking for a good place to quickly populate your iBooks Library, tap Top Charts and then tap the Top Free tab.

Follow these steps to download and install a free eBook:

1. **Locate the eBook you want to read, and tap it.** The book's Info screen appears.

2. **Tap the FREE icon.** The Free icon changes to the Get Book icon.

3. **Tap Get Book.** The iBookstore might ask for your iTunes Store account password.

4. **Tap the Password box, type your password, and tap OK.** The iBooks app switches back to the Library bookcase, places your book on the top shelf, and displays a progress bar that tracks the download (most eBooks download in just a few seconds).

5. **When the download is complete, tap the eBook's cover to start reading.**

Note If the app is quite big and you're surfing the Internet over a cellular connection — particularly an EDGE connection — your iPad may abort the installation and tell you that you need to connect to a Wi-Fi network to download the app.

Sampling an eBook

You'll see in the next section that paid books will set you back anywhere from $4.99 to $14.99 on average. (Textbooks and specialized technical books can easily run you well over $100!) Before forking over that kind of cash, you may want to make sure you really want the book. Checking out other readers' ratings and reviews can help, but there's nothing like checking out the book itself. In an offline bookstore, you can just leaf through the pages; in the online iBookstore, you can do the next best thing: read a sample of the book. Here's how:

1. **In the iBooks app, locate the eBook you want to purchase.** Browse the categories or charts, or use the Search box to track down the book.

2. **Tap the eBook.** The eBook's Info screen appears.

3. **Tap the Get Sample icon.** The iBookstore might ask for your iTunes Store account password.

4. **Tap the Password box, type your password, and tap OK.** The iBooks app switches back to the bookcase and adds the sample.

5. **When the download is complete, tap the sample to start reading.**

Purchasing an eBook

If you're sure you want to purchase a paid eBook — that is, you've read the book's description, checked out the rating, read the reviews, and perhaps even read a sample of the book — then you're ready to follow these steps to purchase and download the book:

1. **In the iBooks app, locate the eBook you want to purchase and tap it.** The eBook's Info screen appears.

2. **Tap the price icon.** The price changes to the Buy Book icon.

3. **Tap the Buy Book icon.** The iBookstore might ask for your iTunes Store account password.

4. **Tap the Password box, type your password, and tap OK.** The iBooks app returns you to the Library, adds your book to the top shelf of the bookcase, and displays a progress bar that tracks the download process (which should take just a few seconds).

5. **When the download is complete, tap the book and start reading.**

Adding other EPUB eBooks to your library

With the apparent ascendance of the EPUB format, publishers and book packagers are tripping over each other to make their titles EPUB-friendly. As a result, the Web is awash in EPUB books, so you don't have to get all your iPad's eBook content from the iBookstore. Here's a short list of some sites where you can download .epub files to your computer:

- **BooksOnBoard.** This site offers a variety of eBooks, although most aren't compatible with iBooks, thanks to DRM. To find non-DRM titles, go to the Advanced Search page and select the Adobe EPUB check box. www.booksonboard.com/.

- **epubBooks.** This is a terrific site for all things related to the EPUB format, and it offers a wide selection of public domain EPUB books. www.epubbooks.com/.

- **eBooks.com.** This site has a variety of books in various eBook formats, although most won't work in the iBooks app because most of the EPUB books use the DRM scheme from Adobe. However, you can go to the Search Options page and search for the "Unencrypted EPUB" file format to see the iBooks-friendly titles they offer. http://ebooks.com/.

- **Feedbooks.** This site offers public domain titles in several formats, including EPUB. www.feedbooks.com/.

- **ManyBooks.** This site offers a nice collection of free eBooks in a huge variety of formats. When you download a book, be sure to choose the EPUB (.epub) format in the Select Format drop-down list. http://manybooks.net/.

- **Smashwords.** This intriguing site offers titles by independent and self-published authors. All eBooks are DRM-free, and each book is available in the EPUB format. www.smashwords.com/.

- **Snee.** This site offers lots of children's picture books in the EPUB format. www.snee.com/epubkidsbooks/.

After you've downloaded an EPUB title to your computer, follow these steps to import the book into iTunes:

1. **In iTunes for the Mac, choose File ⇨ Add to Library or press ⌘+O.** In iTunes for Windows, choose File ⇨ Add File to Library or press Ctrl+O. The Add to Library dialog appears.

2. **Locate and click the EPUB file you downloaded.**

3. **In iTunes for the Mac, click Choose.** In iTunes for Windows, click Open. iTunes adds the eBooks to the Books section of the library.

Editing the iBooks Library

When you add a book to the iBooks Library, the app clears a space for the new title on the left side of the top shelf of the bookcase. The rest of the books get shuffled to the right and down.

This is a sensible way to go about things if you read each book as you download it because it means the iBooks Library displays your books in the order you read them. Of course, life isn't always that orderly, and you might end up reading your eBooks more haphazardly, which means the order the book appears in the Library won't reflect the order you read them.

Similarly, you may have one or more books in your iBooks Library that you refer to frequently for reference, or because you're reading them piecemeal (such as a book of poetry, for example, or a collection of short stories). In that case, it would be better to have such books near the top of the bookcase where they're slightly easier to find and open.

For these and similar Library maintenance chores, iBooks lets you shuffle the books around to get them into the order you prefer. Here's how it works:

1. **Display the iBooks Library.**
   - If you haven't loaded the app yet, tap the iBooks icon to open the iBooks app.
   - If you're in the iBooks app and reading a book, tap the screen to display the controls and then tap Library.

2. **Tap Edit.** iBooks opens the Library for editing.

3. **Tap and drag the book covers to the bookcase positions you prefer.**

4. **If you want to remove a book from your library, tap the X icon in the upper left corner of the book's cover, and then click Delete when iBooks asks you to confirm.**

5. **Tap Done.** iBooks closes the Library for editing.

Syncing Your iBooks Library

If you've used your computer to grab an eBook from the iBookstore or add a downloaded eBook to the iTunes library, you'll want to get that book onto your iPad as soon as possible. Similarly, if you've downloaded a few eBooks on your iPad, it's a good idea to back them up to your computer.

You can do both by syncing eBooks between your computer and your iPad:

1. **Connect your iPad to your computer.** iTunes opens and accesses the iPad. If you added eBooks to your iPad, be sure to wait until iTunes syncs them to your computer.

2. **In iTunes, click your iPad in the Devices list.**

3. **Click the Books tab.**

4. **Select the Sync Books check box.**

5. **To sync only some of your books, select the Selected Books option.**

6. **In the book list, select the check box beside each book that you want to sync, as shown in Figure 7.3.**

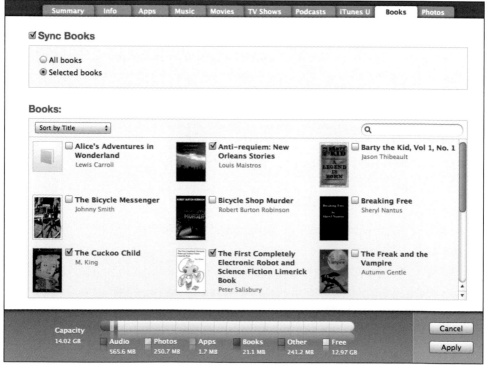

7.3 You can sync selected books with your iPad.

7. **Click Apply.** iTunes syncs the iPad using your new book's settings.

Reading eBooks with the iBooks App

If you're a book-lover like me, when you have your iBooks Library bookcase groaning under the weight of all your eBooks, you may want to spend some time just looking at all the covers sitting prettily in that beautiful bookcase. Or not. If it's the latter, then it's time to get some reading done. The next few sections show you how to control eBooks and modify the display for the best reading experience.

Controlling eBooks on the reading screen

When you're ready to start reading a book using iBooks, getting started couldn't be simpler:

1. **Display the iBooks Library.**

   - If you haven't loaded the app yet, tap the iBooks icon to open the iBooks app.

   - If you're in the iBooks app and reading a book, tap the screen to display the controls and then tap Library.

2. **Tap the book you want to read.** iBooks opens the book.

Here's a list of techniques you can use to control an eBook while reading it:

- **To view one page at a time, orient the iPad in portrait mode.**

- **To view two pages at a time, orient the iPad in landscape mode.**

- **To flip to the next page, tap the right side of the screen.**

- **To flip to the previous page, tap the left side of the screen.**

- **To "manually" turn a page, flick the page with your finger.** Flick left to turn to the next page; flick right to turn to the previous page.

- **To access the iBooks controls, tap the middle of the screen.** To hide the controls, tap the middle of the screen again.

- **To access the book's Table of Contents, display the controls and tap the Contents icon, pointed out in Figure 7.4.** You can then tap an item in the Table of Contents to jump to that section of the book.

- **To go to a different page in the book, display the controls and tap a dot at the bottom of the screen.**

- **To search the book, display the controls, tap the Search icon in the upper-right corner, type your search text, and tap Search.** In the search results that appear, tap a result to display that part of the book.

- **To return to the iBooks Library, display the controls and tap Library in the upper-left corner.**

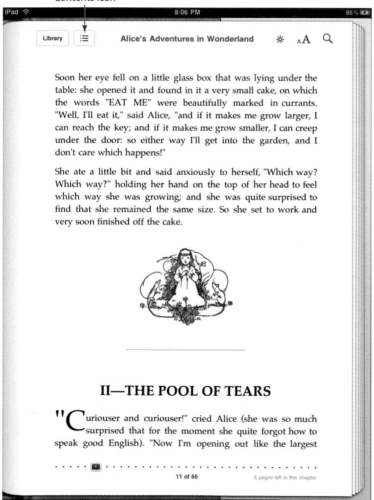

Contents icon

7.4 Tap the middle of the screen to display the controls, and then tap the Contents icon to display the book's Table of Contents.

Formatting eBook text

I mentioned near the top of the show that the EPUB format supports multiple text sizes and multiple fonts, and that the text "reflows" seamlessly to accommodate the new text size. The iBooks app takes advantage of these EPUB features, as shown here:

1. **While reading an eBook, tap the middle of the screen to display the controls.**

2. **Tap the Font icon, pointed out in Figure 7.5.** iBooks displays the Font options.

3. **Tap the larger "A" to increase the text size.** Tap the smaller "A" to reduce the font size.

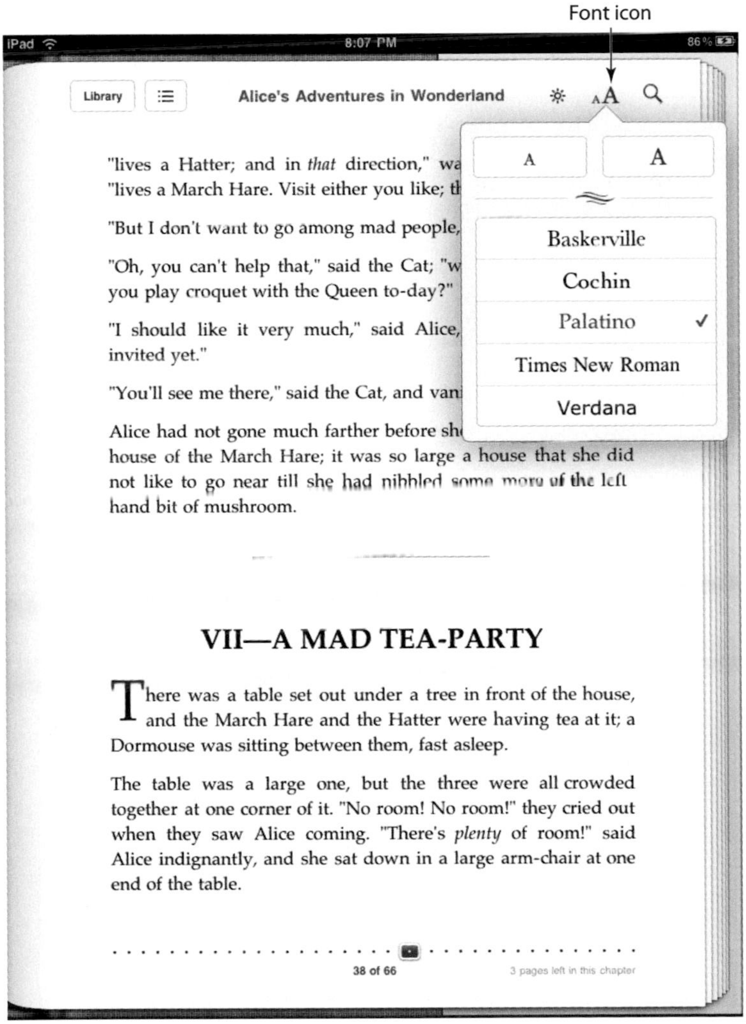

Font icon

7.5 Tap the Font icon to display the iBooks Font options.

4. **Tap Fonts.** iBooks displays a list of typefaces.

5. **Tap the typeface you want to use.** iBooks reformats the eBook for the new typeface.

6. **Tap the middle of the screen to hide the controls.**

Looking up a word in the dictionary

While you're perusing an eBook, you may come across an unfamiliar word. You can look it up using any of the umpteen online dictionaries, but there's no need for that with iBooks:

1. **Tap and hold the word you're furrowing your brow over.** iBooks displays a set of options.

2. **Tap Dictionary.** iBooks looks up the word and then displays its definition.

3. **Tap outside of the definition to close it.**

Saving your spot with a bookmark

Reading an eBook with the iBooks app is so pleasurable you may not want to stop! You have to eat sometime, however, so when it's time to set aside the book, mark your location with a bookmark:

1. **Tap and hold on the spot you want to mark.** iBooks displays a set of options.

2. **Tap Bookmark.** iBooks saves your spot by creating a bookmark at the location you chose.

To return to your place, follow these steps:

1. **Tap the page.** iBooks displays the reading controls.

2. **Tap the Contents icon.** iBooks displays the reading controls.

3. **Tap the Bookmarks tab**. iBooks offers up a list of the saved bookmarks.

4. **Tap the bookmark.** iBooks returns you to the bookmarked page.

Reading Other eBooks on Your iPad

In this chapter, I focused on the iBooks app, mostly because it's an excellent app that's optimized for the iPad and integrates seamlessly with iTunes. But the iPad is arguably the best eReader available today, so it seems a shame to ignore the massive universe of eBooks that aren't iBooks-compatible. If you want to turn your iPad into the ultimate eReader that's capable of reading practically *any* eBook in practically *any* format, then just head for the App Store and install the appropriate eReader apps.

A complete list of eReader apps would extend for pages, so I'll just hit the highlights here:

- **Barnes & Noble eReader.** If you don't have the Nook, Barnes & Noble's eReading device, you can still read Barnes & Noble eBooks by installing the company's eReader app, which supports the EPUB format protected by Adobe's DRM scheme.

- **eReader.** This app supports the eReader format.

- **iSilo.** This app supports the iSilo and Palm Doc formats.

- **Kindle.** Amazon's Kindle app is the way to go if you want to read Kindle eBooks on your iPad.

- **Stanza.** This powerful app supports an amazing variety of eBook formats, including EPUB (protected by Adobe DRM), eReader, and Mobipocket.

How Can I Get More Out of Listening to Audio on My iPad?

The iPod app on your iPad is built with audio in mind, and it lets you crank music, music videos, audiobooks, and podcasts. If you have a fast Wi-Fi connection going (a 3G cellular connection will do in a pinch), you can even use your iPad to purchase music directly from the iTunes Store (tap the iTunes icon in the Home screen). Playing the track you want is a snap on your iPad: Tap iPod, tap a browse button, locate the track, and then tap it. However, your iPad is more than a simple tap-and-play device, and the following sections show you how to take advantage of some of the iPad's more useful audio features.

Getting iTunes Audio Ready for Your iPad

Although you can purchase and download songs directly from the iTunes Store on your iPad, I'm going to assume that the vast majority of your music library is cooped up on your Mac or PC, and that you're going to want to transfer that music to your iPad. Or perhaps I should say that you're going to want to transfer *some* of that music to the iPad. Most of us now have multi-gigabyte music collections, so depending on the storage capacity of your iPad (and the amount of other content you've stuffed into it, particularly videos and movies), it's likely that you'll only want to copy a subset of your music library.

If that's the case, then iTunes gives you three choices when it comes to selecting which tunes to transfer: artist, genre, and playlists. The first two are self-explanatory (and, in any case, I give you the audio syncing details a bit later in this chapter), but it's the last of these three where you can take control of syncing music to your iPad.

A *playlist* is a collection of songs that are related in some way, and using your iTunes library, you can create customized playlists that include only the songs that you want to hear. For example, you might want to create a playlist of upbeat or festive songs to play during a party or celebration. Similarly, you might want to create a playlist of your current favorite songs.

Playlists are the perfect way to control music syncing for the iPad, so before you start transferring tunes, consider creating a playlist or three in iTunes. As the next three sections show, you can create three different types of playlists: standard, Smart, and Genius.

Building a standard playlist

A standard playlist is one where you control which songs are in the playlist (as opposed to the automatic Smart and Genius playlists that I talk about in the next two sections). A standard playlist is a bit more work to maintain, but it gives you complete control over the contents of the playlist.

Follow these steps to build a standard playlist:

1. **Choose File ⇨ New Playlist.** You can also press ⌘+N (Ctrl+N in Windows) or click the Create a Playlist button (+). iTunes adds a new item to the Playlists section, and adds an edit box around the item.

2. **Type the name you want to give the playlist and then press Return (Enter in Windows).**

3. **In the iTunes Music library, display the song, album, artist, or genre that you want to include in the playlist.**

4. **Drag the song, album, artist, or genre and drop it on the playlist.**

5. **Repeat Steps 3 and 4 to populate the playlist.**

Genius

If you're looking for a faster way to create and populate a standard playlist, iTunes offers another technique that lets you select some or all of the songs in advance. Press and hold the ⌘ key (Ctrl key in Windows) and then click each song that you want to include in your playlist. When you're done, choose File ⇨ New Playlist from Selection or press ⌘+Shift+N (Ctrl+Shift+N in Windows).

Building a Smart Playlist

A standard playlist gives you a satisfying amount of control over the list contents, but it can often be a hassle. For example, if you've created a playlist for a particular genre, then every time you add new music from that genre you must then drag the new tunes to the playlist. Similarly, if you assign a particular album or artist to a genre that's different than the one in your playlist, you have to remove the album or artist from the playlist by hand.

To avoid this kind of digital music drudgery, you can create a *Smart Playlist* where the songs that appear in the list have one or more properties in common, such as the genre, rating, artist, or text in the song title. The key here is iTunes populates and maintains a Smart Playlist automatically. For example, if you build a Smart Playlist based on a particular genre, then every time you add new music from the genre, iTunes automatically includes that music in the playlist. Similarly, if you change the genre of some music in your playlist, iTunes automatically removes the music from the playlist.

Here are the steps to follow to build a Smart Playlist:

1. **Choose File ⇨ New Smart Playlist.** You can also press ⌘+Option+N (Ctrl+Alt+N in Windows) or hold down Option (Shift in Windows) and click the Create a Playlist button (+). iTunes displays the Smart Playlist dialog.

2. **Set up the condition for the playlist.**

   ● **Use the first pop-up menu to choose the field you want to use for the first condition.**

   ● **Use the second pop-up menu to choose an operator for the condition.** Your choices here depend on the field you selected in the first pop-up menu. For example, if you chose a text field, the available operators include "contains," "is", and "starts with"; for a numeric field, the operators include "is greater than," "is less than," and "is in the range."

179

● **Use the third control (or set of controls) to enter the details of the condition.** Again, the controls you see depend on the type of field, although in most cases you see a single text box. If you chose "is in the range" as the operator, you see two text boxes so that you can enter the beginning and end values for the range.

3. **If you want to add another condition, click the Add button (+) to the right of the controls.** iTunes adds another set of condition controls to the dialog.

4. **Repeat Step 2 to specify the settings for the new condition.**

5. **Repeat Steps 3 and 4 to add as many conditions as you need.** Figure 8.1 shows an example Smart Playlist dialog with four conditions added.

8.1 Select the Selected playlists option, and then select the playlists you want to sync.

6. **If you want to limit the playlist to a certain length or number of songs, select the Limit To check box and specify the limit:**

   ● Type the number in the first box, and then choose Minutes, Hours, MB, GB, or Items in the first pop-up menu.

   ● In the second pop-up menu, choose how to select the songs — for example, by least often played, by highest rating, or at random.

7. **Select the Match Only Checked Items check box if you want to include only songs whose check boxes you've selected.** This setting lets you clear a song's check box and be sure it won't show up in your Smart Playlists.

8. **Select the Live Updating check box if you want iTunes to update the Smart Playlist for you automatically.**

9. **Click OK.** iTunes creates the playlist and displays an edit box around the name.

10. **Type the name you want to give the playlist, and then press Return (or Enter).**

Building a Genius playlist

You may be familiar with the iTunes Genius Sidebar, which shows you songs from the iTunes Store that are similar to a particular song in your library. A closely related feature is the Genius playlist. The idea here is that you pick a song in your music library, and iTunes creates a playlist of other songs in your library that are similar. It's a ridiculously easy way to ride a particular sonic groove.

Follow these steps to set up a Genius playlist:

1. **In your music library or in a playlist, select the song you want to use as the starting point for the Genius playlist.**

2. **Click the Start Genius button in the lower-right corner of the iTunes window or the Genius symbol in the iTunes track readout at the top of the window.**

3. **iTunes creates the Genius playlist and starts it playing.**

4. **To change the number of songs in the playlist, open the Limit To pop-up menu and choose a different number: 25 songs, 50 songs, 75 songs, or 100 songs.**

5. **Click Save Playlist.** iTunes adds the playlist to the Genius section of the sidebar.

Creating a favorite tunes playlist for your iPad

Your iTunes library includes a Rating field that enables you to supply a rating for your tracks: one star for songs you don't like so much, up to five stars for your favorite tunes. You click the song you want to rate and then click a dot in the Rating column (click the first dot for a one-star rating, the second dot for a two-star rating, and so on). Rating songs is useful because it enables you to organize your music. For example, the Playlists section includes a My Top Rated playlist, which includes all your four- and five-star-rated tunes, ordered by the Rating value.

Rating tracks comes in particularly handy when deciding which music to use to populate your iPad. If you have tens of gigabytes of tunes, only some of them will fit on your iPad. How do you choose? Later in this chapter, I show you how to sync the playlists you want to hear on your iPad. Another possibility is to rate your songs and then just sync the My Top Rated playlist to your iPad.

The problem with the My Top Rated playlist is that it includes only your four- and five-star-rated tunes. You can fit thousands of tracks on your iPad, but it's unlikely that you've got thousands of songs rated at four stars or better. To fill out your playlist, you should also include songs rated at three stars, a rating that should include lots of good, solid tunes.

To set this up, you have two choices:

- **Modify the My Top Rated playlist.** Right-click (or Control+click on a Mac) the My Top Rated playlist, and then click Edit Playlist. In the Smart Playlist dialog, click the second star and then click OK.

- **Create a new playlist.** This is the way to go if you want to leave My Top Rated as your best music. Choose File ⇨ New Smart Playlist to open the Smart Playlist dialog. Choose Rating in the Field list, choose Is Greater Than in the Operator list, and then click the second star. Click OK, type a title for the playlist (such as Favorite Tunes), and then press Return (or Enter).

The next time you sync your iPad, be sure to include either the My Top Rated playlist or the Smart Playlist you created.

Syncing Music and Other Audio Content

The brainy iBooks app and the sleek Safari browser may get the lion's share of kudos for the iPad, but many people reserve their rave reviews for its iPod app. The darn thing is just so versatile: It can play music, of course, but it also happily cranks out audiobooks and podcasts on the audio side and music videos, movies, and TV shows on the video side. Ear candy and eye candy in one package!

If there's a problem with this digital largesse, it's that the iPod player might be *too* versatile. Even if you have a big 64GB iPad, you may still find its confines a bit cramped, particularly if you're also loading up your iPad with photos, contacts, and calendars, and you just can't seem to keep your hands out of the iBooks Store and App Store cookie jars.

All this means that you probably have to pay a bit more attention when it comes to syncing audio to your iPad, and the following sections show you how to do just that.

Syncing music and music videos

The iPad is a digital music player at heart, so you've probably loaded up your iPad with lots of audio content and lots of music videos. To get the most out of the iPod app's music and video capabilities, you need to know all the different ways you can synchronize these items. For example, if you use the iPod app primarily as a music player and the iPad has more disk capacity than you need for all your digital audio, feel free to throw all your music onto the player. On the other hand, your iPad may not have much free space, or you may want only certain songs and videos on the player to make it easier to navigate. Not a problem! You need to configure iTunes to sync only the songs or playlists that you select.

Genius

Something I like about syncing playlists is that you can estimate in advance how much space your selected playlists will usurp on the iPad. In iTunes, click the playlist and examine the status bar, which tells you the number of songs in the playlist, the total duration, and, most significantly for our purposes, the total size of the playlist.

Before getting to the specific sync steps, you need to know the three ways to manually sync music and music videos:

- **Playlists.** With this method, you specify the playlists you want iTunes to sync. Those playlists also appear on the iPod app. This is by far the easiest way to manually sync music and music videos, because you usually just have a few playlists to select. The down side is that if you have large playlists and you run out of space on your iPad, the only way to fix the problem is to remove an entire playlist. Another bummer: With this method, you can only sync *all* of your music videos or *none* of your music videos.

- **Check boxes.** With this method, you specify which songs and music videos get synced by selecting the little check boxes that appear beside every song and video in iTunes. This is fine-grained syncing for sure, but because your iPad can hold thousands of songs, it's also lots of work.

- **Drag-and-drop.** With this method, you click and drag individual songs and music videos, and drop them on your iPad's icon in the iTunes Devices list. This is an easy way to get a bunch of tracks on your iPad quickly, but iTunes doesn't give you any way of tracking which tracks you've dragged and dropped.

Genius

What do you do if you want to select only a few tracks from a large playlist? Waste a big chunk of your life deselecting a few hundred check boxes? Pass. Here's a better way: Press ⌘+A (Mac) or Ctrl+A (Windows) to select every track, right-click (or Control+click on a Mac) any track, and then click Uncheck Selection. Voila! iTunes deselects every track in seconds flat. Now you can select just the tracks you want. You're welcome.

Follow these steps to sync music and music videos using playlists:

1. **Connect your iPad to your computer.**

2. **In iTunes, click your iPad in the Devices list.**

3. **Click the Music tab.**

4. **Select the Sync Music check box.** iTunes asks you to confirm that you want to sync music.

5. **Click Sync Music.**

6. **Select the Selected Playlists, Artists, and Genres option.**

7. **Select the check box beside each playlist, artist, and genre you want to sync, as shown in Figure 8.2.**

8.2 Select the Selected Playlists, Artists, and Genres option, and then select the items you want to sync.

8. **Select the Include Music Videos check box if you also want to add your music videos into the sync mix.**

9. **Select the Include Voice Memos check box if you also want to sync voice memos that you recorded on your iPad.**

10. **If you want iTunes to fill up any remaining free space on your iPad with a selection of related music from your library, select the Automatically Fill Free Space With Songs check box.**

11. **Click Apply.** iTunes syncs your iPad using the new settings.

Follow these steps to sync using the check boxes that appear beside each track in your iTunes Music library:

1. **Click your iPad in the Devices list.**

2. **Click the Summary tab.**

3. **Select the Sync Only Checked Songs and Videos check box.**

4. **Click Apply.** If iTunes starts syncing your iPad, drag the Slide to Cancel slider on the iPad to stop it.

5. **Either click Music in the Library list or click a playlist that contains the tracks you want to sync.** If a track's check box is selected, iTunes syncs the track with your iPad. If a track's check box is deselected, iTunes doesn't sync the track with your iPad; if the track is already on your iPad, iTunes removes the track.

6. **In the Devices list, click your iPad.**

7. **Click the Summary tab.**

8. **Click Sync.** iTunes syncs just the checked tracks.

You also can configure iTunes to let you drag tracks from the Music library (or any playlist) and drop them on your iPad. Here's how this works:

1. **Click your iPad in the Devices list.**

2. **Click the Summary tab.**

3. **Select the Manually Manage Music and Videos check box.**

4. **Click Apply.** If iTunes starts syncing your iPad, drag the Slide to Cancel slider on the iPad to stop it.

5. **Either click Music in the Library list or click a playlist that contains the tracks you want to sync.**

6. **Choose the tracks you want to sync:**

   - If all the tracks are together, Shift-click the first track, hold down Shift, and then click the last track.

   - If the tracks are scattered all over the place, hold down ⌘ (Mac) or Ctrl (Windows) and click each track.

7. **Click and drag the selected tracks to the Devices list, and drop them on the iPad icon.** iTunes syncs the selected tracks.

Note

When you select the Manually Manage Music and Videos check box, iTunes automatically deselects the Sync Music check box in the Music tab. However, iTunes doesn't mess with the music on your iPad. Even when it syncs after a drag and drop, it only adds the new tracks; it doesn't delete any of your iPad's existing music.

Caution

If you decide to return to playlist syncing by selecting the Sync Music check box in the Music tab, iTunes removes all tracks that you added to your iPad via the drag-and-drop method.

Syncing podcasts

In many ways, podcasts are the most problematic of the various media you can sync with your iPad. It's not that the podcasts themselves pose any concern. Quite the contrary: They're so addictive that it's not unusual to collect them by the dozens. Why is that a problem? Because most professional podcasts are at least a few megabytes in size, and many are tens of megabytes. A large enough collection can put a serious dent in your iPad's remaining storage space. All the more reason to take control of the podcast syncing process. Here's how you do it:

1. **Connect your iPad to your computer.**

2. **In iTunes, click your iPad in the Devices list.**

3. **Click the Podcasts tab.**

4. **Select the Sync Podcasts check box.**

5. **If you want iTunes to choose some of the podcasts automatically, select the Automatically Include check box and proceed to Steps 6 and 7.** If you prefer to choose all the podcasts manually, deselect the Automatically Include check box and skip to Step 8.

6. **Choose an option from the first pop-up menu:**

   - **All.** Choose this item to sync every podcast.

   - *X* **Most Recent.** Choose this item to sync the *X* most recent podcasts.

   - **All Unplayed.** Choose this item to sync all the podcasts you haven't yet played.

   - *X* **Most Recent Unplayed.** Choose this item to sync the *X* most recent podcasts that you haven't yet played.

   - *X* **Least Recent Unplayed.** Choose this item to sync the *X* oldest podcasts that you haven't yet played.

- **All New.** Choose this item to sync all the podcasts published since the last sync.

- **X Most Recent New.** Choose this item to sync the X most recent podcasts published since the last sync.

- **X Least Recent New.** Choose this item to sync the X oldest podcasts published since the last sync.

7. **Choose an option from the second pop-up menu:**

   - **All Podcasts.** Choose this option to apply the option from Step 5 to all your podcasts.

   - **Selected Podcasts.** Choose this option to apply the option from Step 5 to just the podcasts you select, as shown in Figure 8.3.

8. **Select the check box beside any podcast or podcast episode you want to sync.**

9. **Click Apply.** iTunes syncs the iPad using your new podcast settings.

8.3 To sync specific podcasts, choose the Selected Podcasts option and then select the check boxes for each podcast you want synced.

Note

A podcast episode is *unplayed* if you haven't yet played at least part of the episode either in iTunes or on your iPad. If you play an episode on your iPad, the player sends this information to iTunes when you next sync. Even better, your iPad also lets iTunes know if you paused in the middle of an episode; when you play that episode in iTunes, it starts at the point where you left off.

To mark a podcast episode as unplayed, in iTunes choose the Podcasts library, right-click (or Control+click on a Mac) the episode and then choose Mark as New.

Syncing audiobooks

The iTunes sync settings for your iPad have tabs for Music, Photos, Podcasts, and Video, but not one for Audiobooks. What's up with that? It's not, as you might think, some sort of anti-book conspiracy, or even forgetfulness on Apple's part. Instead, iTunes treats audiobook content as a special type of playlist, which, confusingly, doesn't appear in the iTunes Playlists section. To get audiobooks on your iPad, follow these steps:

1. **Connect your iPad to your computer.**

2. **In iTunes, click your iPad in the Devices list.**

3. **Click the Music tab.**

4. **Select the Sync Music check box, if you haven't done so already, and then click Sync Music when iTunes asks you to confirm.**

5. **Select the Selected Playlists, Artists, and Genres option.**

6. **Select the check box beside Audiobooks.** Note that you see this playlist only if you have at least one audiobook in your iTunes library.

7. **Click Apply.** iTunes syncs your audiobooks to your iPad.

If you've opted to manually manage your music and video, you need to choose the Audiobooks category of the iTunes library and then drag and drop on your iPad the audiobooks you want to sync.

Getting More Out of Your iPad's Audio Features

Your iPad is a living, breathing iPod thanks to its built-in iPod app, which you can fire up anytime you want by tapping the iPod icon in the Home screen's Dock. The iPod app looks much like its desktop iTunes cousin, with a Library pane on the left and the library content on the right. When you tap the Music section of the Library, you can then browse your tunes using the five tabs on the bottom of the screen: Songs, Artists, Albums, Genres, and Composers. When you see something you want to play, tap it and then tap the first song you want to play.

It's all quite civilized on the surface, but like most of the iPad apps, the iPod has hidden depths, and in the rest of this chapter, I introduce you to the most useful of these features.

Genius

If you use the iPod app all the time, go ahead and customize the Home button to launch iPod. Tap Settings, tap General, tap Home Button to open the Home Button screen, and then tap iPod. Now you can switch to the iPod super-fast by double-clicking the Home button from any screen.

Using audio accessories with your iPad

When Apple announced the iPad, they also announced a few accessories, including an iPad-only dock, a keyboard dock, and a case. Of course, third-party vendors want a piece of the iPad pie, so expect to see a rather large cottage industry of iPad accessories, including headsets (wired and Bluetooth), external speakers, FM transmitters, and all manner of cases, car kits, cables, and cradles. Many places scattered all over the Web sell iPad accessories, but the following sites are my faves:

- **Apple.** http://store.apple.com/us/browse/home/shop_iPad
- **Belkin.** www.belkin.com/ipod/iPad/
- **Griffin.** www.griffintechnology.com/devices/iPad/
- **NewEgg.** www.newegg.com/
- **EverythingiCafe.** http://store.everythingicafe.com/

Keep these notes in mind when shopping for and using audio-related accessories for your iPad:

- **Look for the logo.** Despite the presence of the iPod app, your iPad is *not* an iPod dressed up in fancy tablet clothes. It's a completely different device that doesn't fit or work with many iPod accessories. To be sure what you're buying is iPad-friendly, look for the "Works with iPad" logo.

- **Headsets, headphones, and earpieces.** The iPad uses a standard headset jack, so just about any headset that uses a garden-variety stereo mini-plug will fit your iPad without a hitch and without requiring the purchase of an adapter.

- **External speakers.** Legions of external speakers are made for the iPod, so you simply dock the iPod in the device and wail away. Unfortunately, the relatively massive dimensions of the iPad's bottom panel are so different from any of the iPod models that you won't be able to use your iPad with an iPod's external speakers. As I write this, no one has come up with some kind of adapter to solve this problem.

- **FM transmitters.** These are must-have accessories for car trips because they send the iPad's output to an FM station, which you then play through your car stereo. The FM transmitters that work with the iPod don't generally work with iPads, so look for one that's designed for the iPad.

- **Electronic interference.** Because your iPad is a transmitter (of Wi-Fi, Bluetooth, and in some cases 3G signals), it generates a nice little field of electronic interference, which is why you need to switch it to Airplane mode when you're flying (see Chapter 3). That same interference can wreak havoc on nearby external speakers and FM transmitters, so if you hear static when playing audio, switch to Airplane mode to get rid of it.

Rating a song on your iPad

If you use song ratings to organize your tunes, you may come across some situations where you want to rate a song that's playing on your iPad:

- You used your iPad to download some music from the iTunes Store, and you want to rate that music.

- You're listening to a song on your iPad and decide that you've given a rating that's either too high or too low and you want to change it.

In the first case, you could sync the music to your computer and rate it there; in the second case, you could modify the rating on your computer and then sync with your iPad. However, these solutions are lame because you have to wait until you connect your iPad to your computer. If you're out and about, you want to rate the song *now*, while it's fresh in your mind.

Yes, you can do that with your iPad:

1. **Locate the song you want to rate, and tap it to start the playback.** Your iPad displays the album art and the name of the artist, song, and album at the top of the screen. If you don't see this info, tap the screen.

2. **Tap the Details icon in the lower-right corner of the screen.** Your iPad "turns" the album art and displays a list of the songs on the album. Above that list are the five rating dots.

3. **Tap the dot that corresponds to the rating you want to give the song.** For example, to give the song a four-star rating, tap the fourth dot from the left, as shown in Figure 8.4.

4. **Tap the album art icon in the upper-right corner.** Your iPad saves the rating and returns you to the album art view.

iPad		8:57 PM		▶ 89%

Nathan
Scarecrow
Key Principles

0:36   -3:48

★ ★ ★ ★ ·

1.	John Paul's Deliveries	Nathan	4:30
▶	Scarecrow	Nathan	4:24
3.	Daffodils	Nathan	2:51
4.	Trans Am	Nathan	3:04
5.	The Boulevard Back Then	Nathan	3:25
6.	The Wind	Nathan	4:43
7.	You Win	Nathan	3:20
8.	Key Principles of Success	Nathan	4:13
9.	Ordinary Day	Nathan	3:47

8.4 Tap the dot that corresponds to the rating you want to give the currently playing track.

The next time you sync your iPad with your computer, iTunes notes your new ratings and applies them to the same tracks in the iTunes library.

Creating a Genius playlist on your iPad

You saw earlier how to create a Genius playlist in iTunes. You also can use this seemingly magical feature right on your iPad. First, however, you have to turn on the Genius feature in iTunes. Here's how:

1. **In the iTunes sidebar, click Genius.** iTunes accesses the iTunes store and then displays the Genius page.

2. **Click Turn on Genius.** iTunes asks you to sign into your iTunes account.

3. **Type your Apple ID and password and then click Continue.** iTunes displays the Genius Terms of Service.

4. **Agree to the terms and then click Continue.** iTunes activates the Genius feature and then gathers the information it needs.

5. **Sync your iPad to activate the Genius feature on the device.**

Here's how to create a Genius playlist:

1. **Click the Start Genius button in the lower-left corner of the iPod window.**

2. **Tap the song you want to use as the basis of the Genius playlist.**

3. **iTunes creates the Genius playlist and starts it playing.**

4. **Click Save.** iTunes adds the playlist to the sidebar, and you can tap it to see the list of songs. Figure 8.5 shows an example.

In the Genius screen, you can perform the following actions to mess around with your shiny, new playlist:

- Tap Refresh to recreate the playlist.
- Tap a song to play it.
- Tap Save to save the playlist to the Playlists screen.
- Tap New to crank out a new Genius playlist.

8.5 An example of a Genius playlist.

Customizing your iPad's audio settings

Audiophiles in the crowd don't get much to fiddle with in the iPad, but you can play with a few audio settings. Here's how to get at them:

1. **Press the Home button to get to the Home screen.**

2. **Tap the Settings icon.** The Settings screen opens.

3. **Tap the iPod icon.** Your iPad displays the iPod settings screen, as shown in Figure 8.6.

You get four settings to try out:

- **Sound Check.** Every track is recorded at different audio levels, so invariably you get some tracks that are louder than others. With the Sound Check feature, you can set your iPad to play all your songs at the same level. This feature affects only the baseline level of the music and doesn't change any of the other levels, so you still get the highs and lows. If you use it, you don't need to worry about having to quickly turn down the volume when a really loud song comes on. To turn on Sound Check, in the iPod settings page, tap the Sound Check switch to the On position.

8.6 Use the iPod screen to muck around with the audio settings.

- **EQ.** This setting controls your iPad's built-in equalizer, which is actually a long list of preset frequency levels that affect the audio output. Each preset is designed for a specific type of audio: vocals, talk radio, classical music, rock, hip-hop, and lots more. To set the equalizer, tap EQ and then tap the preset you want to use (or tap None to turn off the equalizer).

- **Volume Limit.** You use this setting to prevent the iPad's volume from being turned up too high and damaging your (or someone else's) hearing. You know, of course, that pumping up the volume while you have your earbuds in is an audio no-no, right? I thought so. However, I also know that when a great tune comes on, it's often a little *too* tempting to go for 11 on the volume scale. If you can't resist the temptation, use Volume Limit to limit the damage. Tap Volume Limit, and drag the Volume slider to the maximum allowed volume.

Genius

If you're setting up an iPad for a younger person, you should set the Volume Limit. However, what prevents the young whippersnapper from setting a higher limit? You can. In the Volume Limit screen, tap Lock Limit Volume. In the Set Code screen, tap out a four-digit code and then tap the code again to confirm. This disables the Volume slider in the Volume Limit screen.

- **Lyrics & Podcast Info.** Leave this setting On to see extra info about songs and podcasts when you click the Details button in the iPod app. For example, if you add lyrics for a song in iTunes (right-click the song, click Get Info, click the Lyrics tab), you see those lyrics in Details view.

How Can I Get More Out of Watching Video on My iPad?

The world has been on a quest for the perfect portable media player for an awfully long time. We seem to have solved the audio part of the hunt rather nicely with the iPod and even the iPhone. However, the video mission has been more problematic, with single-purpose video players being too, well, single-purpose, and more versatile tools such as the iPod touch and the iPhone being just a tad too small for proper video viewing (particularly if more than one person is involved). Now the iPad is making a bid for portable media perfection, and its case is strong: large, high-definition screen, touchscreen interface, talking-cat video support (also known as YouTube). This chapter puts the case to the test as I take you inside the iPad's video features.

Syncing Videos

Although you can use the iTunes app on your iPad to rent movies, or to purchase movies, TV shows, and music videos, it's more likely that the bulk of your video content resides on your computer. If watching any of that video on your computer while sitting in your office chair is unappealing, then you need to transfer it to your iPad for viewing in more comfy circumstances. The next few sections provide the not-even-close-to-gory details.

Converting video content into an iPad-compatible format

Your iPad is very video-friendly, but only certain formats are compatible with the iPad. Here's the list:

- H.264 video, up to 720 pixels, 30 frames per second, H.264 Main Profile Level 3 with AAC-LC audio up to 160 Kbps, 48 kHz, stereo audio in M4V, MP4, and MOV file formats

- MPEG-4 video, up to 2.5 Mbps, 640×480 pixels, 30 frames per second, Simple Profile with AAC-LC audio up to 160 Kbps, 48 kHz, stereo audio in M4V, MP4, and MOV file formats

If you have a video file that doesn't match either of these formats, you may think you're out of luck. Not so. You can use iTunes to convert that video to an MPEG-4 file that's iPad-friendly. Here's how:

1. **If the video file isn't already in iTunes, choose File ⇨ Add to Library or press ⌘+O.** (In Windows, choose File ⇨ Add File to Library or press Ctrl+O.) The Add To Library dialog appears. If the file is already in iTunes, skip to Step 3.

2. **Locate and choose your video file, and click Open.** iTunes copies the file into the library, which may take a while depending on the size of the video file. In most cases, iTunes adds the video to the Movies section of the library.

3. **In iTunes, click your movie.**

4. **Choose Advanced ⇨ Create iPad or Apple TV version.** iTunes begins converting the video to the MPEG-4 format. This may take some time for even a relatively small video. When the conversion is complete, a copy of the original video appears in the iTunes library.

Genius

Because the converted video has the same name as the original, you should probably rename one of them so you can tell them apart when it comes to syncing your iPad. If you're not sure which file is which, right-click (or Control+click on a Mac) one of the videos and then click Get Info. In the Summary tab, read the Kind value. The iPad-friendly file has a Kind setting of MPEG-4 Video File.

Syncing movies

The iPad's screen is large (9.7 inches on the diagonal) and sharp (1024×768 resolution at 132 pixels per inch), which makes it ideal for watching a flick while sitting on the front porch with a mint julep at hand. The major problem with movies is that their file size tends to be quite large — even short films lasting just a few minutes weigh in at dozens of megabytes, and full-length movies are several gigabytes. Clearly there's a compelling need to manage your movies to avoid filling up your iPad and leaving no room for the latest album from your favorite band.

Syncing rented movies

If you've rented a movie from iTunes, you can move that movie to your iPad and watch it there. (Note that you're *moving* the rented movie, not copying it; you can store rented movies in only one location at time, so if you sync the movie to your iPad it is no longer available on your computer.)

Follow these steps to sync a rented movie to your iPad:

1. **Connect your iPad to your computer.**

2. **In iTunes, click your iPad in the Devices list.**

3. **Click the Movies tab.**

4. **In the Rented Movies section, shown in Figure 9.1, click the Move button beside the rented movie you want to shift to your iPad.** iTunes adds the movie to the On *"iPad"* list (where *iPad* is the name of your iPad).

5. **Click Apply.** iTunes syncs the iPad using your new movie settings.

9.1 In the Rented Movies section of the Movies tab, click Move to move a rented movie to your iPad.

Syncing purchased or downloaded movies

If you've purchased a movie from iTunes or added a video to your iTunes library, follow these steps to sync some or all of those movies to your iPad:

1. **Connect your iPad to your computer.**

2. **In iTunes, click your iPad in the Devices list.**

3. **Click the Movies tab.**

4. **Select the Sync Movies check box.**

5. **If you want iTunes to choose some of the movies automatically, select the Automatically Include check box and proceed to Step 6.** If you prefer to choose all the movies manually, deselect the Automatically Include check box and skip to Step 7.

6. **Choose an option from the pop-up menu:**

   - **All.** Choose this item to sync every movie.

   - *X* **Most Recent.** Choose this item to sync the *X* most recent movies you've added to iTunes.

   - **All Unwatched.** Choose this item to sync all the movies you haven't yet played.

   - *X* **Most Recent Unwatched.** Choose this item to sync the *X* most recent movies you haven't yet played.

   - *X* **Least Recent Unwatched.** Choose this item to sync the *X* oldest movies you haven't yet played.

Note A movie is unwatched if you haven't yet viewed it either in iTunes or on your iPad. If you watch a movie on your iPad, the player sends this information to iTunes when you next sync.

7. **Select the check box beside any other movie you want to sync, as shown in Figure 9.2.**

8. **Click Apply.** iTunes syncs the iPad using your new movie settings.

Genius To mark a movie as unwatched, in iTunes, choose the Movies library, right-click (or Control+click on a Mac) the movie, and choose Mark as Unwatched.

9.2 In the Movies tab, select Sync Movies and choose the films you want to sync.

Syncing TV show episodes

If the average iPad is at some risk of being filled up by a few large movie files, it probably is at grave risk of being overwhelmed by a large number of TV show episodes. A single half-hour episode eats up approximately 250MB, so even a modest collection of shows consumes multiple gigabytes of precious iPad disk space.

This means it's crucial to monitor your collection of TV show episodes and keep your iPad synced with only the episodes you need. Fortunately, iTunes gives you a decent set of tools to handle this:

1. **Connect your iPad to your computer.**

2. **In iTunes, click your iPad in the Devices list.**

3. **Click the TV Shows tab.**

4. **Select the Sync TV Shows check box.**

5. **If you want iTunes to choose some of the episodes automatically, select the Automatically Include check box and proceed to Steps 6 and 7.** If you prefer to choose all the episodes manually, deselect the Automatically Include check box and skip to Step 8.

6. **Choose an option from the drop-down menu.**

   - **All.** Choose this item to sync every TV show episode.

   - **X Most Recent.** Choose this item to sync the X most recent episodes.

   - **All Unwatched.** Choose this item to sync all the episodes you haven't yet viewed.

- **X Most Recent Unwatched.** Choose this item to sync the X most recent episodes you haven't yet viewed.

- **X Least Recent Unwatched.** Choose this item to sync the X oldest episodes you haven't yet viewed.

Note

A TV episode is unwatched if you haven't yet viewed it either in iTunes or on your iPad. If you watch an episode on your iPad, the player sends this information to iTunes when you next sync.

7. **Choose an option from the second pop-up menu:**

- **All Shows.** Choose this option to apply the choice from Step 5 to all your TV shows.

- **Selected Shows.** Choose this option to apply the choice from Step 5 to just the TV shows you select, as shown in Figure 9.3.

8. **Select the check box beside any TV show or TV show episode you want to sync.**

9. **Click Apply.** iTunes syncs the iPad using your new TV show settings.

9.3 To sync specific TV shows, select the Selected Shows option and then select the check boxes for each show you want synced.

Genius

To mark a TV episode as unwatched, in iTunes, choose the TV Shows library, right-click (or Control+click on a Mac) the episode, and choose Mark as Unwatched.

Syncing music videos

In the iTunes sync settings for your iPad, you can scour the Movies tab until your mouse hand goes numb and you won't find any mechanism for syncing music videos. That's because you're focusing on the "video" part of the phrase *music video*; iTunes focuses on the "music" part of that phrase, so it considers all such videos to be music instead of movies.

Therefore, to include music videos in the sync, you need to head for the Music tab, as described in the following steps:

1. **Connect your iPad to your computer.**

2. **In iTunes, click your iPad in the Devices list.**

3. **Click the Music tab.**

4. **Select the Sync Music check box.**

5. **Select the Include Music Videos check box.**

6. **Click Apply.** iTunes includes your music videos in the iPad sync.

Genius

If you download a music video from the Web and then import it into iTunes (by choosing File ⇨ Import), iTunes adds the video to its Movies library. To display it in the Music library instead, open the Movies library, right-click (or Control+click on a Mac) the music video, and then click Get Info. Click the Video tab, and use the Kind list to choose Music Video. Click OK. iTunes moves the music video to the Music folder.

Getting More Out of Your iPad's Video Features

With a few movies and TV shows finally residing on your iPad, you get to kick back and watch some moving pictures in comfort. Your commute (meaning, of course, your commute as a *passenger*) doesn't have to be boring anymore. Just connect your headphones, and fire up a show. The next few sections take you through a few techniques and tips that help you get a bit more out of your iPad's video capabilities.

Playing videos, movies, and TV shows

In an ideal world, you'd watch all your videos on a comfy couch in front of a flat-screen TV with a rockin' surround-sound system. Unfortunately, all that equipment isn't exactly portable. However, your iPad is *very* portable, and what's more, you probably carry it with you just about everywhere. Throw that nice large screen into the mix, and you have yourself a great portable video player.

To watch a video on your iPad, follow these steps:

1. **Tap the Videos icon on the Home screen.** The Videos app appears.

2. **Tap the tab for the type of video you want to watch: Movies, TV Shows, or Music Videos.**

3. **Tap the video you want to watch.** Your iPad displays information about the video; for a TV show, you also see a list of the show's episodes.

4. **Choose what you want to watch.**

    - **Entire movie or music video, or all episodes of a TV show.** Tap the Play button.

    - **Movie chapter.** Tap Chapters to display a list of the movie's chapters, and then tap the chapter you want to watch.

    - **TV show episode.** Tap the episode you want to watch.

5. **Turn the screen to the landscape position to watch the video.**

When you first see an iPad video, you may think you have no way to control the playback because no controls are in sight. Fortunately for you, Apple realized that watching a movie with a bunch of buttons pasted on the screen wouldn't exactly enhance the movie-watching experience. I agree. The buttons are actually hidden, but you can force them out of hiding by tapping the screen, as you can see in Figure 9.4. When you're finished with the controls, tap the screen again to hide them.

Here's what you see:

- **Progress Bar.** This bar shows you where you are in the video playback. The white ball shows you the current position, and you can drag the ball left (to rewind) or right (to fast forward). To the right is the time remaining in the video, and on the left is the time elapsed.

- **Fill/Fit the Screen.** This button in the upper-right corner toggles the video between filling the entire screen, which may crop the outside edges of the video, and fitting the video to the screen width, which gives you letterboxed video with black bars above and below the video.

 You also can switch between filling the screen and fitting the screen by double-tapping the screen.

Note

9.4 Tap the video to reveal the playback controls.

- **Previous.** Tap this button (the left-pointing arrows) to return to the beginning of the video or, if you're already at the beginning, to jump to the previous chapter (if the video has multiple chapters, as do most movies). Tap and hold this button to rewind the video.

- **Next.** Tap this button (the right-pointing arrows) to jump to the next chapter (if the video has multiple chapters). Tap and hold this button to fast-forward the video.

- **Pause/Play.** Tap this button to pause the playback, and then tap it again to resume.

- **Chapter Guide.** Tap this button to see a list of chapters in the video. (You don't see this button if the video doesn't have multiple chapters.)

- **Volume Bar.** This bar controls the video volume level. Drag the white ball to change the level. You also can use volume controls on the side of the iPad.

- **Done.** Tap this button to stop the video and return to the list of videos on your iPad. You also can press the Home button to stop the video and wind up on the Home screen.

You can use your iPad headset to control video playback. Click the mic button once to play or pause. Click it twice to skip to the next chapter.

Note

If you stop the video before the end, the next time you tap the video, it resumes the playback from the spot where you stopped it earlier. Nice!

Playing just the audio portion of a music video

When you play a music video, you get a two-for-one media deal: great music and (hopefully) a creative video. That's nice, but the only problem is you can't separate the two. For example, sometimes it might be nice to listen to just the audio portion of the music video. Why? Because you can't do anything else on your iPad while a video is playing. If you press the Home button, for example, the video stops and the Home screen appears. That certainly makes sense, so it would be nice to be able to play just the audio portion, because your iPad *does* let you perform some other tasks while playing audio.

Unfortunately, your iPad doesn't give you any direct way to do this. You may think your only hope is to rip or purchase the song separately, but I've figured out a workaround. The secret is that if you add a music video to a regular music playlist, iPad treats the music video like a regular song. When you play it on your iPad using that playlist, you hear just the audio portion (and see just the first frame of the video as the album art).

To add a music video to a playlist in iTunes, follow these steps:

1. **Open iTunes on your computer.**

2. **It's best to use a custom playlist for this, so create your own playlist if you haven't done so already.** See Chapter 8 to learn how to create playlists in iTunes.

3. **In Playlists, click Music Videos.** A list of all your music videos appears.

4. **Right-click (or Control+click on a Mac) the video you want to work with, click Add to Playlist, and then click a playlist.** iTunes adds the music video to the playlist.

5. **Repeat Step 4 for any other music videos you want to just listen to.**

Sync your iPad to download the updated playlist. Then on your iPad, tap iPod, tap the playlist you used, and then tap the music video. Your iPad plays the audio portion and displays the first frame of the video. You're now free to move about the iPad cabin while listening to the tune.

Playing iPad videos on your TV

You can carry a bunch of videos with you on your iPad, so why shouldn't you be able to play them on a TV if you want? Well, you can. You have to buy another cable, but that's the only investment you have to make to watch iPad videos right on your TV.

To hook your iPad up to your TV, you have three choices:

- **Apple Dock Connector to VGA Adapter.** This $29 cable has a 30-pin connector on one end that connects to the iPad or an iPad dock and a VGA connector on the other end. It's unlikely your TV has a VGA port, so you also need an adapter that converts the VGA output to the corresponding inputs on your TV (usually component inputs).

- **Apple Component AV cable.** This $49 cable has a dock connector on one end that plugs into the iPad's dock connector and component connectors on the other end that connect to the component inputs of your TV.

- **Apple Composite AV cable.** This $49 cable has a dock connector on one end that plugs into the iPad's dock connector and composite connectors on the other end that connect to the composite inputs of your TV.

The cable you choose depends on the type of TV you have. Older sets have AV inputs or possible composite inputs, while most newer flat-screen TVs have component inputs.

After setting up your cables, set your TV to the input and play your videos as you normally would.

Note

Your iPad offers a couple of settings that affect the TV output. See the next section to learn more about them.

Customizing your iPad's video settings

Your iPad offers a few video-related settings that you can try on for size. Follow these steps to get at them:

1. **Press the Home button to get to the Home screen.**
2. **Tap Settings to open the Settings app.**
3. **Tap the Videos icon.** The Video screen opens.

You get four settings to meddle with:

- **Start Playing.** This setting controls what your iPad does when you stop and restart a video. You have two choices: Where Left Off (the default), which picks up the video from the same point where you stopped it, and From Beginning, which always restarts the video from scratch. Tap Start Playing, and then tap the setting you prefer.

- **Closed Captioning.** This setting toggles support for closed captioning on and off, when it's available. To turn on this feature, tap the Closed Captioning switch to the On position.

- **Widescreen.** This setting toggles support for widescreen TV output. If you have a widescreen TV and you want to play iPad videos on the set, tap the Widescreen switch to the On position.

- **TV Signal.** This setting specifies the TV output signal. If you're going to play videos on a TV, tap TV Signal and then tap either NTSC or PAL.

Watching YouTube Videos

As if all those movie, TV show, and music video shenanigans weren't enough, your iPad also comes with a YouTube app right on the Home screen, so you can watch whatever video everyone's talking about or just browse around for interesting finds.

YouTube videos tend to be in Flash, a video format that the iPad doesn't recognize. However, many of YouTube's videos have been converted to a format called H.264, which is a much higher-quality video format and is playable on your iPad. The YouTube app plays only these H.264 videos.

To fire up the YouTube app, press the Home button to return to the Home screen and tap the YouTube icon.

Finding a YouTube video

YouTube's collection of talking cats, stupid human tricks, and TV snippets is vast, to say the least. To help you apply at least a bit of order to the YouTube chaos, your iPad organizes the YouTube app with a collection of browse buttons in the menu bar, as shown in Figure 9.5.

Here's a summary of what each browse button does for you:

- **Featured.** Tap this button to display a list of videos picked by the YouTube editors. The list shows each video's name, star rating, popularity, and length.

- **Top Rated.** Tap this button to display the videos that have the highest user ratings.

● **Most Viewed.** Tap this to see the videos with the most views. At the top, you can tap Today, This Week, and All. This chooses the top-viewed videos of today, this week, or of all time. At the bottom of the list, you can tap Load 25 More, which loads 25 more Most Viewed.

Note To get more detailed information about a video, tap the blue More Info icon. The screen that appears gives you a description of the video, tells you when it was added, and shows a list of related videos.

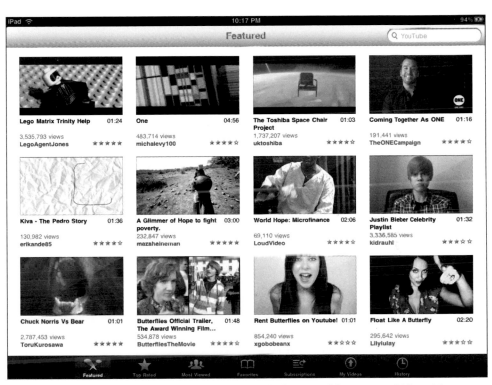

9.5 The YouTube app offers several browse buttons at the bottom of the screen, which enable you to locate and manage YouTube's videos.

● **Favorites.** Tap this button to see a list of videos that you've bookmarked as being favorites. This screen also has a Playlists tab, which you can tap to log on to YouTube and see the video playlists you've created.

● **Subscriptions.** Tap this button to log on to YouTube and see a list of your video subscriptions.

- **My Videos.** Tap this button to log on to YouTube and see a list of the videos you've uploaded.

- **History.** Give this a tap to see the videos that you've viewed.

Note

Don't want someone passing by to know that you're addicted to lonelygirl15? I can't blame you. Tap the History button, tap Clear, and when your iPad asks you to confirm, tap Clear History.

You also can locate videos by using the Search box in the top-right corner of the screen. Tap inside the box, enter a search phrase, and then tap Return. YouTube sends back a list of videos that match your search term.

Saving a video as a favorite

Just like finding a great site on the Web, finding a gem in the mountain of cut glass that is YouTube is a rare and precious thing. Chances are good that you'll want to play that video again later, but you can't always rely on it being in your History list or your being able to find it using the Search feature. Fortunately, the YouTube app saves you such frustration by enabling you to save a video as a bookmark. You can then run the video anytime you want by tapping the Bookmarks button.

Follow these steps to create a bookmark for a video:

1. **In the YouTube app, locate the video you want to save.**

2. **Tap the video to start the playback.**

3. **Tap the Bookmark icon.** The Bookmark icon is on the left side of the playback controls. (If you don't see the controls, tap the screen.) iPad creates a bookmark for the video.

Sending a link to a video via e-mail

If you come across yet another amazing guitar player video that you simply must share with a friend, the YouTube app makes it easy by enabling you to send that person an e-mail message that includes the video address as a link. Here's how it works:

1. **In the YouTube app, locate the video you want to share.**

2. **Tap the video to start the playback.**

3. **Tap the Fullscreen icon.** The Fullscreen icon is on the right side of the playback controls (if you don't see the controls, tap the screen). YouTube displays the video in a window.

4. **Tap the video.** YouTube displays several icons on the video.

5. **Tap the Share icon.** iPad creates a new message with the video title as the subject and the YouTube address in the body.

6. **Choose your message recipient.**

7. **Modify the Subject line and body text as you see fit.**

8. **Tap Send.** iPad sends the message and returns you to the video.

Can I Use iPad to Manage My Contacts?

One of the paradoxes of modern life is that as your contact information becomes more important, you store less and less of that information in the easiest database system of them all — your memory. That is, instead of memorizing phone numbers like you used to, you now store your contact info electronically. This isn't all that surprising because it's not just a landline number that you have to remember for each person; it might also be a cell number, an e-mail address, a Web site address, and more. That's a lot to remember, so it makes sense to go the electronic route. And for the iPad, "electronic" means the Contacts app, which is loaded with useful features that can help you organize the contact management side of your life.

Syncing Your Contacts

Although you can certainly add contacts directly on your iPad — and I show you how to do just that a bit later in this chapter — adding, editing, grouping, and deleting contacts is a lot easier on a computer. So a good way to approach contacts is to manage them on your Mac or Windows PC, and then sync your contacts with your iPad.

Creating contact groups

However, do you really need to sync *all* your contacts? For example, if you only use your iPad to contact friends and family, then why clog your iPad's Contacts app with work contacts? I don't know!

You can control which contacts are sent to your iPad by creating groups of contacts, and then syncing only the groups you want. Here are some quick instructions for creating groups:

- **Address Book (Mac).** Choose File ⇨ New Group, type the group name, and then press Return. Now populate the new group by dragging and dropping contacts on it.

- **Contacts (Windows 7 and Windows Vista).** Click New Contact Group, type the group name, and then click Add to Contact Group. Choose all the contacts you want in the group and then click Add. Click OK.

Note

If you're an Outlook user, note that iTunes doesn't support Outlook-based contact groups, so you're stuck with syncing everyone in your Outlook Contacts folder.

Running the sync

With your group (or groups) all figured out, follow these steps to sync your contacts with your iPad:

1. **Connect your iPad to your computer.**

2. **In iTunes, click your iPad in the Devices list.**

3. **Click the Info tab.**

4. **Turn on contacts syncing by using one of the following techniques:**
   - **Mac.** Select the Sync Address Book Contacts check box.
   - **Windows.** Select the Sync Contacts With check box, and then use the list to choose the program you want to use (such as Outlook).

5. **Select an option:**

   - **All Contacts.** Select this option to sync all your Address Book contacts.

   - **Selected Groups.** Select this option to sync only the groups you pick. In the group list, select the check box beside each group that you want to sync, as shown in Figure10.1.

10.1 You can sync selected contact groups to your iPad.

6. **If you want to make the sync a two-way street, select the Add Contacts Created Outside of Groups on this iPad To check box, and then choose a group from the menu.**

7. **(Mac only) If you have a Yahoo! account and you also want your Yahoo! Address Book contacts in on the sync, select the Sync Yahoo! Address Book Contacts check box, type your Yahoo! ID and password, and click OK.**

8. **(Mac only) If you have a Google account and you also want your Google Contacts in on the sync, select the Sync Google Contacts check box, type your Google and password, and click OK.**

9. **Click Apply.** iTunes syncs the iPad using your new contacts settings.

Getting Started with the Contacts App

You'll need the Contacts app up and running for this chapter, so head for your iPad's Home screen and tap the Contacts icon. Figure 10.2 shows the Contacts app.

The Contacts app displays the All Contacts list on the left, and the info for the currently selected contact on the right. If you've got a healthy number of contacts, you'll need to know how to navigate the list. You have four choices:

| iPad 🛜 | 10:34 PM | 96 % 🔋 |

All Contacts

Groups

Q Search

A B C D E F G H I J K L M N O P Q R S T U V W X Y Z #

A

Accessories

Paolo **Accorti**

Secret **Address**

Pedro **Afonso**

Maria **Anders**

Apple Inc.

Victoria **Ashworth**

Gary **Aslett**

Andrea **Aster**

#AUTO

B

Bernardo **Batista**

Victoria Ashworth
Sales Representative
B's Beverages

work   1 (715) 551-212

work   vashworth@bsbeverages.co.uk

work   **Fauntleroy Circus**
       London EC2 5NT
       UK

notes

+   Edit   Share

10.2 The iPad's handsome Contacts app.

- By default the Contacts app displays the All Contacts list. To view a group of contacts, instead, tap the Groups icon in the upper left corner of the screen, and then tap the group you want to view.
- Flick up and down to scroll through the list.
- Tap a letter to leap directly to the contacts whose last names begin with that letter.
- Use the Search box at the top of the All Contacts list to type a few letters from the name of the contact you want to work with, and then tap the contact in the search results.

Creating and Editing Contacts

Syncing your computer's contacts program (such as Address Book on the Mac, or Outlook's Contacts folder) is by far the easiest way to populate your iPad Contacts app with a crowd of people, but it might not include everyone in your posse. If someone's missing and you're not around your computer, you can add that person directly to the Contacts app. Similarly, you might be messing around with the Contacts app and notice an error or old info for someone. No problem: you can edit a contact right on the iPad.

Best of all, any changes you make within the Contacts app are automatically synced back to your computer the next time your iPad and iTunes get together for a sync session.

Creating a new contact

The next time you realize someone's missing from your contacts, you can fire up your trusty iPad and tap that person's vital statistics right into the Contacts app. Here are the steps to follow:

1. **In the Home screen, tap the Contacts icon.** Your iPad opens the Contacts app.

2. **Tap the + button at the bottom right of the screen.** The New Contact screen appears and your iPad displays the keyboard, as shown in Figure10.3.

10.3 Use the New Contact screen to tap in the details of your contact.

3. **The cursor starts off in the First box, so enter the person's first name.** If you're jotting down the contact data for a company or some other inanimate object, skip to Step 5.

4. **Tap the Last box and then enter the person's surname.**

5. **If you want to note where the person works (or if you're adding a business to your Contacts list), tap the Company box and enter the company name.**

Yup, I know there are still plenty of other fields to fill in, and we'll get to those in a second. For now, though, I want to interrupt your regularly scheduled programming to show you how to edit an existing contact. It will all make sense soon, trust me.

Editing an existing contact

Now that your new contact is off to a flying start, you can go ahead and fill in details such as phone numbers, addresses (e-mail, Web, and real world), and anything else you can think of (or have the patience to enter into your iPad; it can be a lot of tapping!). The next few sections take you through the steps for each type of data.

Note

The one technique that I don't get into here is how to spruce up your contact with a photo. That's because I already covered that earlier in Chapter 6.

However, the steps I show also apply to any contact that's already residing in your iPad. Here, then, are the steps required to open an existing contact for editing:

1. **In the Home screen, tap the Contacts icon to open the All Contacts screen.**

2. **Tap the contact you want to edit.**

3. **Tap Edit.** Your iPad displays the contact's data in the Info screen.

4. **Make your changes, as described in the next few sections.**

5. **Tap Done.** Your iPad saves your work and returns you to the All Contacts screen.

Assigning phone numbers to a contact

Everyone has a phone number, so you'll want to augment a contact by entering their phone data. Sure, but *which* number? Work? Home? Cell? Pager? Fax? Fortunately, there's no need to choose just one, because your iPad is happy to store all these numbers, plus a few more if need be.

Here are the steps to follow to add one or more phone numbers for a contact:

1. **In the contact editing screen, examine the Phone field's label box to see if the default label is the one you want.** For a new contact, the default label is "mobile," but you might see a different label if you're editing an existing contact. If you're okay with the existing label, skip to Step 4.

2. **Tap the Phone field label.** The Contacts app displays a list of phone labels, as shown in Figure 10.4.

3. **Tap the label that best applies to the phone number you're adding, such as mobile, iPhone, home, or work.** The Contacts app displays the new label.

4. **Tap inside the Phone field and then enter the phone number with area code first.** Note that you only need to enter the numbers; Contacts helpfully adds extra stuff like parentheses around the area code and the dash. When you begin entering the phone number, the Contacts app automatically adds another Phone field below the current field.

5. **Repeat Steps 1 to 4 to add any other numbers you want to store for this contact.**

Assigning e-mail addresses to a contact

It makes sense that you might want to add multiple phone numbers for a contact, but would you ever need to enter multiple e-mail addresses? Well, sure you would! Most people have at least a couple of addresses — usually home and work addresses — and some Type A e-mailers have a dozen or more. Life is too short to enter that many e-mail addresses, but you need at least the important ones if you want to use your iPad's Mail application to send a note to your contacts.

10.4 Tap a phone number label and then tap the label you want to use for the contact's phone number.

Follow these steps to add one or more e-mail addresses for a contact:

1. **In the contact editing screen, check out the Email field's default label.** For a new contact, the default label is "home," but you might see a different label if you're editing an existing contact. If you want to use the existing label, skip to Step 4.

2. **Tap the Email field label to display a list of e-mail labels.**

3. **Tap the e-mail label you want to use, such as home or work.** The Contacts app applies the new label.

4. **Tap inside the Email field and type the person's e-mail address.** Note that the onscreen keyboard now displays the handy @ and . keys; you need those. While you're entering the e-mail address, the Contacts app sneakily adds another Email field below the current field.

5. **Feel free to repeat Steps 1 to 4 as often as necessary to add other e-mail addresses for this contact.**

Assigning Web addresses to a contact

Who on Earth doesn't have a Web site these days? It could be a humble home page, a blog, a Facebook page, a Twitter feed, a home business site, or it could be someone's corporate Web site. Some busy Web beavers may even have all six! Whatever Web home a person has, it's a good idea to toss the address into his or her contact data because later on you can simply tap the address and your iPad (assuming it can see the Internet from here) immediately fires up Safari and takes you to the site. Does your pal have multiple Web sites? No sweat: Your iPad is happy to take you to them all.

You can add one or more Web addresses for a contact by making your way through these steps:

1. **In the contact editing screen, eyeball the URL field's current label.** If you're okay with the existing label, skip to Step 4.

2. **Tap the URL field label to get yourself a list of Web address labels.**

3. **Tap the label that suits the Web address you're entering, such as home page, home, or work.** The Contacts app adds the new label.

4. **Tap inside the URL field and then tap the person's Web address.** In Figure 10.5, note that the onscreen keyboard now includes several useful URL-friendly keys, including slash (/), dot (.), underscore (_), dash (-), and .com. Note, too, that when you start tapping the Web address, the Contacts app surreptitiously inserts another URL field below the current field.

5. **Repeat Steps 1 to 4 to add other Web addresses for this contact, as you see fit.**

10.5 When you're tapping away at a Web address, don't forget to take advantage of the onscreen keyboard URL-related keys, such as slash (/) and .com.

Genius

To save some wear and tear on your tapping finger, don't bother adding the http:// stuff at the beginning of the address. Your iPad adds those characters automatically anytime you tap the address to visit the site. Same with the www. prefix. So if the full address is http://www.wordspy.com, you need only enter wordspy.com.

Assigning physical addresses to a contact

With all this talk about cell numbers, e-mail addresses, and Web addresses, it's easy to forget that people actually live and work somewhere. You may have plenty of contacts where the location of that somewhere doesn't much matter, but if you ever need to get from here to there, taking the time to insert a contact's physical address really pays off. Why? Because you need only tap the address and your iPad displays a Google map that shows you the precise location. From there you can get directions, see a satellite map of the area, and more. (I talk about all this great map stuff in Chapter 12.)

Tapping out a full address is a bit of work, but as the following steps show, it's not exactly painful:

1. **In the contact editing screen, tap Add New Address.** The Contacts app displays fields for the street address, city, state, postal code, and country, as shown in Figure 10.6.

home	Street	
	City	State
	ZIP	**United States**

   10.6 Use the fields shown here to tap out your contact's physical coordinates.

2. **Examine the address label to see if the default "home" label is the one you want.** If you're okay with the existing label, skip to Step 5.

3. **Tap the address label.** The Contacts app displays a list of address labels.

4. **Tap the label that best applies to the address you're entering, such as home or work.** The Contacts app displays the new label.

5. **Tap the Street field and then enter the person's street address.** When Contacts realizes you're entering a street address, it automatically adds a second Street field.

6. **If necessary, tap the second Street field, and then enter even more of the person's street address.**

7. **Tap the City field, and then enter the person's city.**

8. **Tap the State field, and then enter the person's state.** Depending on what you later select for the country, this field might have a different name, such as Province.

9. **Tap the ZIP field, and then enter the ZIP code.** Again, depending on what you later select for the country, this field might have a different name, such as Postal Code.

10. **Tap the Country field to open the Country list, and then tap the contact's country.**

11. **Repeat Steps 1 to 10 if you feel like entering another address for your contact.**

Getting More Out of the Contacts App

Adding and editing data using the Contacts app is blissfully linear: Tap a field label to change the label, and then tap inside a field to add the data. If you remember to take advantage of the onscreen keyboard's context-sensitive keys (such as the .com key that materializes when you're entering a Web address), then contact data entry becomes a snap.

The Contacts app is straightforward on the surface, but if you dig down a bit, you find some useful tools and features that can make your contact management duties even better.

Creating a custom label

When you fill out your contact data, your iPad insists that you apply a label to each tidbit: home, work, mobile, and so on. If none of the predefined labels fits, you can always just slap on the generic label: other. You could do that, but it seems so, well, dull. If you've got a phone number or address that you can't shoehorn into any of your iPad's prefab labels, get creative and make up a label. Here's how:

1. **In the contact editing screen, tap the label for the field you want to work with.** The Label list appears.

2. **Tap Add Custom Label.** The Custom Label dialog appears, as shown in Figure 10.7.

3. **Type the custom label.**

4. **Tap Save.** The Contacts app saves your custom label and returns you to the contact editing screen.

10.7 Use the Custom Label dialog to forge your very own custom label for your contacts.

You can apply your custom label to any type of contact data. For example, you can create a label named college and apply it to a phone number, e-mail address, Web address, or physical address.

Deleting a custom label

If a custom label wears out its welcome, follow these steps to delete it:

1. **In the contact editing screen, tap the label for any field.** The Label list appears.
2. **Tap Edit.** The Contacts app puts the Label list into Edit mode.
3. **Tap the red Delete icon to the left of the custom label you want to remove.** The Contacts app displays a Delete button to the right of the field.
4. **Tap Delete.**
5. **Tap outside the Label list.** The Contacts app returns you to the editing screen.

Adding extra fields to a contact

The New Contact screen (which appears when you add a contact) and the Info screen (which appears when you edit an existing contact) display just the fields you need for basic contact info. However, these screens lack quite a few common fields. For example, you might need to specify a contact's prefix (such as Dr. or Professor), suffix (such as Jr., Sr., or III), or job title.

Thankfully, your iPad is merely hiding these and other useful fields where you can't see them. There are 11 hidden fields that you can add to any contact:

- Prefix
- Phonetic First Name
- Phonetic Last Name
- Middle
- Suffix
- Nickname
- Job Title
- Department
- Instant Message
- Birthday
- Date

The iPad is only too happy to let you add as many of these extra fields as you want. Here are the steps involved:

1. **In the contact editing screen, tap Add Field.** The Add Field list appears, as shown in Figure 10.8.

2. **Tap the field that you want to add.** The Contacts app adds the field to the contact.

3. **If the field has a label, tap the label box to choose a new label, if needed.**

4. **Enter the field data.**

5. **Repeat Steps 1 to 4 to add more fields as needed.**

Keeping track of birthdays and anniversaries

Do you have trouble remembering birthdays? If so, then I feel your pain because I, too, used to be pathetically bad at keeping birthdays straight. And no wonder: These days you not only have to keep track of birthdays for your family and friends, but increasingly often you have to remember birthdays for staff, colleagues, and clients, as well. It's too much! My secret is that I simply gave up and outsourced the job to my iPad's Contacts app, which has a hidden field that you can use to store birth dates.

10.8 The Add Field list shows the hidden fields that you can add to any contact.

To add the Birthday field to a contact, follow these steps:

1. **In the Contacts app, tap the contact you want to work with.**

2. **Tap Edit.** The Info screen appears.

3. **Tap Add Field.** The Contacts app opens the Add Field list.

4. **Tap Birthday.** The Contacts app adds a birthday field to the contact and displays the nifty scroll wheels shown in Figure 10.9.

10.9 Use these fun scroll wheels to set the contact's birth date.

5. **Scroll the left wheel to set the day of the month for the birth date.**

6. **Scroll the middle wheel to set the month for the birth date.**

7. **Scroll the right wheel to set the year of the birth date.**

8. **Tap outside of the scroll wheels.** The Contacts app saves the birthday info.

Everyone has a birthday, naturally, but lots of people have anniversaries, too. It could be a wedding date, a quit-smoking date, or the date that someone started working at the company. Whatever the occasion, you can add it to the contact info so that it's staring you in the face as a friendly reminder each time you open that contact.

Follow these steps to include an anniversary with a contact:

1. **In the Contacts app, tap the contact you want to edit.**

2. **Tap Edit.** The Contacts app shows the Info screen.

3. **Tap Add Field.** The Add Field list appears.

4. **Tap Date.** The Contacts app adds a Date field to the contact and displays the same scroll wheels that you saw earlier in Figure 10.9.

5. **Scroll the left wheel to set the day of the month for the anniversary.**

6. **Scroll the middle wheel to set the month for the anniversary.**

7. **Scroll the right wheel to set the year of the anniversary.**

8. **The label box should already show the anniversary label, but if not, tap the label box, and then tap the anniversary.**

9. **Tap outside of the scroll wheels.** The Contacts app saves the anniversary.

Note

Although you can only add one birthday to a contact (not surprisingly), you're free to add multiple anniversaries.

Adding notes to a contact

The standard contact fields all are designed to hold specific data: a name, an address, a date, and so on. Sometimes, however, you might need to enter more free-form data:

- The highlights of a recent client meeting
- A list of things to do for the contact

- How you met the contact or why you added the person to your Contacts list

- Contact data that doesn't have a proper field: spouse's or partner's name, kids' names, account numbers, gender, hobbies, and on and on

Whatever it is, your iPad offers a Notes field that you can add to a contact and then scribble away in as needed. To add the Notes field to a contact, follow these steps:

1. **In the Contacts list, tap the contact you want to work with.**

2. **Tap Edit.** The Info screen appears.

3. **Tap inside the Notes field.**

4. **Type the note data.**

Creating a new contact from an electronic business card

Entering a person's contact data by hand is a tedious bit of business at the best of times, so it helps if you can find a faster way to do it. If you can cajole a contact into sending his or her contact data electronically, then you can add that data with just a couple of taps. What do I mean when I talk about sending contact data electronically? The world's contact management gurus long ago came up with a standard file format for contact data: the vCard. It's a kind of digital business card that exists as a separate file. People can pass this data along by attaching their (or someone else's) card to an e-mail message.

If you get a message with contact data, you see an icon for the VCF file, as shown in Figure 10.10.

To get this data into your Contacts list, follow these steps:

1. **In the Home screen, tap Mail to open the Mail application.**

2. **Tap the message that contains the vCard attachment.**

3. **Tap the icon for the vCard file.** Your iPad opens the vCard.

4. **Tap Create New Contact.** If the person is already in your Contacts list, but the vCard contains new data, tap Add to Existing Contact, and then tap the contact.

10.10 If your iPad receives an e-mail message with an attached vCard, an icon for the file appears in the message body.

Sorting your contacts

By default, the Contacts app displays your contacts sorted by last name (or company name, for businesses), and then by first name (to resolve cases where people have the same last name). That makes sense in most cases, but you might prefer a more friendly approach that sorts contacts by first name and then by last name. Here's how to make it so:

1. **Return to the iPad's Home screen and tab Settings.** The Settings screen appears.
2. **Tap Mail, Contacts, Calendars.** The Mail, Contacts, Calendars screen appears.
3. **Scroll down to the Contacts section.**
4. **Tap Sort Order to display the Sort Order options.**
5. **Tap First, Last.** The Contacts app will now sort your contacts by first name.

Deleting a contact field

People change, and so does their contact info. Most of the time these changes require you to edit an existing field, but sometimes people actually shed information. For example, they might get rid of their pager or fax machine, or they might shutter a Web site. Whatever the reason, you should delete that data from the contact to keep the Info screen tidy and easier to navigate.

To delete a contact field, follow these steps:

1. **In the Contacts list, tap the contact you want to work with.**

2. **Tap Edit.** The Info screen appears.

3. **Tap the red Delete icon to the left of the field you want to trash.** The Contacts app displays a Delete button to the right of the field.

4. **Tap Delete.** The Contacts app removes the field.

5. **Tap Done.** The Contacts app closes the Info screen.

Deleting a contact

It feels good to add new contacts but, life being what it is, you don't get a lifetime guarantee with these things: friends fall out or fade away; colleagues decide to make a new start at another firm; clients take their business elsewhere; and some of your acquaintances simply wear out their welcome after a while. You move on, and so does your Contacts list, and the best way to do that is to delete the contact to help keep the list trim and tidy.

Follow these steps to delete a contact:

1. **In the Contacts list, tap the contact you want to get rid of.**

2. **Tap Edit.** The Info screen appears.

3. **Tap the Delete Contact button at the bottom of the screen.** The Contacts app asks you to confirm the deletion.

4. **Tap Delete Contact.** The Contacts app removes the contact and returns you to the All Contacts screen.

Can I Use iPad to Track My Appointments?

Do you, like the White Rabbit in Lewis Carroll's book *Alice's Adventures in Wonderland*, find yourself constantly saying, "My ears and whiskers, how late it's getting!"? I suspected as much. Well, you've come to the right place because your iPad can help. No, not because you can use it to read *Alice's Adventures in Wonderland* (great book, but reading it will just make you later than you already are). Instead, you can take advantage of the beautiful and efficient Calendar app that turns your iPad into a kind of electronic administrative assistant that stores your appointments and even reminds you when they're coming up. My ears and whiskers, how punctual you'll be!

Syncing Your Calendar

When you're tripping around town with your trusty iPad at your side, you certainly don't want to be late if you have a date. The best way to ensure that you don't miss an appointment, meeting, or rendezvous is to always have the event details at hand, which means adding those details to your iPad's Calendar app. You could add the appointment to Calendar right on the iPad (a technique I take you through later in this chapter), but it's easier to create it on your computer and then sync it to your iPad. This gives you the added advantage of having the appointment listed in two places, so you're sure to arrive on time.

Most people sync all their appointments, but it's not unusual to keep track of separate schedules — for example, business and personal. You can control which schedule is synced to your iPad by creating separate calendars and then syncing only the calendars you want:

- **Mac.** In your Mac's iCal application, choose File ➪ New Calendar, type the calendar name, and press Return.

- **Windows.** In Outlook, click the Calendars tab, choose Folder ➪ New Calendar, type the calendar name, and click OK.

Now follow these steps to sync your calendar with your iPad:

1. **Connect your iPad to your computer.**

2. **In iTunes, click your iPad in the Devices list.**

3. **Click the Info tab.**

4. **Turn on calendar syncing by using one of the following techniques:**

   - **Mac.** Select the Sync iCal Calendars check box.

   - **Windows.** Select the Sync Calendars With check box, and use the list to choose the program you want to use (such as Outlook).

5. **Select an option:**

   - **All Calendars.** Select this option to sync all your calendars.

   - **Selected Calendars.** Select this option to sync only the calendars you pick. In the calendar list, select the check box beside each calendar that you want to sync, as shown in Figure 11.1.

Note iTunes doesn't support Windows Live Calendar or Windows Calendar (available with Windows Vista), so you're out of luck if you use that to manage your schedule.

| Summary | Info | Apps | Music | Movies | TV Shows | Podcasts | iTunes U | Books | Photos |

☑ Sync iCal Calendars

○ All calendars
◉ Selected calendars:

☐ Home
☑ Work

☑ Do not sync events older than 30 days
Your calendars are being synced over the air. Your calendars will also sync directly with this computer.

11.1 You can sync selected calendars with your iPad.

6. **To control how far back the calendar sync goes, select the Do Not Sync Events Older Than X Days check box, and then type the number of days of calendar history you want to see on your iPad.**

7. **Click Apply.** iTunes syncs the iPad using your new calendar settings.

Genius Your iPad syncs completed events so you have a record of them. By default, your iPad syncs events that happened up to one month back. To change this, go to the Home screen, tap Settings, and then tap Mail, Contacts, Calendars. Scroll down to the Calendars section, tap Sync, and then tap how far back you want to go: Events 2 Weeks Back, Events 1 Month Back, Events 3 Months Back, Events 6 Months Back, or All Events.

Getting Started with the Calendar App

When you meet someone and ask "How are you?", the most common reply these days is a short one: "Busy!" We're all bee-busy nowadays, and that places-to-go, people-to-see feeling is everywhere. All the more reason to keep your affairs in order, and that includes your appointments. Your iPad comes with a Calendar app that you can use to create items, called *events*, which represent your appointments, meetings, lunch dates, and so on. Calendar keeps track of all this stuff for you, leaving your brain free to concentrate on more important things.

You need the Calendar app up and running for this chapter, so head for your iPad's Home screen and tap the Calendar icon. Figure 11.2 shows the Calendar app in landscape mode.

11.2 The iPad's administrative assistant: The beautiful and talented Calendar app.

The key to getting around in the Calendar app efficiently is to take advantage of its various views, represented by the four buttons at the top of the screen:

- **Day.** This view shows a single day's appointment, with the day's schedule on the right and a list of the day's appointments on the left.

- **Week.** This view shows all your appointments for the selected week.

- **Month.** This view shows the titles of all your appointments for a given month.

- **List.** This view shows a list of all your upcoming appointments on the left and the details of the selected appointment on the right.

The Calendar app also provides you with a navigation bar at the bottom of the screen, and this bar changes depending on the current view. For example, in Day view you can use the Navigation bar to tap a different day, and in Month view you can tap a different month.

Genius

Month view shows just the title of each appointment, along with a color-coded bullet that tells you which calendar the appointment resides in. To see more details for the appointments, drag your finger over them. Each time your finger passes over an appointment, Calendar displays details such as the event time, location, notes, and attendees.

Tracking Your Appointments

I showed you how to sync your computer's calendar application (such as iCal on the Mac, or Outlook's Calendar folder) earlier in this chapter, and that's the easiest way to fill your iPad with your appointments. However, something always comes up when you're running around, so you need to know how to add and edit appointments directly in your iPad Calendar. The next few sections provide the details.

Adding an appointment to your calendar

Follow these steps to add a basic appointment:

1. **Select the date on which the appointment occurs.** In Day view, navigate to the date; in Week view or Month view, tap the date.

2. **Tap the + button in the bottom-right corner of the screen.** The Add Event screen appears, as shown in Figure 11.3.

3. **Tap the Title box, and enter a title for the appointment.**

4. **Tap the Location box, and enter a location for the appointment.**

5. **Tap Start/End.** Calendar displays the Start & End screen.

6. **Tap Starts, and use the scroll wheels to set the date and time that your appointment begins.**

7. **Tap Ends, and use the scroll wheels to set the date and time that your appointment finishes.**

8. **If you have multiple calendars, tap Calendar and then tap the calendar in which you want this appointment to appear.**

9. **Tap the Notes box, and enter your notes for the appointment.**

10. **Tap Done.** The Calendar app saves the appointment info and displays the new appointment in the calendar.

11.3 Use the Add Event screen to create your appointment.

Editing an existing appointment

Whether you've scheduled an appointment by hand or synced the appointment from your computer, the event details might change: a new time, a new location, and so on. Whatever the change, you need to edit the appointment to keep your schedule accurate.

Follow these steps to edit an existing appointment:

1. **Display the date that contains the appointment you want to edit.** In Day view, navigate to the date; in Week view or Month view, open the week or month that contains the date.

2. **Tap the appointment.**

3. **Tap Edit.** Your iPad displays the appointment data in the Edit screen.

4. **Make your changes to the appointment.**

5. **Tap Done.** Your iPad saves your work and returns you to the event details.

Setting up a repeating event

One of Calendar's truly great timesavers is the repeat feature, which enables you to set up a single event and get Calendar to automatically repeat the same event at a regular interval.

For example, if you set up an event for a Friday, you can repeat the event every week, which means that Calendar automatically sets up the same event to occur on subsequent Fridays. You can continue the events indefinitely or end them after a certain number of repeats or on a specific date.

Follow these steps to configure an existing event to repeat:

1. **Display the date that contains the appointment you want to edit.** In Day view, navigate to the date; in Week view or Month view, open the week or month that contains the date.

2. **Tap the appointment.** Calendar opens the event info.

3. **Tap Edit.** Calendar displays the event data in the Edit screen.

4. **Tap Repeat.** The Repeat Event list appears, as shown in Figure 11.4.

11.4 Use the Repeat Event list to decide how often you want your event to recur.

5. **Tap the repeat interval you want to use.**

6. **Tap Done.** Calendar returns you to the Edit Event screen.

7. **Tap End Repeat.** The End Repeat list appears, as shown in Figure 11.5.

11.5 Use the End Repeat list to decide how long you want the event to repeat.

8. **You have three choices here:**

   - **To have the event repeat indefinitely, tap Repeat Forever.**

   - **To have the event repeats stop on a particular day, tap End Repeat.** Use the scroll wheels to set the day, month, and year that you want the final event to occur.

9. **Tap Done.** Calendar returns you to the Edit Event screen.

10. **Tap Done.** Calendar saves the repeat data and returns you to the event details.

Converting an event to an all-day event

Some events don't really have specific times that you can pin down. These include birthdays, anniversaries, sales meetings, trade shows, conferences, and vacations. What all these types of events have in common is that they last all day: In the case of birthdays and anniversaries, literally so; in the case of trade shows and the like, "all day" refers to the entire work day.

Why is this important? Well, suppose you schedule a trade show as a regular appointment that lasts from 9 a.m. to 5 p.m. When you examine that day in the Calendar app's Day or Week view, you see a big fat block that covers the entire day. If you also want to schedule meetings that occur at the trade show, Calendar lets you do that, but it shows these new appointments "on top" of this existing trade show event. This makes the schedule hard to read, so you might miss an appointment.

To solve this problem, configure the trade show (or whatever) as an all-day event. Calendar clears it from the regular schedule and displays the event separately, near the top of the Day view, or on the top part of the Week view.

Follow these steps to configure an event as an all-day event:

1. **Display the date that contains the appointment you want to edit.** In Day view, navigate to the date; in Week view or Month view, open the week or month that contains the date.

2. **Tap the appointment.** Calendar opens the event info.

3. **Tap Edit.** Calendar switches to the Edit screen.

4. **Tap Start/End.** Calendar displays the Start & End screen.

5. **Tap the All-day switch to the On position.**

6. **Tap Done.** The Calendar app saves the event, returns you to the calendar, and now shows the event as an all-day event.

Figure 11.6 shows Calendar in Day view with an all-day event added.

11.6 All-day events appear in the all-day section, which is near the top of the Day view (as shown here) and the Week view.

Adding an alert to an event

One of the truly useful secrets of stress-free productivity in the modern world is what I call the set-it-and-forget-it school of time management. That is, you set up an appointment electronically and then get the same technology to remind you when the appointment occurs. That way, your mind doesn't have to waste energy fretting about missing the appointment because you know your technology has your back.

With your iPad, the technology of choice for doing this is the Calendar app and its alert feature. When you add an alert to an event, Calendar automatically displays a reminder of the event, which is a dialog that pops up on the screen. Your iPad also vibrates and sounds a few beeps to get your attention. You also get to choose when the alert triggers (such as a specified number of minutes, hours, or days before the event), and you can even set up a second alert just to be on the safe side.

Follow these steps to set an alert for an event:

1. **Display the date that contains the appointment you want to edit.** In Day view, navigate to the date; in Week view or Month view, open the week or month that contains the date.

2. **Tap the appointment.** Calendar opens the event info.

3. **Tap Edit.** Calendar displays the event data in the Edit screen.

4. **Tap Alert.** The Event Alert list appears, as shown in Figure 11.7.

11.7 Use the Event Alert screen to tell Calendar when to remind you about your event.

5. **Tap the type of alert you want to use.**

6. **Tap the number of minutes, hours, or days before the event you want to see the alert.**

7. **To set up a backup alert, tap the Second Alert option, and then tap the number of minutes, hours, or days before the event you want to see the second alert.**

8. **Tap Done.** The Calendar app saves your alert choices and returns you to the calendar.

Figure 11.8 shows an example of an alert. Tap View Event to see the details, or tap OK to dismiss the alert.

11.8 Your iPad displays an alert similar to this when it's time to remind you of an upcoming event.

Genius

You can disable the alert chirps if you find them annoying. On the Home screen, tap Settings, tap Sounds, and then tap the Calendar Alerts switch to the Off position.

Getting More Out of the Calendar App

The Calendar app's basic features — multiple views, color-coded calendars, repeating events, all-day events, and event alerts — make it an indispensible time management tool. But the Calendar app has a few more tricks up its sleeve that you ought to know about, and that's just what happens in the rest of this chapter.

Setting the default calendar

If you have multiple calendars on the go, each time you create a new appointment, the Calendar automatically chooses one of your calendars by default. It's no big whoop if every now and then you have to tap the Calendar setting and choose a different calendar. However, if you have to do this most of the time, it gets old in a hurry, particularly when I tell you there's something you can do about it. That is, you can configure the Calendar app to use a different default calendar. Here's how it's done:

1. **Return to the iPad's Home screen, and tap Settings.** The Settings screen appears.
2. **Tap Mail, Contacts, Calendars.** The Mail, Contacts, Calendars screen appears.
3. **In the Calendars section, tap Default Calendar.** The Default Calendar screen appears.
4. **Tap the calendar you prefer to use as the default.** The Calendar app now uses that calendar as the default for each new event.

Setting a birthday or anniversary reminder

If someone you know has a birthday coming up, you certainly don't want to forget! You can use your iPad's Contacts app to add a Birthday field for that person, and that works great if you actually look at the contact. If you don't, you're toast. The best way to remember is to get your iPad to do the remembering for you.

Follow these steps to set up a reminder about a birthday (or anniversary or some other important date):

1. **Display the date that contains the appointment you want to edit.** In Day view, navigate to the date; in Week view or Month view, open the week or month that contains the date.
2. **Tap the + button in the bottom right of the screen.** The Add Event screen appears.

3. **Tap the Title box, and type a title for the event ("Karen's Birthday", for example).**

4. **Tap the All-day switch to the On position.**

5. **Tap Starts, and use the scroll wheels to choose the birthday.**

6. **Tap Repeat, and then tap Every Year.**

7. **Tap Alert, and then tap On Date of Event.**

8. **Tap the second Alert, and then tap 2 Days Before.** This gives you a couple of days' notice, so you can go out and shop for a card and a present!

9. **Tap Done.** Calendar saves the event, and you have another load off your mind.

Subscribing to a calendar

If you know someone who has published a calendar, you might want to keep track of that calendar within your iPad's Calendar app. You can do that by subscribing to the published calendar. iPad sets up the published calendar as a separate item in the Calendar app, so you can easily switch between your own calendars and the published calendar.

To pull this off, you need to know the address of the published calendar. This address usually takes the following form: *server*.com/*calendar*.ics.

Here, *server*.com is the address of the calendar server, and *calendar*.ics is the name of the iCalendar file (almost always preceded by a folder location). For calendars published to MobileMe, the address always looks like this: ical.me.com/*member*/*calendar*.ics.

Here, *member* is the MobileMe member name of the person who published the calendar. Here's an example address:

ical.me.com/aardvarksorenstam/aardvark.ics

Follow these steps to subscribe to a published calendar:

1. **On the Home screen, tap Settings.** Your iPad opens the Settings screen.

2. **Tap Mail, Contacts, Calendars.** The Mail, Contacts, Calendars screen appears.

3. **Tap Add Account.** The Add Account screen opens.

4. **Tap Other.** Your iPad displays the Other screen.

5. **Tap Add Subscribed Calendar.** You see the Subscription screen, as shown in Figure 11.9.

6. **Use the Server text box to enter the calendar address.**

11.9 Use the Subscription screen to specify the address of the calendar you want to subscribe to.

7. **Tap Next.** Your iPad connects to the calendar.

8. **Tap Save.** Your iPad adds an account for the subscribed calendar.

To view the subscribed calendar, tap Calendar on the Home screen to open the Calendar app, and then click Calendars to open the Calendars screen. Your new calendar appears in the Subscribed section, as shown in Figure 11.10. Tap the calendar to view its appointments.

11.10 Your calendar subscriptions appear in the Subscribed section of the Calendars screen.

Handling Microsoft Exchange meeting requests

If you've set up a Microsoft Exchange account in your iPad, there's a good chance you're using its push features, where the Exchange Server automatically sends incoming e-mail messages to your iPad, as well as new and changed contacts and calendar data. If someone back at headquarters adds your name to a scheduled meeting, Exchange generates an automatic meeting request, which is an e-mail message that tells you about the meeting and asks if you want to attend.

How will you know? Tap Calendar in the Home screen, and examine the top left of the screen. In the Calendar's apps toolbar, the Invitations icon tells you how many meeting requests you have waiting for you, as shown in Figure 11.11.

Note

If you don't see the Invitations icon, you need to turn on syncing for your Exchange calendar. I show you how to do this in Chapter 5.

iPad 📶	12:22 AM	100%

| 📅 Calendars | ⬆ Invitations (1) | Day | Week | **Month** | List | 🔍 Search |

May 2010

Sun 25	Mon 26	Tue 27	Wed 28	Thu 29	Fri 30	Sat 1
	● Training Sess...					

11.11 Calendar's Invitations icon shows you how many Exchange meeting requests you have.

It's best to handle such requests as soon as you can, so here's what you do:

1. **Tap the inbox-like icon in the bottom-right corner of the screen.** Calendar displays your pending meeting requests.

2. **Tap the meeting request you want to respond to and then tap Details.** Calendar displays the meeting details, as shown in Figure 11.12.

11.12 The details screen for an Exchange meeting request.

3. **Tap your response:**

- **Accept.** Tap this button to confirm that you can attend the meeting.

- **Maybe.** Tap this button if you're not sure and will decide later.

- **Decline.** Tap this button to confirm that you can't attend the meeting.

Note Meeting requests show up as events in your calendar, and you can recognize them thanks to their gray background. Another way to open the meeting details is to tap the meeting request in your calendar.

How Do I Use iPad to Navigate My World?

Dedicated GPS (Global Positioning System) devices have become gasp-inducingly popular over the past few years because it's not easy finding your way around in a strange city or an unfamiliar part of town. The old way — hastily scribbled directions or scratching your head over a possibly out-of-date map — was just too hard and error-prone, so having a device tell you where to go (so to speak) was a no-brainer. However, dedicated devices, whether they're music players, eBook readers, or GPS receivers, are going the way of the Dodo. They're being replaced by multifunction devices that can play music, read books, and display maps. In this chapter, you take advantage of your iPad's own multifunction prowess to learn about two navigation tools: the Maps app and the Compass.

Finding Your Way with Maps and GPS

When you're out in the real world trying to navigate your way between the proverbial points A and B, the questions often come thick and fast. "Where am I now?" "Which turn do I take?" "What's the traffic like on the highway?" "Can I even get there from here?" Fortunately, the answers to those and similar questions are now just a few finger taps away. That's because your iPad comes loaded not only with a way-cool Maps app brought to you by the good folks at Google, but it also has a GPS receiver built in. (Just to be clear about this: Note that your iPad only has GPS if you have the 3G model; if you have the Wi-Fi only version, there's no GPS for you!) Now your iPad knows exactly where it is (and so, by extension, you know where you are, too), and it can help you get where you want to go.

To get the Maps app on the job, tap the Maps icon in your iPad's Home screen. Figure 12.1 shows the Maps screen.

12.1 Use your iPad's Maps app to navigate your world.

Viewing your destination

When you want to locate a destination using Maps, the most straightforward method is to search for it:

1. **Tap inside the Search box in the upper-right corner of the screen.**

2. **Type the name, address, or a keyword or phrase that describes your destination.**

3. **In the on-screen keyboard, tap Search.** The Maps app locates the destination, moves the map to that area, and drops a pin on the destination, as shown in Figure 12.2.

Google Street View

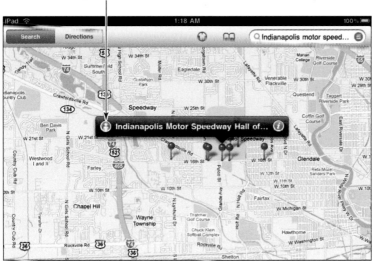

12.2 When you search for a destination, Maps displays a pin to mark its location on the map.

Now that you have your destination pinpointed (literally!), you can read the map to find your way — by looking for street names, local landmarks, nearby major intersections, and so on. (You also can use the Maps app to get specific directions, and I show you how that works later in this chapter.) However, it's always hard to transfer the abstractions of a map to the real-world vista you see outside your car window (or whatever) when you're close to the destination.

Fortunately, Maps can bridge that gap. If Google Street View is available in that area, you see a red icon on the left side of the destination pushpin (pointed out in Figure 12.2). Tap that icon, and Maps immediately shows you the destination in all its Street View glory, as shown in Figure 12.3. To get your bearings, flick the screen left or right to get a full 360-degree view of the area surrounding your destination.

12.3 Tap the Google Street View icon to see a real-world representation of your destination.

Displaying your current location

When you arrive at an unfamiliar shopping mall and you need to get your bearings, your first instinct might be to seek out the nearest mall map and look for the inevitable "You Are Here" marker. This gives you a sense of your current location with respect to the rest of the mall, so locating The Gap shouldn't be all that hard.

When you arrive at an unfamiliar part of town or a new city, have you ever wished you had something that could provide you with that same "You Are Here" reference point? If so, you're in luck because you have exactly that waiting for you right in your iPad. Tap the Tracking button in the Maps app menu bar, as pointed out in Figure 12.4. That's it! Your iPad examines GPS coordinates, Wi-Fi hot spots, and — if your iPad is 3G-equipped — nearby cellular towers to plot your current position. When it completes the necessary processing and triangulating, your iPad displays a map of your current city, zooms in on your current area, and then adds a blue dot to the map to pinpoint your current location, as shown in Figure 12.4. Amazingly, if you happen to be in a car, taxi, or other moving vehicle, the blue dot moves in real time.

Tracking button

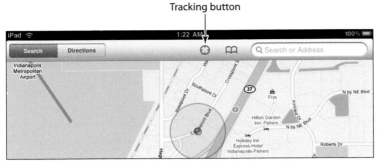

12.4 Tap the Tracking button to see your precise location as a blue dot on a map.

Genius

Knowing where you are is a good thing, but it's even better to know what's nearby. For example, suppose you're in a new city and you're dying for a cup of coffee. Tap Search in the Search box, type **coffee** (or perhaps **café** or **espresso**, depending on what you're looking for), and then tap Search. The Maps app drops a bunch of pins that correspond to nearby locations that match your search. Tap a pin to see the name, and tap the blue More Info icon to see the location's phone number, address, and Web site.

Displaying a map of a contact's location

In the old days (a few years ago!), if you had a contact located in an unfamiliar part of town or even in another city altogether, visiting that person required a phone call or e-mail asking for directions. You'd then write down the instructions, get written directions via e-mail, or perhaps even get a crudely drawn map faxed to you. Those days, fortunately, are long gone thanks to a myriad of online resources that can show you where a particular address is located and even give you driving directions to get there from here (wherever "here" may be).

Even better, your iPad takes it one step further and integrates with Google Maps to generate a map of a contact's location based on the person's contact address. So, as long as you've typed in (or synced) a contact's physical address, you can see where he or she is located on the map.

To display a map of a contact's location, follow these steps:

1. **In the Home screen, tap the Contacts icon to open the Contacts application.**

2. **Tap the contact you want to work with.** Your iPad displays the contact's data.

3. **Tap the address you want to map.** Your iPad switches to the Maps app and drops a pushpin on the contact's location.

Mapping an address embedded in an e-mail

Addresses show up in all kinds of e-mail messages these days. Most commonly, folks will include their work or home addresses in their e-mail signature at the bottom of each message. Similarly, if the e-mail is an invitation to an event, your correspondent will almost certainly include the event's address somewhere in the message.

If you need to know where an address is located, you might think that you need to copy the address from the message and then paste it into the Maps app. Sure, that'll work, but it's way too much effort! Instead, just do this:

1. **In the Mail app, locate the message that includes the address.** If your iPad is in portrait mode, tap Inbox to see the messages.

2. **Tap and hold on the address in the message.** Your iPad displays a list of actions.

3. **Tap Open in Maps.** The Maps app opens and drops a pushpin on the address.

Saving a location as a bookmark for easier access

If you know the address of the location you want to map, you can add a pushpin for that location by opening the Maps app and running a search on the address. That is, you tap the Search box in the menu bar, type the address, and then tap the Search button.

That's no big deal for one-time-only searches, but what about a location you refer to frequently? Typing that address over and over gets old in a hurry, I assure you. You can save time and tapping by telling the Maps app to save that location on its Bookmarks list, which means you can access the location usually with just a few taps.

Follow these steps to add a location to the Maps app's Bookmarks list:

1. **Search for the location you want to save.** The Maps app marks the location with a pushpin and displays the name or address of the location in a banner above the pushpin.

2. **Tap the blue More Info icon in the banner.** The Maps app displays the Info screen with details about the location:

    - If the location is in your Contacts list, you see the contact's data.

- If the location is a business or institution, you see the address as well as other data such as the organization's phone number and Web address.

- For all other locations, you see just the address.

3. **Tap Add to Bookmarks.** The Maps app displays the Add Bookmarks screen.

4. **Edit the name of the bookmark, if you want to, and then Tap Save.** The Maps app adds the location to the Bookmarks list.

Genius

The Bookmarks screen also comes with a Recents button in the menu bar. Tap this button to see your last few searches, locations entered, and driving directions requested. To get the Maps app to run any item again, just tap it.

To map a bookmarked location, follow these steps:

1. **Tap the Bookmark icon in the menu bar.** The Maps app opens the Bookmarks screen.

2. **Tap Bookmarks in the menu bar.** The Maps app displays your list of bookmarked locations, as shown in Figure 12.5.

3. **Tap the location you want to map.** The Maps app displays the appropriate map and adds a pushpin for the location.

12.5 You can access frequently used locations with just a few taps by saving them as bookmarks.

Specifying a location when you don't know the exact address

Sometimes you have only a vague notion of where you want to go. In a new city, for example, you might decide to head downtown and then look for any good coffee shops or restaurants. That's fine, but how do you get downtown from your hotel in the suburbs? Your iPad can give you directions, but it needs to know the endpoint of your journey, and that's precisely the information you don't have. Sounds like a conundrum, for sure, but there's a way to work around it. You can drop a pin on the map in the approximate area where you want to go. The Maps app can then give you directions to the dropped pin.

Follow these steps to drop a pin on a map:

1. **In the Maps app, display a map of the city you want to work with:**

   - If you're in the city now, tap the Tracking icon in the lower-left corner of the screen.

   - If you're not in the city, tap the Search box, enter the name of the city (and perhaps also the name of the state or province), and then tap the Search button.

2. **Use finger flicks to pan the map to the approximate location you want to use as your destination.**

3. **Tap the Action button in the lower-right corner of the screen.** The Maps app displays a list of actions.

4. **Tap Drop Pin.** The Maps app drops a purple pin in the middle of the current map.

5. **Drag the purple pin to the location you want.** The Maps app creates a temporary bookmark called Dropped Pin that you can use when you ask the iPad for directions (as described next).

Getting directions to a location

One possible navigation scenario with the Maps app is to specify a destination (using a contact, an address search, a dropped pin, or a bookmark), and then tap the Tracking button. This gives you a map that shows both your destination and your current location. (Depending on how far away the destination is, you may need to zoom out — by pinching the screen or tapping the screen with two fingers — to see both locations on the map.) You can then eyeball the streets to see how to get from here to there.

"Eyeball the streets"? Hah, how primitive! The Maps app can bring you into the 21st century not only by showing you a route to the destination, but also by providing you with the distance and time it should take, *and* giving you street-by-street, turn-by-turn instructions. It's one of your iPad's sweetest features, and it works like so:

1. **Use the Maps app to add a pushpin for your journey's destination.** Use whatever method works best for you: the Contacts list, an address search, a dropped pin, or a bookmark.

2. **Tap Directions in the menu bar.** The Maps app opens the Directions screen. As shown in Figure 12.6, you should see Current Location in the Start box and your destination address in the End box.

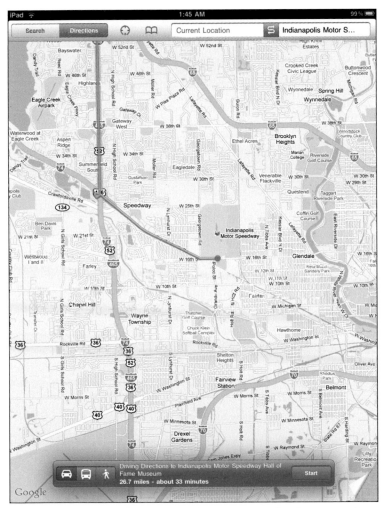

12.6 Use the Directions screen to specify the starting and ending points of your trip.

Genius

Instead of getting directions *to* the destination, you might need directions *from* the destination. No sweat. When you map the destination, tap the blue More Info icon, and then tap Directions From Here. If you're already in the Directions screen, tap the Swap button to the left of the Start and End boxes. The Maps app swaps the locations.

3. **If you want to use a starting point other than your current location, tap Current Location in the Start box and then type the address of the location you want to use.**

4. **In the Overview area at the bottom of the screen, tap the mode of transportation: car, transit, or walking.** The Maps app shows the trip distance and approximate time.

5. **Tap Start.** The Maps app displays the directions for the first leg of the journey.

6. **Tap the Next (right arrow) key.** You see the directions for the next leg of the journey. Repeat to see the directions for each leg. You also can tap the Previous (left arrow) key to go back.

Note

Instead of seeing the directions one step at a time, you may prefer to see them all at once. On the left side of the Overview area at the bottom of the screen, tap the List icon.

Getting live traffic information

Okay, it's pretty darn amazing that your iPad can tell you precisely where you are and precisely how to get somewhere else. However, in most cities, it's the getting somewhere else part that's the problem. Why? One word: traffic. The Maps app may tell you the trip should take 10 minutes, but that could easily turn into a half hour or more if you run into a traffic jam.

That's life in the big city, right? Maybe not. If you're on a highway in a major North American city, the Maps app can most likely supply you with — wait for it — real-time traffic conditions. This is really an amazing tool that can help you avoid traffic messes and find alternative routes to your destination.

To see the traffic data, tap the Action icon in the lower-right corner of the screen and then tap the Traffic switch to the On position. As you can see in Figure 12.7, the Maps app uses four colors to illustrate the traffic flow:

- **Green.** Routes where the traffic is moving at 50 miles per hour or faster.
- **Yellow.** Routes where the traffic is moving between 25 and 50 mph.

● **Red.** Routes where the traffic is moving at 25 mph or slower.

● **Gray.** Routes that currently have no traffic data.

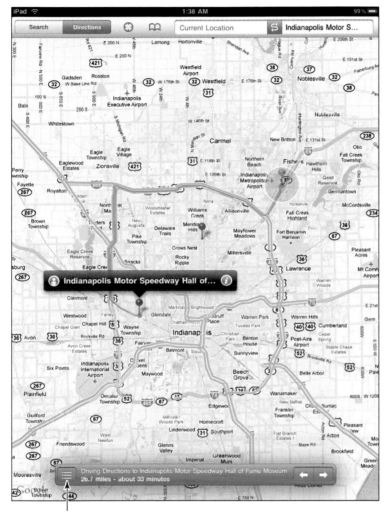

List icon

12.7 For most North American metropolitan highways, the color of the route tells you the current speed of the traffic.

Now you don't have to worry about finding a news radio station and waiting for the traffic report. You can get real-time traffic information whenever you need it.

Sharing Map Data

If you want to show someone where you live, where you work, or where you want to meet, you could just send the address, but that's *so* last century. The more modern way is to send your friend a digital map that shows the location. Your iPad makes this a snap, as the following sections show.

E-mailing a map location

Practically everyone has an e-mail address (everyone online, that is), so sending someone a map attached to an e-mail message makes sense. Here are the steps to follow:

1. **Use the Maps app to add a pushpin for the location you want to send.** Use whatever method works best for you: the Contacts list, an address search, a dropped pin, or a bookmark. If you want to send your current location, display it and then tap the beacon.

2. **Tap the blue More Info icon.**

3. **Tap Share Location.** Your iPad creates a new e-mail message that includes a Google Maps link to the location.

4. **Fill in the rest of your message and send it.**

The iPad's out-of-the-box collection of apps is pretty impressive, and most of us could happily while away our days playing around with nothing but the default apps. That, of course, would be silly. After all, when Apple announced the iPad in early 2010, they also announced that the App Store — the online marketplace of all things app — had more than 140,000 apps available. (The total is no doubt significantly higher as you read this.) That's a mind-boggling, eye-goggling number, and it means that you're bound to find fistfuls of apps that will make your life easier, cooler, more efficient, and more fun. Best of all, tons of the apps won't cost you a dime, so you can bulk up your iPad without draining your bank account.

Apps and Your iPad

You've seen that your iPad comes loaded with not only a basketful of terrific technology, but also a decent collection of truly amazing apps, all of which take advantage of the iPad's special features. But it won't escape your notice that the iPad's suite of apps is, well, incomplete. Where are the news and sports headlines? Why isn't there an easy way to post a short note to your blog or a link to your de.licio.us account? And why on Earth isn't there a game in sight?

Fortunately, it's possible to fill in these and many other gaping holes in the iPad app structure by using the App Store. Here you'll find a raft of high-quality apps in categories such as business, education, social networking, games, and many more. The vast majority of these apps were created for the iPhone, but that's okay because most of those apps run on the iPad too. When you open an iPhone app on your iPad, at first you see the app in its default iPhone size, similar to the one shown in Figure 13.1.

Feel free to use the app like this, but it does seem odd to waste that big, beautiful iPad screen. Fortunately, you don't have to. Tap the 2x button in the bottom-right corner, and your iPad automatically doubles the size of the app (an operation that Apple calls "pixel doubling") so it takes up the entire iPad screen, as shown in Figure 13.2. The image is a bit fuzzier, and if you don't like it, you can always tap the 1x button to return to the standard iPhone view.

Fortunately, you're not stuck with using only iPhone apps on your iPad. In the months before the release of the iPad in the spring of 2010, software developers from all over the world were busy either tweaking existing apps or cobbling together new apps expressly designed to take advantage of the iPad's awesome screen. This means you'll see plenty of apps designed specifically for the iPad.

Accessing the App Store on Your Computer

Your one-stop source for iPad apps is the famous App Store. In the same way that you use the iTunes Store to browse and purchase songs and albums, you use the App Store to browse and purchase apps (although many of them are free for the downloading). It's done using the familiar iTunes software on your Mac or Windows PC. (You also can connect to the App Store directly from your iPad, which I explain later.)

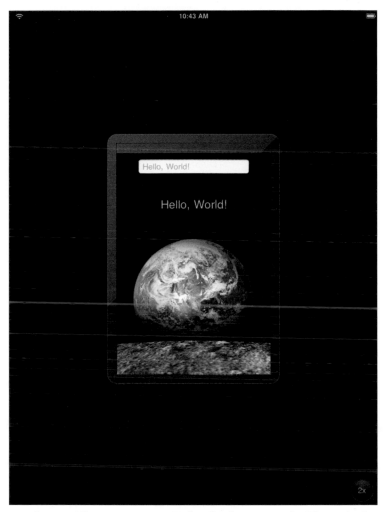

13.1 Open an iPhone app on your iPad, and at first you see the iPhone-sized version of the app.

13.2 Tap the 2x button to enjoy your app at a larger size.

To access the App Store on your computer, follow these steps:

1. **Launch iTunes.**

2. **Click iTunes Store.** The iTunes Store interface appears.

3. **Click App Store.** iTunes loads the main App Store page, as shown in Figure 13.3.

From here, use the links to browse the apps, or use the iTunes Store search box to look for something specific.

13.3 The main App Store page is the start of your search for iPad apps.

Downloading free apps

Early in the development process of the App Store, Apple made a pledge to the software developers: If you make your app free, then Apple will host it in the App Store without charging you a cent. Getting to show off your digital handiwork in front of a few million people is the dream of any developer, but to get that access for nothing is almost too good to be true. Almost. The App Store does, indeed, boast a large collection of apps that are free for the downloading.

Note In most cases, you can't tell just by looking whether an app is free. However, the App Store does have a handy Top Free Apps list on the right side (just below the Paid Apps list), so that's often a good place to start if you're looking for free stuff.

Follow these steps to download and install a free app:

1. **In iTunes, click the App Store link.** Your computer opens the App Store for business.
2. **Use the App Store interface to locate the app you want to download.**

267

3. **Click the app.** The App Store displays a description of the app, along with its ratings, some screen shots, and some user reviews, as shown in Figure 13.4.

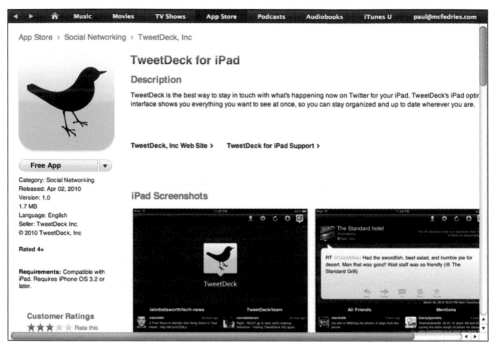

13.4 Click an app to see its details.

4. **Click Free App.** The App Store asks for your iTunes account password.

5. **Type your password, and click Get.** iTunes downloads the app and stores it in the Library's Apps category.

Purchasing apps

Even software developers have to make a living, so giving away apps might make good marketing sense, but it doesn't put Jolt Colas on the table in the short term. So, yes, many of the programs you see in the App Store will cost you a few dollars. That's okay if the app is decent, and hopefully you'll see a few reviews that let you know whether the app is worth shelling out the bucks.

Follow these steps to purchase and install a commercial App Store app:

1. **In iTunes, click the App Store link.** Your computer opens the App Store for business.

2. **Use the App Store interface to locate the app you want to download.**

3. **Click the app.** The App Store displays a description of the app. Pay particular attention to the app's rating and to the reviews that users have submitted.

4. **Click Buy App.** The App Store asks for your iTunes account password.

5. **Type your password, and click Buy.** iTunes downloads the app and stores it in the Library's Apps category.

Subscribing to apps

When you purchase an app, the vast majority of the time that's the only payment you ever make for that program because, sensibly, most apps offer free updates. That payment model works well for your typical apps such as games and utilities, but it's not ideal for apps that constantly replenish their content, such as magazines and newspapers. In those cases, a subscription-based model is more appropriate, and that's just what Apple has now added to the App Store.

Follow these steps to subscribe to and install an app:

1. **In iTunes, click the App Store link.** Your computer opens the App Store for business.

2. **Use the App Store interface to locate the app you want to use.**

3. **Click the app.** The App Store displays a description of the app. Pay particular attention to the app's rating and to the reviews that users have submitted.

4. **Click Subscribe.** The App Store asks for your iTunes account password.

5. **Type your password, and click Buy.** iTunes downloads the app and stores it in the Library's Apps category.

Viewing and updating your apps

When you click Apps in the iTunes Library, you see a list of icons that represent all the apps you've downloaded from the App Store, as shown in Figure 13.5.

13.5 In the iTunes Library, click the Apps category to see your downloaded apps.

Notice that at the bottom of the screen, iTunes tells you how many updates are available. When the developer releases a new version of an app, the App Store compares the new version with what you have. If you have an earlier version, it offers to update the app for you (usually without charge). To see which apps need updating, click *X* Updates Available (where *X* is the number of updates). iTunes takes you to the App Store and displays the list of available updates, as shown in Figure 13.6. To update an app, click the app's Get Update button, type your iTunes Store password and click Get.

13.6 To update an app, click its Get Update button.

Accessing the App Store on Your iPad

Getting apps synced to your iPad from iTunes is great, but what if you're away from your desk and you hear about an amazing iPad game, or you realize that you forgot to download an important app using iTunes? This isn't even remotely a problem because your iPad can establish a wireless connection to the App Store anywhere you have Wi-Fi access or a cellular signal (ideally 3G for faster downloads, assuming you have a 3G version of the iPad). You can browse and search the apps, check for updates, and purchase any app you want (unless it's free, of course). The app downloads to your iPad and installs itself on the Home screen. You're good to go!

To access the App Store on your iPad, follow these steps:

1. **Tap the Home button to return to the Home screen.**

2. **Tap the App Store icon.**

As you can see in Figure 13.7, your iPad organizes the App Store similar to the iTunes Store. That is, you get five browse buttons in the menu bar: Featured, Genius, Categories, Top Charts, and Updates. You use these buttons to navigate the App Store.

Here's a summary of what each browse button does for you:

- **Featured.** Tap this button to display a list of apps picked by the App Store editors. The list shows each app's name, icon, star rating, number of reviews, and price. Tap New to see the latest apps, and tap What's Hot to see the most popular items.

- **Genius.** Tap this button to access the Genius feature, which gives you a list of apps that are similar to the ones already on your iPad.

- **Categories.** Tap this button to see a list of app categories, such as Games and Business. Tap a category to see a list of the apps available.

- **Top Charts.** Tap this button to see a collection of charts, including the Top Paid apps, the Top Free apps, and the Top Grossing apps.

- **Updates.** Tap this button to install updated versions of your apps.

Note Tap an app to get more detailed information about it. The Info screen that appears gives you a description of the app, shows a screen shot, and may even offer some user reviews.

13.7 Use the browse buttons in the App Store's menu bar to locate and manage apps for your iPad.

When you're perusing the apps, you'll come across many where the price button or the FREE button has a little plus (+) in the top left corner, as shown in Figure 13.8. This tells you that the app works with both the iPad and the iPhone.

13.8 A plus sign (+) in an app's price or FREE icon tells you the app works with both the iPad and the iPhone.

When you're wandering around the App Store and you're just not sure what you want, probably the best thing to do is tap Categories in the Menu bar to display the Choose a Category screen shown in Figure 13.9. This can really help you narrow down your search and often help you find hidden gems.

Downloading free apps

Amazingly, quite a few of the App Store apps cost precisely nothing. Nada. Zip. You may think these freebies would be amateurish or too simple to be useful. It's true that some of them are second-rate, but a surprising number are full-fledged apps that are as polished and feature-rich as the commercial apps.

Note   In your iPad's App Store, the free apps say FREE on the right side of the app link. If you're looking for a good place to get your collection of free apps off the ground, tap Top Charts and then tap the Top Free tab.

13.9 Tap Categories and use the App Store's 20 categories to find what you're looking for, even if you didn't know you were even looking for it.

Follow these steps to download and install a free app:

1. **On the Home screen, tap App Store.** Your iPad opens the App Store.

2. **Locate the app you want to download, and tap it.** The app's Info screen appears.

3. **Tap the FREE icon.** The Free icon changes to the Install icon.

4. **Tap Install App.** The App store asks for your iTunes account password.

5. **Type your password, and tap OK.** The App Store begins downloading the app. An icon for the app appears on the Home screen, and you see a progress bar that tracks the download and install process. (The icon title changes from Loading to Installing and finally to the name of the app itself.)

6. **When the installation is complete, tap the new icon on the Home screen to start using your new app.**

Note If the app is quite big and you're surfing the Internet over a cellular connection — particularly an EDGE connection — your iPad may abort the installation and tell you that you need to connect to a Wi-Fi network to download the app.

Purchasing apps

Many of the iPad apps are extremely sophisticated, so it's not surprising that some of them will set you back a few bucks. To make sure you don't waste your money, read the description of the app, and be sure to read any reviews that other folks have submitted.

If a commercial app looks like something you want, follow these steps to purchase and install it:

1. **On the Home screen, tap App Store.** Your iPad connects to the App Store.

2. **Locate the app you want to purchase, and tap it.** The app's Info screen appears.

3. **Tap the price icon.** The price changes to a Buy Now icon.

4. **Tap the Buy App icon.** The App Store asks for your iTunes account password.

5. **Tap the Password box, type your password, and tap OK.** The App Store begins downloading the app. An icon for the app appears on the Home screen, and you see a progress bar that tracks the download and install process. (The icon title changes from Loading to Installing and finally to the name of the app itself.)

6. **When the installation is complete, tap the new icon on the Home screen to launch the app.**

Note The App Store may not let you download a huge app if you're connected over a cellular signal. Instead of downloading the app, your iPad displays a message telling you to try again using a Wi-Fi connection.

Subscribing to apps

If you have a sudden desire to read a particular magazine, newspaper, or other content that you get through a paid App Store subscription, you can conveniently and quickly subscribe right from your iPad. Here's how:

1. **On the Home screen, tap App Store.** Your iPad connects to the App Store.

2. **Use the App Store interface to locate the app you want to subscribe to.**

3. **Click the app.** The App Store displays a description of the app. Pay particular attention to the app's rating and to the reviews that users have submitted.

4. **Click Subscribe.** The App Store asks for your iTunes account password.

5. **Type your password, and click Buy.** iPad downloads and installs the app.

Updating your apps

When you access the App Store with your iPad, look at the Updates browse button in the menu bar. If you see a red dot with a white number inside it superimposed over the Updates button, it means some of your installed apps have updated versions available. The number inside the dot tells you how many updates are waiting for you. It's a good idea to update your apps whenever a new version becomes available. The new version usually fixes bugs, but it also may supply more features, give better performance, or beef up the app's security.

Follow these steps to install an update:

1. **On the Home screen, tap App Store.** Your iPad connects to the App Store.

2. **Tap the Updates button.** Remember that you can tap this button only if you see the red dot with a number that indicates the available updates. You see the Updates screen.

3. **Tap an update.** The App Store displays a description of the update.

4. **Tap Free.** The Free button changes to Install. (In the unlikely event that the update isn't free, you'd tap the price instead, and then tap Buy Now.)

5. **Tap Install.** Your iPad downloads and installs the app update.

Syncing Your Apps

After you download an app or two into iTunes, they won't do you much good just sitting there. To actually use the apps, you need to get them on your iPad. Similarly, if you've grabbed an app or three on your iPad, it's a good idea to back them up to your computer.

You can accomplish both goals by syncing apps between your computer and your iPad:

1. **Connect your iPad to your computer.** iTunes opens and accesses the iPad.

2. **In iTunes, click your iPad in the Devices list.**

3. **Click the Apps tab.**

4. **Select the Sync Apps check box.**

5. **In the app list, select the check box beside each app that you want to sync, as shown in Figure 13.10.**

13.10 You can sync selected apps with your iPad.

6. **To remove an app from the iPad, click the Home screen that contains the app, hover the mouse pointer over the app's icon, and then click the X that appears in the upper-left corner of the icon.**

7. **Click Apply.** iTunes syncs the iPad using your new app settings.

How Do I Fix My iPad?

Your iPad may *look* like an iPod touch on steroids, but the iPad's sophisticated innards tell a different story: This is one fancy device that's on an order of magnitude more complex than an iPod touch. The good news about this is that the iPad is a full-blown computer, and given the iPad's fast processor, extra memory, and large solid state hard drive, you can use it to perform some pretty amazing tricks. The bad news about this is that the iPad is a full-blown computer, and most computers eventually have problems. So there's a good chance that someday your iPad will behave strangely or not at all. When that day comes, this chapter gives you some general troubleshooting techniques for iPad woes and also tackles a few specific problems.

General Techniques for Troubleshooting Your iPad

If your iPad is behaving oddly or erratically, it's possible that a specific component inside the device is the cause, and in that case you don't have much choice but to ship your iPad back to Apple for repairs. Fortunately, however, most glitches are temporary and can often be fixed by using one or more of the following techniques:

- **Restart your iPad.** By far the most common solution to an iPad problem is to shut down and restart the device. By rebooting the iPad, you reload the entire system, which is often enough to solve many problems. You restart your iPad by pressing and holding the Sleep/Wake button for a few seconds, until you see the Slide to Power Off screen (at which point you can release the button). Drag the Slide to Power Off slider to the right to start the shutdown. When the screen goes completely black, your iPad is off. To restart, press and hold the Sleep/Wake button until you see the Apple logo, and then release the button.

- **Reboot your iPad's hardware.** When you restart your iPad by pressing and holding Sleep/Wake for a while, what you're really doing is rebooting the system software. If that still doesn't solve the problem, you may need to reboot the iPad's hardware as well. To do that, press and hold the Sleep/Wake button *and* the Home button. Keep them pressed until you see the Apple logo (it takes about eight seconds or so), which indicates a successful restart.

Genius

The hardware reboot is also the way to go if your iPad is *really* stuck and holding down just the Sleep/Wake button doesn't do anything.

- **Recharge your iPad.** It's possible that your iPad just has a battery that's completely discharged. Connect your iPad to your computer or to the dock. If it powers up and you see the battery logo (note that this may take 10 or 20 seconds), then it's charging just fine and will be back on its feet in a while.

- **Shut down a stuck application.** If your iPad is frozen because an application has gone haywire, you can usually get the iPad back in the saddle by forcing the application to quit. Press and hold the Home button for about six seconds. Your iPad shuts down the application and returns you to the Home screen.

- **Check for iPad software updates.** If Apple knows about the problem you're having, it will fix it (eventually!) and make the patch available in a software update. I tell you how to update your iPad a bit later in this chapter.

● **Check for application updates.** It's possible that a bug in an application is causing your woes. On the Home screen, tap App Store and check the Updates icon to see if any updates are available. If so, tap Updates, tap each application, and tap the Free button (or, in the unlikely event that the update costs money, tap the Buy button) to make it so.

● **Erase and restore your content and settings.** This may seem like drastic advice, but it's possible to use iTunes to perform a complete backup of everything on your iPad. You can then reset the iPad to its original, pristine state, and then restore the backup. I explain this rather lengthy process later in the chapter.

● **Reset your settings.** Sometimes your iPad goes down for the count because its settings have become corrupted. In that case, you can restore the iPad by restoring its original settings. If iTunes doesn't recognize your iPad, then the backup-and-restore option is out. However, you can still reset the settings on the iPad itself. Tap Settings in the Home screen, tap General, tap Reset, and then tap Reset All Settings. When your iPad asks you to confirm, tap Reset All Settings.

Genius

If resetting the settings doesn't get the job done, it could be some recalcitrant bit of content that's causing the problem. In that case, tap Settings in the Home screen, tap General, tap Reset, and then tap Erase All Content and Settings. When your iPad asks you to confirm, tap Erase iPad.

Troubleshooting connected devices

You can connect devices to your iPad in only a few ways: using the headset jack, using the Dock connector, and using Bluetooth. So although the number of devices you can connect is relatively limited, that doesn't mean you might never have problems with those devices.

If you're having trouble with a device attached to your iPad, the good news is that a fair chunk of those problems have a relatively limited set of causes, so you may be able to get the device back on its feet by attempting a few tried-and-true remedies that work quite often for many devices. If it's not immediately obvious what the problem is, then your hardware troubleshooting routine should always start with these very basic techniques:

● **Check connections, power switches, and so on.** Some of the most common (and some of the most embarrassing) causes of hardware problems are the simple physical things: making sure that a device is turned on and checking that cable connections are secure. For example, if you can't access the Internet through your iPad's Wi-Fi connection, make sure your network's router is turned on, and make sure that the cable between your router and the ISP's modem is properly connected.

- **Replace the batteries.** Wireless devices such as headsets really chew through batteries, so if such a device is working intermittently or not at all, always try replacing the batteries to see if that solves the problem.

- **Turn the device off and then on again.** You *power cycle* a device by turning it off, waiting a few seconds for its innards to stop spinning, and then turning it back on again. You'd be amazed how often this simple procedure can get a device back up and running. For a device that doesn't have an on/off switch, try either unplugging the device from the power outlet or removing and replacing the batteries.

- **Reset the device's default settings.** If you can configure a device, then perhaps some new setting is causing the problem. If you recently made a change, try returning the setting to its original value. If that doesn't do the trick, most configurable devices have some kind of Restore Default Settings option that enables you to quickly return the device to its factory settings.

- **Upgrade the device's firmware.** Many a device comes with *firmware*, a small program that runs inside the device and controls its internal functions. For example, all routers have firmware. Check with the manufacturer to see if a new version exists. If it does, download the new version and then see the device's manual to learn how to upgrade the firmware.

Updating the iPad operating system

The iPad's operating system should update itself from time to time when you connect it to your computer, provided the computer has an Internet connection. This is another good reason to sync your iPad regularly. The problem is, you might hear about an important update that adds a feature you're really looking forward to or perhaps fixes a gaping security hole. What do you do if iTunes isn't scheduled to check for an update for a few days?

In that case, you take matters into your own hands and check for updates yourself:

1. **Connect your iPad to your computer.** iTunes opens and connects to your iPad.

2. **Click your iPad in the Devices list.**

3. **Click the Summary tab.**

4. **Click Check for Update.** iTunes connects to the Apple servers to see if any iPad updates are available. If an update exists, you see the iPad Software Update dialog, which offers a description of the update.

5. **Click Next.** iTunes displays the Software License Agreement.

6. **Click Agree.** iTunes downloads the software update and installs it.

Backing up and restoring the iPad's data and settings

Sometimes your iPad goes down for the count because its settings have become corrupted. In that case, you can restore the iPad by restoring its original settings. The best way to go about this is to use the Restore feature in iTunes, because that enables you to make a backup of your settings. However, it does mean that your iPad must be able to connect to your computer and be visible in iTunes.

If that's not the case, see the instructions for resetting in the next section. Otherwise, follow these steps to do a backup and restore on your iPad:

1. **Connect your iPad to your computer.**

2. **In iTunes, click your iPad in the Devices list.**

3. **Click Sync.** This ensures that iTunes has copies of all the data from your iPad.

4. **Check that your iPad is backed up by choosing iTunes ⇨ Preferences, and clicking the Devices tab.** You should see your iPad in the Devices Backup list, as shown in Figure 14.1.

5. **Click the Summary tab.**

Caution   If you have confidential or sensitive data on your iPad, that data becomes part of the backup files and could be viewed by some snoop. To prevent this, select the Summary tab's Encrypt iPad backup check box, and then use the Set password dialog to specify your decryption password.

6. **Click Restore.** iTunes asks you to confirm you want to restore.

7. **Click Restore.**

8. **If the iPad Software Update dialog appears, click Next and then click Agree.** iTunes downloads the software, backs up your iPad, and then restores the original software and settings. When your iPad restarts, iTunes connects to it and displays the Set Up Your iPad screen.

9. **Select the Restore from the backup of option.**

10. **If you happen to have more than one iPad backed up, use the list to choose yours.**

11. **Click Continue.** iTunes restores your backed-up data, restarts your iPad, and then syncs the iPad.

14.1 In the iTunes preferences, use the Devices tab to double-check that your iPad is backed up.

12. **Go through the tabs, and check the sync settings to make sure they're set up the way you want.**

13. **If you made any changes to the settings, click Sync.** This ensures that your iPad has all its data restored.

Taking Care of the iPad Battery

Your iPad comes with a large lithium-ion battery, and Apple claims the iPad gives you up to 10 hours of continuous usage and holds a charge in standby mode for 30 days. Those are impressive times, although count on getting less in the real world.

The biggest down side to the iPad battery is that it's not, in Apple parlance, a *user-installable* feature. If your battery dies, you have no choice but to return it to Apple to get it replaced. Which is all the more reason to take care of your battery and try to maximize battery life.

Tracking battery use

Your iPad doesn't give much battery data, but you can monitor both the total usage time (this includes all activities: surfing, reading eBooks, gaming, playing media, and so on) and standby time (time when your iPad was in Sleep mode). Here's how:

1. **On the Home screen, tap Settings.** The Settings screen appears.

2. **Tap General.** Your iPad displays the General screen.

3. **Tap the Battery Percentage On/Off switch to the On position.** Your iPad shows you the percentage of battery life left in the status bar beside the battery icon, as shown in Figure 14.2.

14.2 In the General screen, turn on the Battery Percentage option to monitor battery life in the iPad status bar.

Tips for extending your battery life

Reducing battery consumption as much as possible on the iPad not only extends the time between charges but also extends the overall life of your battery. Here are a few suggestions:

- **Dim the screen.** The touch screen drains lots of battery power, so dimming it reduces that power. On the Home screen, tap Settings, tap Brightness & Wallpaper, and then drag the slider to the left to dim the screen.

- **Cycle the battery.** All lithium-based batteries slowly lose their charging capacity over time. If you can run your iPad on batteries for 8 hours today, later on you'll be able to run it for only 6 hours on a full charge. You can't stop this process, but you can delay it significantly by periodically *cycling* the iPad battery. Cycling — also called reconditioning or recalibrating — a battery means letting it completely discharge and then fully recharging it again. To maintain optimal performance, you should cycle your iPad's battery every one or two months.

- **Slow the auto-check on your e-mail.** Having your e-mail poll the server for new messages eats up your battery. Don't set it to check every 15 minutes if possible. Ideally, set it to Manual check if you can. See Chapter 5 for information on how to do this.

- **Turn off push.** If you have a MobileMe account, consider turning off the push feature to save battery power. Tap Settings; tap Mail, Contacts, Calendars; and then tap Fetch New Data. In the Fetch New Data screen, tap the Push setting to Off and tap Manually in the Fetch section, as shown in Figure 14.3.

14.3 You can save battery power by turning off your iPad's push features.

Genius
Paradoxically, the *less* you use your iPad, the *more* often you should cycle its battery. If you often go several days or even a week or two without using your iPad (I can't imagine!), you should cycle its battery at least once a month.

- **Minimize your tasks.** If you won't be able to charge your iPad for a while, avoid background chores such as playing music or secondary chores such as organizing your contacts. If your only goal is to read all your e-mail, stick to that until it's done because you don't know how much time you have.

- **Put your iPad into Sleep mode by hand, if necessary.** If you're interrupted — for example, the pizza delivery guy shows up on time — don't wait for your iPad to put itself to sleep because those few minutes use up precious battery time. Instead, put your iPad to sleep manually right away by pressing the Sleep/Wake button.

- **Avoid temperature extremes.** Exposing your iPad to extremely hot or cold temperatures reduces the long-term effectiveness of the battery. Try to keep your iPad within a reasonable range of temperatures.

- **Turn off Wi-Fi if you don't need it.** When Wi-Fi is on, it regularly checks for available wireless networks, which drains the battery. If you don't need to connect to a wireless network, turn off Wi-Fi to conserve energy. Tap Settings, tap Wi-Fi, and then tap the Wi-Fi setting to Off.

- **Turn off GPS if you don't need it.** When GPS is on, the receiver exchanges data with the GPS system regularly, which uses up battery power. If you have a Wi-Fi + 3G version of the iPad and you don't need the GPS feature for the time being, turn off the GPS antenna. Tap Settings, tap General, and then tap the Location Services setting to Off.

- **Turn off Bluetooth if you don't need it.** When Bluetooth is running, it constantly checks for nearby Bluetooth devices, which drains the battery. If you aren't using any Bluetooth devices, turn off Bluetooth to save energy. Tap Settings, tap General, tap Bluetooth, and then tap the Bluetooth setting to Off.

Genius
If you don't need all three of your iPad's antennas for a while, a faster way to turn them off is to switch your iPad to Airplane mode. Tap Settings, and then tap the Airplane Mode switch to the On position.

Sending Your iPad in for Repairs

To get your iPad repaired, you could take your device to an Apple store or send it in. Visit www.apple.com/support and follow the prompts to find out how to send your iPad in for repairs. Remember that the memory comes back wiped, so be sure to sync with iTunes, if you can. Also, don't forget to remove your SIM card before you send it in.

Solving Specific Problems

The generic troubleshooting and repair techniques that you've seen so far can solve all kinds of problems. However, specific problems always require specific solutions. The rest of this chapter takes you through a few of the most common of these problems.

Your battery won't charge

If you find that your battery won't charge, here are some solutions:

- **If the iPad is plugged into a computer to charge via the USB port, it may be that the computer has gone into standby.** Waking the computer should solve the problem.

- **The USB port may not be transferring enough power.** For example, the USB ports on most keyboards don't offer much in the way of power. If you have your iPad plugged into a keyboard USB port, plug it into a USB port on the computer itself.

- **Attach the USB cable to the USB power adapter, and then plug the adapter into an AC outlet.**

- **Double-check all connections to make sure everything is plugged in properly.**

- **Try an iPod cord if you have one.**

If you can't seem to locate the problem after these steps, you may need to send your iPad in for service. A replacement battery will cost you US$99 plus $6.95 shipping.

You have trouble accessing a Wi-Fi network

Wireless networking adds a whole new set of potential snags to your troubleshooting chores because of problems such as interference and device ranges. Here's a list of a few troubleshooting items that you should check to solve any wireless connectivity problems you're having with your iPad:

- **Make sure the Wi-Fi antenna is on.** Tap Settings, tap Wi-Fi, and then tap the Wi-Fi switch to the On position.

- **Make sure the iPad isn't in Airplane mode.** Tap Settings, and then tap the Airplane Mode switch to the Off position.

- **Check the connection.** The iPad has a tendency to disconnect from a nearby Wi-Fi network for no apparent reason. Tap Settings. If the Wi-Fi setting shows as Not Connected, tap Wi-Fi and then tap your network in the list.

- **Renew the lease.** When you connect to a Wi-Fi network, the access point gives your iPad a Dynamic Host Control Protocol (DHCP) lease that allows it to access the network. You can often solve connectivity problems by renewing that lease. Tap Settings, tap Wi-Fi, and then tap the blue More Info icon to the right of the connected Wi-Fi network. Tap the DHCP tab, and then tap the Renew Lease button, as shown in Figure 14.4.

- **Reconnect to the network.** You can often solve Wi-Fi network woes by disconnecting from the network and then reconnecting. Tap Settings, tap Wi-Fi, and then tap the blue More Info icon to the right of the connected Wi-Fi network. Tap the Forget This Network button to disconnect, and then reconnect to the same network.

14.4 Open the connected Wi-Fi network's settings, and tap Renew Lease to get a fresh lease on your Wi-Fi life.

Caution

You should keep your iPad and wireless access point well away from microwave ovens; microwaves can jam wireless signals.

- **Reset your iPad's network settings.** This removes all stored network data and resets everything to the factory state, which might solve the problem. Tap Settings, tap General, tap Reset, and then tap Reset Network Settings. When your iPad asks you to confirm, tap Reset Network Settings.

- **Reboot and power cycle devices.** Reset your hardware by performing the following tasks, in order: restart your iPad, reboot your iPad's hardware, power cycle the wireless access point, and power cycle the broadband modem.

- **Look for interference.** Devices such as baby monitors and cordless phones that use the 2.4 GHz radio frequency (RF) band can play havoc with wireless signals. Try either moving or turning off such devices if they're near your iPad or wireless access point.

- **Check your range.** If you're getting no signal or a weak signal, your iPad could be too far away from the access point. If you have an 802.11n access point, the theoretical range is about 230 feet; if you have an older access point (such as 802.11g), you usually can't get much farther than about 115 feet away from it before the signal begins to degrade. Either move closer to the access point or turn on the access point's range booster feature, if it has one. You also could install a wireless range extender.

- **Update the wireless access point firmware.** The wireless access point firmware is the internal program that the access point uses to perform its various chores. Wireless access point manufacturers frequently update their firmware to fix bugs, so you should see if an updated version of the firmware is available. See your device documentation to learn how this works.

- **Reset the router.** As a last resort, reset the router to its default factory settings (see the device documentation to learn how to do this). Note that if you do this, you need to set up your network from scratch.

iTunes doesn't see your iPad

When you connect your iPad to your computer, iTunes should start and you should see the iPad in the Devices list. If iTunes doesn't start when you connect your iPad, or if iTunes is already running but the iPad doesn't appear in the Devices list, it means that iTunes doesn't recognize your iPad. Here are some possible fixes:

- **Check the connections.** Make sure the USB connector and the Dock connector are fully seated.

- **Try a different USB port.** The port you're using may not work, so try another one. If you're using a port on a USB hub, trying using one of the computer's built-in USB ports.

- **Restart your iPad.** Press and hold the Sleep/Wake button for a few seconds until the iPad shuts down, and then press and hold Sleep/Wake until you see the Apple logo.

- **Restart your computer.** This should reset the computer's USB ports, which might solve the problem.

- **Check your iTunes version.** You need at least iTunes version 9 to work with the iPad.

- **Check your operating system version.** On a Mac, your iPad requires OS X 10.5.8 or later; on a Windows PC, your iPad requires Windows 7, Windows Vista, or Windows XP Service Pack 3 or later.

iTunes doesn't sync your iPad

If iTunes sees your iPad, but you can't get it to sync, you probably have to adjust some settings. See Chapter 2 for some troubleshooting ideas related to syncing. Another possibility is that your iPad is currently locked. That's not usually a problem for iTunes, but it sometimes gets confused by a locked iPad. The easy remedy is to unplug the iPad, unlock it, and then plug it in again.

You have trouble syncing music or videos

You may run into a problem syncing your music or videos to your iPad. The most likely culprit here is that your files are in a format that the iPad can't read. WMA, MPEG 1, MPEG 2, and other formats aren't readable to the iPad. First, convert them to a format that the iPad does understand using converter software. Then put them back on iTunes and try to sync again. This should solve the problem.

iPad-supported audio formats include AAC; AIFF; Audible Formats 2, 3, and 4; Apple Lossless; MP3; MP3 VBR; and WAV. iPad-supported video formats include H.264 and MPEG-4.

Your iPad doesn't recognize your SIM card

If you have an iPad Wi-Fi + 3G model and your iPad doesn't detect your SIM card, try this:

1. **Eject the SIM card tray from the top of your iPad using the tool that came with your iPad or a paper clip or pin.** Press the tool into the little hole on the tray, and it should pop out.

2. **Make sure the SIM card is free of dirt and debris.**

3. **Reseat the SIM card in the tray, and slide the tray back in.**

If this doesn't solve the problem, then your problem is a larger one and you need to contact Apple or your cellular provider.

Glossary

3G A third-generation cellular network that's faster than the old EDGE network and is supported in iPad Wi-Fi + 3G models for data delivery over the cellular network.

802.11 See *Wi-Fi*.

accelerometer The component inside the iPad that senses the device's orientation in space and adjusts the display accordingly (such as switching Safari from portrait view to landscape view).

access point A networking device that enables two or more devices to connect over a Wi-Fi network and to access a shared Internet connection.

ad hoc wireless network A wireless network that doesn't use an access point.

Airplane mode An operational mode that turns off the transceivers for the iPad's 3G, Wi-Fi, and Bluetooth features, which puts the device in compliance with federal aviation regulations.

app An application that is designed for and runs on an iPad.

authentication See *SMTP authentication*.

Bluetooth A wireless networking technology that enables you to exchange data between two devices using radio frequencies when the devices are within range of each other (usually within about 33 feet/10 meters).

bookmark An Internet site saved in Safari so you can access the site quickly in future browsing sessions.

cloud The collection of me.com networked servers that store your MobileMe data and push any new data to your iPad, Mac, or Windows PC.

cycling Letting the iPad battery completely discharge and then fully recharging it again.

data roaming A cellular provider feature that enables you to perform activities such as checking for e-mail when you're outside of your provider's normal coverage area.

digital rights management Technology that restricts the usage of content to prevent piracy.

discoverable Describes a device that has its Bluetooth feature turned on so other Bluetooth devices can connect to it.

double-tap To use a fingertip to quickly press and release the iPad screen twice.

DRM See *digital rights management*.

EDGE (Enhanced Data rates for GSM [Global System for Mobile communication] Evolution) A cellular network that's older and slower than 3G, although still supported by the iPad.

event An appointment or meeting that you've scheduled in your iPad's Calendar.

flick To quickly and briefly drag a finger across the iPad screen.

FM transmitter A device that sends the iPad's output to an FM station, which you then play through your car stereo.

GPS (Global Positioning System) A satellite-based navigation system that uses wireless signals from a GPS receiver — such as the one in the iPad — to accurately determine the receiver's current position.

group A collection of Address Book contacts. See also *smart group*.

headset A combination of headphones for listening and a microphone for talking.

Home screen The main screen on your iPad, which you access by pressing the Home button.

IMAP (Internet Message Access Protocol) A type of e-mail account where incoming messages, as well as copies of messages you send, remain on the server.

Internet tethering Using your iPad as a kind of Internet gateway device where you connect your iPad to your notebook — either directly via a USB cable or wirelessly via Bluetooth — and your notebook can then use the iPad's cellular Internet connection to get online.

keychain A list of saved passwords on a Mac.

magnetometer A device that measures the direction and intensity of a magnetic field.

memory effect The process where a battery loses capacity over time if you repeatedly recharge it without first fully discharging it.

MMS (Multimedia Messaging Service) A technology that enables the iPad to accept and send a text message with an embedded media file, such as a photo, video, or map.

multitouch A touchscreen technology that can detect and interpret two or more simultaneous touches, such as two-finger taps, spreads, and pinches.

pair To connect one Bluetooth device with another by entering a passkey.

pan To slide a photo or other image up, down, left, or right.

passcode A four-digit code used to secure or lock an iPad.

piconet An ad hoc wireless network created by two Bluetooth devices.

pinch To move two fingers closer together on the iPad screen. See also *spread*.

playlist A collection of songs that you create using iTunes.

POP (Post Office Protocol) A type of e-mail account where incoming messages are only stored temporarily on the provider's mail server, and when you connect to the server, the messages are downloaded to the iPad and removed from the server. See also *IMAP*.

power cycle A method of rebooting your iPad, in which you turn the device off, wait a few seconds for its inner components to stop spinning, and then turn it back on again.

preferences The options, settings, and other data that you've configured for your Mac via System Preferences.

push To send data immediately without being prompted.

ringtone A sound that plays when an incoming call is received.

RSS feed A special file that contains the most recent information added to a Web site.

silent mode An operational state where the iPad plays no sounds, except alerts set with the Clock application.

slide To drag a finger across the iPad screen.

smart group A collection of Address Book contacts where each member has one or more things in common, and where Address Book adds or deletes members automatically as you add, edit, and delete contacts.

SMS (Short Message Service) A wireless messaging service that enables the exchange of short text messages between mobile devices.

SMTP (Simple Mail Transfer Protocol) The set of protocols that determines how e-mail messages are addressed and sent.

SMTP authentication The requirement that you must log on to a provider's SMTP server to confirm that you're the person sending the mail.

SMTP server The server that an Internet service provider uses to process outgoing e-mail messages.

spread To move two fingers apart on the iPad 3G screen. See also *pinch*.

SSID (Service Set Identifier) The name that identifies a network to Wi-Fi devices.

synchronization A process that ensures that data such as contacts, e-mail accounts, and events on your computer is the same as the data on your iPad.

tap To use a fingertip to quickly press and release the iPad screen.

tethering See *Internet tethering*.

touchscreen A screen that responds to touches such as finger taps and finger slides.

transceiver A device that transmits and receives wireless signals.

trim To edit the start point and end point of a video recording or a voice memo.

two-fingered tap To use two fingertips to quickly press and release the iPad screen.

vCard A file that contains a person's contact information.

.vcf The file extension used by a vCard.

wallpaper The background image you see when you unlock your iPad.

Web Clip A Home screen icon that serves as a link to a Web page that preserves the page's scroll position and zoom level.

Wi-Fi (Wireless Fidelity) A wireless networking standard that enables wireless devices to transmit data and communicate with other devices using radio frequency signals that are beamed from one device to another.

Index

The Genius is in.